Lyn Peterson's
Real Life
Renovating

Lyn Peterson's Real Life Renovating

Lyn Peterson

Clarkson Potter/Publishers
New York

Copyright © 2006 by Lyn Peterson

All rights reserved.
Published in the United States
by Clarkson Potter/Publishers,
an imprint of the Crown Publishing Group,
a division of Random House, Inc., New York.

Clarkson N. Potter is a trademark
and Potter and colophon are registered
trademarks of Random House, Inc.

ISBN: 1-4000-5300-5

Printed in the U.S.A.

Design by Jennifer Napier and Grace Lee

All photographs are by Mick Hales except those on pages
14 (above), 15 (below), 16 (left and below), 23, 24 (below), 26
(right), 27 (below), 30 (below), 35 (above), 36, 37, (below),
48 (middle and below), 53 (below), 58 (left), 70, 71 (below),
80 (below), 90, 112, 114 (right), 118 (right), 142, 172, 213, 250,
253, and 255, which are courtesy of the author, and those
on pages 102, 105, and 108, which are by Veronica
Cagliero. All illustrations and floor plans are courtesy of
the author. Cover photograph location courtesy of
Sunningdale Development LLC.

Acknowledgments

Real Life Renovating arose from the need to share two decades' worth of personal and professional renovating experience. I wanted to pass on to all of you once-and-future renovators the facts about the process, the pitfalls, and ultimately the divine pleasure of renovating a home. The urge to improve one's surroundings is, after all, a basic human instinct. Since we must do it, why not learn from the experiences of those who have gone before us?

IT TOOK FAR MORE THAN A VILLAGE TO PRODUCE THIS BOOK. It took my entire world—my nights, my days, my spring, summer, fall, and winter. And it took all these wonderful people who helped me along the way:

BJ Sharpe, my summer sister, my always-does-everything-perfectly assistant. If only I could clone you and have you by my side 24/7.

Susan Carlton, my writing refiner, my word designer, my lighthearted friend. If only I could *be* you.

Natalie Kaire, my push-to-make-it-right and push-to-make-it-better editor. And you succeeded.

Keith Girard, my pinch hitter, my data supplier, my late-night buddy.

Andi Ross, my invaluable, resourceful, and amusing research assistant.

The McMahons, Cullen and Diana, my in-laws, for their input and for acting as my sounding board.

Thanks also to all the wonderful families whose homes are pictured in our pages: Leah and Leo Mullin, Tom and Laurie Saylak, Veronica and Bob Cagliero, Barbara and Jack Quinlan, Linda and Frank Fialkoff, Joan and Ralph Ammirati, Tena and Hayes Kavanaugh, Jane and Arnold Adlin, Laura Lee and John Samford, Mae and Webb Robertson, Susan and Ralph Carlton, Sue and Bart Blatt, and Kristiina Ratia.

SPECIAL THANKS TO:

The Whitneys—Liz, Ken, Rachel, Allison, Chloe, and Potter—for letting me photograph their home while they were still in the midst of a massive renovation.

The Krases—Chrystie, Scott, and the kids—for always letting me barge through their door virtually unannounced and usually with a camera in hand.

The Cyganowskis—Katie, David, Megan, and Davey—

for letting me vent and vent and vent. Being with you guys always means a good day!

To all of my decorating clients over the years, to their architects and contractors for educating me, letting me learn, and sharing your renovations.

To the (very large, and that's the way I like it) crew at 54 Park Road: my family, Amer, Kris, Erik, PF, Rusty, and Grampa (and Harry)—the bachelor boys in the bunkhouse, and Uncle Bob for coping with my beastly sleep-deprived personality for far too many months and then graciously (well, there was *some* reluctance) saving my place at the dinner table.

TO THE PROS:

Pam Krauss, we did a book—finally, eighteen years after we first talked about it.

Carla Glasser, my agent, who was always gracious, smart, kind, and incredibly chic to boot.

Aliza Fogelson, my eleventh-inning editor, for carrying the ball over the finish line. (I'm sure I'm mixing my sports metaphors.)

To Mick Hales, my delightful photographer, who does it with such ease and grace, accomplishing the impossible without a ruffled feather. A cup of tea at 11 A.M. and 5 P.M. and the man will do anything.

To my coworkers at Motif Designs—Fran Principe, JoAnn, Colette, Lisa, Linda, Keith, Gayle, Fran Smith, Ron Fairey, Charles, John, Jennifer, and Ron Schneider—for all of the countless times you have all pitched in wherever and whenever necessary.

To Pat Sadowsky for her incredible expertise and for getting me noticed.

To Sara Gioavanitti for teaching me about the beauty of design.

To my husband, Karl Friberg, for fostering in me that most invaluable asset—confidence in myself.

Thank you all again and again and again.

Contents

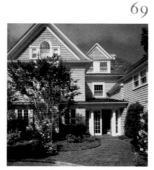

The Details . . . Room by Room | 149

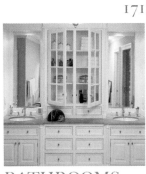

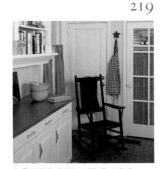
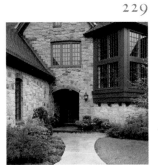

Introduction

I am a passionate renovator. I believe deeply in the value of restoring a home—resurrecting it or reimagining it to be something better, if not always bigger. Renovating is an artful endeavor. It takes creativity and energy, intuition and intellect. The payoff for putting so much of yourself into this kind of all-encompassing project is that you get to actually live and breathe (and appreciate) it when it's complete.

I'M NOT THE ONLY WHO FEELS THIS WAY ABOUT RENOVATION. Fixing up houses—from old Victorians to midcentury split-levels—is at an all-time high. And little wonder. The homes most of us live in are becoming obsolete. What was considered an adequate, even luxurious, house twenty years ago is often missing a lot of what we want today: the fully loaded cook's kitchen, the tech-savvy media room, and the spa-like master bath. Our homes are obsolete in other, more hidden, ways, too, with outdated wiring and heating and cooling systems.

So why not just build something new? Because maybe, just maybe, you're like me, and you still love your home. You have history there, memories. Renovating lets you stay put and retrofit. Replace the tubs and tiles, relocate the driveway, refinish the floors. You can also, land permitting, increase your square footage to accommodate your family's growing needs and wants. Add a piano room for budding musicians, a guest wing for out-of-town relatives, a home office for you, and, along the way, more light, more sun, more sharing. Renovating also means you don't have to change dry cleaners and shoemakers, let alone schools and soccer fields. I happen to like my neighborhood, my street. I've known my mail carrier for years.

My love affair with restoration began long before I owned a house. In college I wanted nothing to do with the sterile and boring new dormitory to which I was assigned. Instead I was attracted to a charming, albeit quirky, older dorm, and I got myself switched. When I moved in and started decorating my room, I realized how much I loved the process of fixing, decorating, and ultimately transforming a space to reflect my taste. I became, no surprise, an interior designer.

THE BEST RENOVATIONS RESTORE, REJUVENATE, OR REVEAL THE INTRINSIC CHARMS OF A HOUSE. IN THIS LIVING ROOM, EXQUISITELY ARTICULATED WINDOWS WERE LEFT BARE, THE BETTER TO SHOW THEIR BEAUTIFUL DETAILS.

Now, three decades and hundreds of renovations for countless clients later, I am no less infatuated with architecture, no less challenged by the prospect of setting a house right, making it work uniquely for a particular family. As with any infatuation, of course, there are bound to be moments of disenchantment. My current home, a mere eighty years young, has many wonderful features, but I am well aware that the slate roof leaks, the doors and windows rattle all night long, the upstairs hall is fun-house crooked, and the bathroom tiles are ancient. Shall I continue?

No one ever said renovating is easy. I had one client recently, an Ivy League graduate and founder of a major investment firm, who said renovating her house was the hardest thing she'd ever done. Every time she turned around, she had to make a decision about something she'd never thought twice about. Red or white oak flooring? Lever or spoke faucets? Incandescent or fluorescent lighting? Oh, and by the way, what exactly are escutcheons?

Once you decide to renovate, it's time to write up your wish list. Start by thinking big. Include not only practical changes and additions but also more luxurious indulgences: his-and-hers walk-in closets, a new master bath, a home office or two, a game room for the kids (big and little), a screened porch, an open kitchen, a ground-floor guest room for visiting family, a new three-car garage. It's not uncommon to go through a punch-drunk phase and decide you must have the 1,500-bottle wine cellar or oiled African mahogany flooring. Inevitably you will scale back, but if you never ask for the dream item or price it, you will never know if it was attainable.

Part of the wish-list process is getting a picture—literally—of the look you want. Collect photographs of rooms you like from magazines, books, friends' places, hotels—whatever. When you lay out the references side by side, you may find a similarity you hadn't noticed before. Maybe almost every kitchen has an ivory granite countertop or nearly every family room has a coffered ceiling; identifying these recurring themes will be helpful as you decide what you want.

With the project taking shape in your mind, it's time to gather the professionals who can turn your vision into walls and floors and windows. The main players will be the architect, the contractor (and his or her subcontractors), and the interior designer, if you choose to use one. Nearly three-quarters of homeowners find their renovation professionals through word of mouth—really the best way. Still, be sure to call all references and pump them for details about scheduling, budgeting, ease of communication, and happiness with the result. Then meet with each prospect at the job site—you'll hear ideas for the project and get a better sense of personality. Chemistry is key. You'll be head to head (sometimes butting heads) with the pros you hire for far longer than you anticipate.

Getting a fix on the project's price for construction typically hinges on a detailed architect's plan. The drawings should leave as little room for interpretation as possible, identifying all materials and products right down to the brand and model number. Get bids from two or three contractors. Start by asking that the bid be broken down by trades—plumber, electrician, plasterer, et cetera—so you can compare apples to apples. If two bids come in close, don't worry about the third, which may reflect either desperation (lowball bidder) or lack of interest (high bidder). If the bids are all over the place, then you may have to ask the contractors to sharpen their pencils in a second bid. Remember, budgets are a best-case scenario; pad them by 20 percent for a more realistic figure. You can count on running into changes to the plan—so-called change orders. A request for a ceiling light fixture can delay an electrical inspection, which in turn delays the insulation, which puts back the Sheetrocker, the taper, and the painter.

Part of the conversation with the contractor should cover a detailed breakdown of financial terms, including total cost and payment schedules; procedures for handling change orders; and specifications for all materials and products. It's also a good idea to go over how you'll all coexist throughout the construction. Where will the carpenters set

Before you pour your heart and soul into the long, sometimes arduous process of renovation, consider a few key issues to be sure the project is a wise investment of time and money.

How long you will be staying.

This affects how much to spend on the project and how much (or how little) to tailor the renovation to your family. If you intend to retire to the house, then make it yours, even if that means turning it into a fantasy with a grotto, like my neighbors'. If you plan to be in the house for just a few years, then Band-Aid fixes might work; installing new kitchen counters and putting up wainscoting are changes with high resale value.

Location, location, location.

Real estate is historically an enduring investment. In an overheated housing market, renovation almost always costs less than moving. Ask a reliable Realtor to assess the price of your home relative to its neighbors. A million-dollar home on a street of half-million-dollar homes won't command as high a price as a million-dollar home on a street of homes selling at $1.5 million.

What's worth saving.

A partial renovation is sometimes as smart as a gut job, especially if the house has a lot of charm to hang onto. Look into what you can fix without tearing down. Too often people take an all-or-nothing approach that may not be necessary. Assess the assets. Can you keep the kitchen cabinets and spray them white? Keep the windows and put up new screens? Keep the old bath fittings and replace the tiles?

up an on-site shop? Will the contractor install a designated phone line for the crew? Rent a portable toilet? Will your site be a smoke-free zone? Resolve issues like this early, and you'll encounter fewer surprises and bumps along the renovation road.

With your dream team on board, it's smart to call a preliminary "blue sky" design meeting of all involved. Renovating is, after all, a collaborative process, and you want to start engendering team spirit right from the beginning. At this first meeting, ideas will be hashed out and solutions proposed. The architect, for example, may suggest a stair tower sheathed in glass. The contractor may object, knowing it will cost a fortune. The decorator may come up with a realistic compromise—a skylit stairwell—instead.

Any renovation is bound to involve compromise, but I believe you should never compromise on your priorities or your personal aesthetic. At the end of the day, when the plumber, the painter, and the tile guy have all gone home, you don't want to be living in someone else's idea of a dream house. You want to be in your own dream—which is now your own reality!

In this book, I set out to give the renovator, novice or not, good ideas, honest advice, and loads of inspiration. Over the course of running my own business, Motif Designs, I've kept reams of notes, thoughts, sketches, scribbles, tips, and product specs. All have been a great resource for me—and now, in this book, for you. Read it and renovate!

IMAGINE A HOME THIS LARGE AND A STAIR THIS MAGNIFICENT WITHOUT A PLACE TO PUT A SINGLE PIECE OF FURNITURE. BOTH A LINEN CLOSET WITH A PAIR OF CURTAINED GLASS DOORS AND AN UPSTAIRS HALL NICHE WERE HARVESTED FROM SPACE GENERATED BY REMOVING AN ATTIC STAIR.

The Houses . . .
and Their Stories

A Colorful Life

Accomplished in six months

- Create a friendlier entry
- Add decorative overdoor moldings to make small doorways appear taller
- Wake up the living room, family room, and sitting room with strong color
- Update and rework the existing kitchen with a custom island and larger windows
- Spruce up a screened-in porch
- Give a child's room character with wainscoting
- Gut a maze of tiny spaces to build a home office

LITTLE DID THE FOLEYS SUSPECT THAT IN A SPAN OF FIVE years they would go from virgin remodelers to veteran renovators. Talk about a learning curve. Job changes took the family from New York up to the coast of Maine and finally down South. Their lives were uprooted—family and friends left behind, dry cleaners, greengrocers, and contractors changed not once, not twice, but three times. The Foleys sometimes felt dispossessed—lonely at worst, intimidated at best by the prospect of acclimating to a new climate, a new group of friends, and a new house.

With each move the Foleys—Henry, Susan, and their two daughters—thought (mistakenly, it turned out) they had found their dream house in their dream location and that they would stay, if not forever, then for many years to come. Each time they spent money like they were in it for the long haul: buying expensive lanterns for the porch on the coast, glass tiles for the children's bath in the suburbs, and Viking stoves for all three kitchens as if they would be enjoying them for years. Their time- and cost-consuming renovations, however, turned out to be savvy investments. Every house was sold in a bidding war.

The Foleys' first renovation endeavor involved their Westchester, New York, colonial on a small piece of property, where they added a bit to the back of the house to

AN OVERSIZED STONE FLOOR (QUARTZ) IN THE ENTRY AND LIBRARY HALL BRACKETS THE LIVING ROOM AND CREATES A NICE SYMMETRY. CEILING PENDANTS, BOTH ANTIQUE AND NEW, BREAK UP THE EXPANSE OF UNDERDETAILED SHEETROCK CEILINGS.

enlarge the kitchen and the family room. Their second renovation, to an 1880s Maine waterfront cottage, required a more significant overhaul. They relocated the kitchen, added bathrooms, and built a semicircular porch.

Their third and most recent renovation tackled an old southern farmhouse that had languished on the market for three years. The Foleys liked that the large house sat far back from the road and that the property encompassed four densely landscaped acres in the city, a pool, a pool house, and a frog pond. Although their plan for the house was not extensive, it was invasive. Here, there, and everywhere they added color and architectural detail, giving the house a lot of personality and a dose of their own style.

The Foleys knew a first impression was important, especially in their southern neighborhood. They hung a handsome new front door and painted it a strong barn red. The

door has become an identifying landmark—"You know, the house with the red door." They replaced flimsy shutters with heavy custom shutters painted a soft mossy green. Right away it was a friendlier house.

Inside, the pretty front hall—with a curved staircase, rounded walls, and an arched entrance to the dining room —had been debased by peel-and-stick parquet-tile flooring. The Foleys pulled up the floor and replaced it with oversized squares of quartzite slate. They had the slate laid on the diagonal to complement the shape of the round room; visually, a diagonal goes in all directions, as does a circle. They put simple jute carpeting on the stairs and warmed the walls with subdued English wallpaper.

Next, they addressed the openings off the entryway to the living room and the sitting room. These entrances seemed low and squat in contrast to the 10-foot ceilings.

Rather than going to the expense of heightening and completely reframing the openings, the architect suggested a visual trick: adding a series of moldings stacked on top of the door frames, a simple but effective way of visually elongating the openings. Removing the actual doors, which served no real purpose, also helped create a grander and more gracious feeling and eliminated awkward door swings.

In the living room, that dinosaur from the days before the family room, the Foleys did a little decorative tweaking, too. They painted the walls a soft pomegranate and enlivened the fireplace with a riotous checkerboard of

COLOR AND PATTERN WAKE UP A SLEEPY SOUTHERN FARMHOUSE. [LEFT] A RED FRONT DOOR AND MOSSY GREEN SHUTTERS GIVE THE EXTERIOR A STRIKING AND VERY PERSONAL LOOK. [OPPOSITE, ABOVE] ADDING DETAILS OVER DOORWAYS "LIFTED" THE OPENINGS IN THE ENTRANCE HALL TO CREATE A BETTER PROPORTION FOR THE 10-FOOT CEILINGS. [OPPOSITE, BELOW] THE FOLEYS REFURBISHED THE LIVING ROOM WITH IMPACT COLORS: POMEGRANATE WALLS, A CHEERY CHECKERBOARD FIREPLACE SURROUND, AND STRONGLY PATTERNED CARPET.

TRADE TIP

SOMETIMES PAINT JUST ISN'T ENOUGH OF A DECORATIVE TRANSFORMER. IF A ROOM HAS A LOT OF DISPARATE FURNITURE PIECES OR BUILT-IN QUIRKS LIKE WINDOWS OF DIFFERENT SIZES AND ODD NOOKS AND CRANNIES, YOU MAY FIND THAT A STRONG WALLPAPER OR PATTERNED CARPET IS THE BEST WAY TO PULL THE LOOK TOGETHER. A BOLD FLORAL OR PAISLEY WILL CREATE A TROMPE L'OEIL (LITERALLY, "TO TRICK THE EYE") AND GIVE A SPACE REAL IDENTITY.

hand-glazed tiles in raspberry, kiwi, mango, and sunflower topped by a prominent new mantel. They removed the recessed lights that pockmarked the ceiling, replacing them with an elegant hanging spear light fixture.

Off the living room was a quirky space, a porch that had long ago been enclosed, with doors on all four sides. The Foleys turned the nearly useless spot into a library. Rather than invest in built-in bookcases, they found a pair of wrought-iron etagères (display shelves) in an antique market and stacked them with piles and piles of books. They hung an old light from a Manhattan theater lobby—one of their favorite objects—over a large reading table, which itself was dressed in a lush fabric embellished with deep, decadent fringe.

In the oversized family room, the Foleys went for a different color mood. The room faced north and got very little light, so they painted it a happy yellow and put up playful wallpaper in a rear inglenook, home to the family's century-old piano. Lighting this behemoth of a room was a problem. A pair of double sconces and two large Swedish ceiling fixtures, all gilded, were installed for a winter palace touch.

The small sitting room located between the entry hall and the kitchen also needed sprucing up. A strong dose of bohemian paisley wallpaper gave the room instant charm. The rich paper, with an inky black background and muted reds and khakis, also married a mix of furnishings, upholstered in checks, twills, and provençal prints. The cozy room quickly became the family's favorite spot to read or crowd on the loveseat to watch TV.

The kitchen had a host of problems. It had an excess of old yellowed cabinets and an island shaped, as daughter Jane pointed out, like the state of California. The appliances

[**OPPOSITE AND THIS PAGE, TOP**] SOMETIMES BIGGER IS NOT BETTER. OVERSIZED COUNTRY SWEDISH LANTERNS AND AN OLD COMMERCIAL CLOCK FACE BREAK UP THE EXPANSE OF AN EARLIER (AND TOO ROOMY) RENOVATION WITH A LIGHTHEARTED PLAYFULNESS. [**ABOVE**] A DIMINUTIVE SITTING ROOM OFF THE KITCHEN HAS BECOME THE FAMILY'S FAVORITE SPOT IN THE EVENINGS. BOHEMIAN PAISLEY WALLPAPER MAKES COZY EVEN COZIER.

TRADE TIP

WHEN IT COMES TO STYLE, YOU *CAN* TAKE IT WITH YOU.
FURNITURE, COLOR SCHEMES, AND FAVORITE OBJECTS
CAN BE PACKED UP AND TRANSPORTED AND TRANSLATED
INTO NEW INTERIORS. CASE IN POINT: THE FOLEYS' MAINE
KITCHEN, ABOVE, AND THEIR ATLANTA KITCHEN SHARE
MANY OF THE SAME ELEMENTS AND IDEAS, FROM VIKING
STOVES TO HONED BLACK COUNTERTOPS.

were ancient, and the oven didn't work at all. The coup de grace, though, was the twenty-year-old-fabric-covered walls—fragrant with two decades of cooking odors and splattered with a generation's spills and splashes. The girls pulled down the fabric themselves and discovered petrified foam beneath.

Susan, a magazine editor, began editing the décor. The cabinets, although worn, were top quality. She evaluated each cabinet as a unit with its own specific purpose. How much room did she need for pots? For mixing bowls? Graph paper in hand, she built her kitchen. In the end, the Foleys took away almost half of the cabinets—including nearly all the upper cupboards—and had the remaining cabinets professionally sprayed the brightest of whites.

The cabinetry reconfigured, Susan took stock of her countertops, made of miles of Corian, a man-made plastic. In each of their previous renovations, Susan had specified stone counters, and she wasn't wild about using Corian this time. Ultimately, though, she decided it would be wasteful to ditch a perfectly good countertop, so she retained the Corian on the counters closest to the sink. On the back wall of the kitchen, where new open-storage shelves replaced heavy upper cabinetry, the Foleys used stainless-steel countertops for a scullery effect. The awkward island

was replaced with a spare table-island topped with black granite honed to a matte finish to resemble soapstone.

To let in more light and views from their pretty garden to the kitchen, the Foleys added new banks of windows over the sink and on the two walls in the adjacent breakfast room. They installed oversized French doors to lead from the table to the kitchen porch. In a move to add charm and texture to the new/old room, they applied wide wainscoting to the ceiling

[ABOVE] TOO MANY CABINETS? IT CAN HAPPEN. HERE, AN OVERABUNDANCE OF CABINETS MADE THE KITCHEN FEEL CROWDED AND COMMERCIAL. THE FOLEYS HAD THE UPPER CABINETS REMOVED FROM TWO WALLS AND REPLACED WITH 4-INCH V GROOVE (AKA WIDE WAINSCOTING). THE REMAINING CABINETS WERE SPRAYED A CRISP, CLEAN WHITE. [OPPOSITE, ABOVE] THE FOLEYS' AIRY, CHEERY MAINE KITCHEN. [OPPOSITE, BELOW] A WORK-TABLE–CUM-ISLAND WAS FABRICATED WITH OVERSIZED TAPERED LEGS AND TOPPED WITH HONED BLACK ABSOLUT GRANITE—GIVING THE LOOK AND FEEL OF SOAPSTONE WITHOUT THE SPOTS AND STAINS.

[ABOVE] IN THE BREAKFAST ROOM, THE FOLEYS REPLACED THE SMALL SINGLE WINDOWS [LEFT], A HOLDOVER OF AN EARLIER FLAWED ADDITION, WITH BANKS OF DOUBLE-HUNG WINDOWS. THE FLAT WHITE SHEETROCK CEILING WAS COVERED WITH 4-INCH V GROOVE—INSTALLED UPSIDE DOWN TO SHOWCASE A DEEPER GROOVE AND CREATE MORE IMPACT. [BELOW] THE ORIGINAL SCREENED-IN PORCH HAD FALLEN INTO A STATE OF NEGLECT.

and to several walls and painted it a fresh, glossy white.

That southern must-have, the screened-in porch, was in good shape but a little dreary. As a weekend project, Henry and daughter Annie took down an old black awning and then painted the existing New Orleans–style trelliswork framing the screens in the same mossy green as the front-of-house shutters. They gave the chimney inside the porch a coat of cheery sunflower paint, which also helped brighten the space. A lively mix of colorful furnishings—yellow wicker sofas, a periwinkle table, and fuchsia-striped cushions—injected vitality into this formerly dark porch.

On the second floor, the remodeling touches were minimal and yet far-reaching. The Foleys rescued daughter Jane's bland box of a bedroom with wainscoting. Four-by-eight sheets of prefabricated wainscoting went up in a snap. A shallow protruding ledge finished the paneling and gave Jane, an inveterate collector, a place to display her tableaux. In the master bath, starved for light and heavy on cabinetry, the Foleys removed a pair of upper cabinets flanking the lone window. Now the light poured in. They built a new countertop over the long run of remaining lower cabinets to make a tiled window seat. The girls have taken to perching there and talking to their dad while he shaves.

Just beyond the master bedroom lay an incomprehensible maze of dressing rooms, even a smoking corner. The Foleys decided that combining these spaces would yield enough space for Susan's office—a modest space, they figured. What they didn't expect was how big the office would feel once the walls were down. With a new triple window installed in the same mullion

pattern as the rest of the house, it's Susan's prettiest and brightest office to date.

The renovation was wrapped up in just six months, and the Foleys felt right at home. They have come to learn that all they need to make the transition to a new home are a few of

TRADE TIP

WHO KNEW THAT CLOSET COMPANIES DO
MORE THAN CLOSETS? MOST OF THE BIGGER
OUTFITS ARE WILLING AND ABLE TO PUT
TOGETHER BEDROOM AND HOME OFFICE
DESIGNS SUCH AS A BUILT-IN DESK, BOOK-
SHELVES, STORAGE BENCHES, AND EVEN A
BATHROOM VANITY OR DRESSING TABLE. FROM
SKETCH TO INSTALLATION OFTEN TAKES ONLY
A COUPLE OF WEEKS. THE PRICES AREN'T BAD,
EITHER—BETTER THAN CUSTOM, CERTAINLY.

their favorite things—their piano, bistro kitchen chairs, painted kitchen hutch covered with children's artwork, and books, books, books. Susan also figured out how to carry over decorating motifs or themes from one house to the next. Each home has had a red room, a pantry with glass doors, wainscoting galore, and bright checkerboard tiles—just the kind of design continuity that gives the family a strong sense of place, even when the place keeps moving.

[ABOVE] A TEENAGE GIRL'S BLAND, BOXY ROOM WAS TRANSFORMED WITH WAINSCOTING INSTALLED THREE-QUARTERS OF THE WAY UP THE WALLS. A THREE-INCH-DEEP LEDGE TOPS THE WAINSCOTING, SERENDIPITOUSLY PROVIDING A DISPLAY LEDGE FOR COLLECTIONS OF ALL SORTS, FROM ELEPHANTS TO TROPHIES. [OPPOSITE, ABOVE] THE FOLEYS MERGED THREE CRAMPED AND NOT VERY USEFUL ROOMS TO CREATE ONE VERY FUNCTIONAL AND HOMEY HOME OFFICE. A NEW TRIPLE-BANK OF WINDOWS ALLOWS A VIEW OF THE GARDEN. A VINTAGE GARDEN LAT-TICEWORK CREATED A CHARMING BULLETIN BOARD. [OPPOSITE, BELOW] THE MASTER BATHROOM HAD A PUBLIC SIDE—IT HAPPENED TO BE ONE WAY TO ACCESS THE HOME OFFICE—WITH THE SINK ON DISPLAY (AND THE TUB AND TOILET THANKFULLY HIDDEN BEHIND A WALL OF MIRRORS). TO GIVE THE BATHROOM MORE POLISH AND PRESENCE, THE "PUBLIC" PORTION GOT A MINI-MAKEOVER WITH CHECKERBOARD TILED COUNTERTOPS, A VINTAGE-INSPIRED SINK AND FAUCET, AND A MIX OF NEW LIGHT FIXTURES FROM SLEEK TO SWEDISH COUNTRY.

HOUSE RULES

NO ONE DETAIL IS THAT IMPORTANT. In the first renovation, Susan and Henry sweated every faucet. Gradually they've come to see that no single item—light fixture, window lock, doorknob—can make or break a look. Rather, it is the coming together of *all* the elements that makes a room successful.

THINK BEYOND THE BLAH. Before they moved in, the Foleys took rolls of pictures of the blah rooms. Susan sat down with a pack of markers and a bottle of Wite-Out and began coloring and erasing, imagining the rooms transformed by the family's favorite bright colors.

A LITTLE CAN GO A LONG WAY. Changing light fixtures, enlarging windows, ripping up carpet—all can dramatically change the way a room feels without adding a square foot.

LET THE KIDS CONTROL SOME DECISIONS. Glitter paint on the bedroom walls, a shelf for the toy elephant collection—why not? Susan found that the buy-in she got from the kids' involvement was worth it. The girls have developed a great eye and now like to tag along on trips to flooring showrooms and antique hardware sources.

Making the Most of Modern

[the program] Accomplished in twelve months

- Expand a small kitchen encompassing a labyrinth of staff rooms to form a large kitchen-cum–art gallery
- Infuse the living room and the dining room with light
- Take a master bath from seventies kitsch to sleek contemporary
- Ditch a conversation pit in favor of a reading room
- Construct his-and-hers home offices, each with its own style

ARNOLD AND JANE ADLIN—HE AN INVESTMENT ANALYST, she a curator of modern art—had raised their two children in a traditional four-square home in a mid-Atlantic suburb. But as the kids got bigger, the Adlins craved more space for them—and their cars, now that there were four drivers in the family. They decided to look for a home that gave each member of the family a bit more privacy.

That was the main agenda. With respect to the style of the house, the Adlins didn't have anything particular in mind. But when they came across a flat-roofed modern house with two garages on a spectacular site, they knew they had found something special. The house, which was built in the early seventies à la Richard Neutra, with a bit of

Frank Lloyd Wright influence in the stacked stonework, stood out in their neck of the woods, where most homes were conventional white clapboard colonials.

The Adlins hadn't exactly pictured themselves in such a contemporary house, but they immediately felt at home with the clean, sleek style and the wall-to-wall windows and glass doors, which almost seemed to bring the outside inside. The Adlins had decorated their previous home in a modern manner, so, in a sense, this house took them in the same direction they were already going.

As they walked through the property and considered

ONCE CONSIDERED TERRIBLY '70S AND ULTRA-DÉMODÉ, THE ADLINS' NEWLY UPDATED MODERN HOUSE NOW ATTRACTS PLENTY OF NEIGHBORHOOD ATTENTION, INCLUDING BONA-FIDE OFFERS STUFFED IN THE MAILBOX FROM PROSPECTIVE BUYERS.

[ABOVE] A SIMPLE RECTANGULAR POOL, IN KEEPING WITH THE OVERALL MODERN AESTHETIC OF THE HOUSE, REPLACED A DATED SWIM-IN/SWIM-OUT GROTTO AFFAIR. [RIGHT] ALTHOUGH THE ACTUAL FOOTPRINT OF THE ADLINS' HOME WAS VIRTUALLY UNCHANGED, THEY HAD THE INTERIOR WALLS MOVED, SOMETIMES JUST A FOOT OR TWO THIS WAY OR THAT, WHICH GAVE THE HOUSE A CLEAN, CONTEMPORARY FEEL.

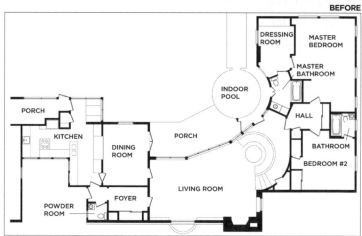

BEFORE

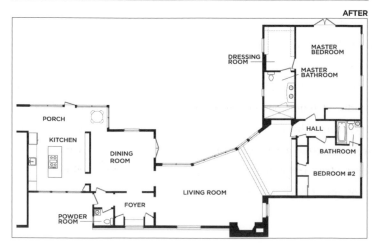

AFTER

putting in a bid, the Adlins' first thought was "What a great house! Maybe we'll just throw some paint around, clean things up, take care of some landscaping, and be *fini*." The house was less than twenty-five years old, so they assumed it was in relatively good condition, especially from their perspective; they were moving from a home that was seventy-five years old, so how bad could this one be? They bought the place and, not long after, took up residence.

Well, as they say, looks can be deceiving. Despite a passing grade from the engineer (which turned out to be inaccurate), the flat-roofed building had a pile of problems. It was raining the day the family moved in, and water was pouring down through the ceiling and into the light fixtures. When the Adlins had the ceiling opened to investigate, methane gas escaped, indicating extensive rot. As it turned out, the entire roof was rotted, the underlying support was rotted, the substructure was rotted—and all of it had to be replaced. "We knew that first day that we were in very big trouble," said Jane.

After the roof fiasco, the Adlins settled in, albeit a little uneasily. Very little time went by before they saw problems in the house that had less to do with leaks than with layout. They decided the house could really use bigger openings between the rooms to create more openness and flow—not to mention an updated kitchen and all new baths. The Adlins decided to renovate after all and began interviewing professionals for the job.

The first person on board was the contractor, who was highly recommended by their former and much-trusted next-door neighbor. Next, the couple started shopping for an architect. They chose someone local on the theory he'd be able to get all the necessary variances through the system faster. After a few months, though, the architect hadn't produced much beyond minor drawings, and the Adlins moved on. This time they went for a big-name Manhattan architect with a SoHo sensibility. He was brimming with great ideas and came up with a terrific plan. The Adlins were impressed. But when the architect constructed a

model of the house, the contractor stepped in and pointed out that it couldn't be built. There were no supporting structures for all the glass he'd added. A second architect bit the dust. Finally, the Adlins decided to hire one of the architects they'd originally interviewed. He went back to the drawing board, literally, and came up with brand-new ideas and plans.

From the day this third and final architect came on board to the end of the project, construction took just over a year. The job was fast-tracked, meaning that certain parts of the house were constructed before the plan for the rest of the house was resolved. This strategy involved risks—the windows might not be in the right location, walls might need to be reopened to accommodate plumbing or electrical wiring that hadn't been anticipated. Luckily, the Adlins' team avoided design redos and mishaps, although the approach made predicting a clear budget next to impossible. The Adlins had to have faith that between their

contractor and architect, they'd be advised when their design decisions and desires were too expensive to implement.

The renovation began in the single-story section of the house, which comprised the kitchen, living spaces, master bedroom, and home offices. With all that entirely sealed off, the family moved into the two-story section, a former staff wing, which contained a side entrance from the driveway, three bedrooms, two baths, a sitting room, and a laundry room. One son had just gone off to college, so the parents took over his room and made do with a pint-size refrigerator and a hot plate. Their daughter, still in high school, lived through the renovation with them.

The first order of construction was the makeover of the small, compartmentalized, L-shaped staff kitchen, which had been designed by the previous owners, an older couple, for their two live-in helpers. The Adlins first moved the wall between the kitchen and the dining room, yielding a lovely square dining room with enough space for a sideboard-server—as *they* did not have live-in servers. The dining room now overlapped the breakfast area at one end, creating a much more integrated connection between the kitchen and the rest of the house. Next, they enlarged the kitchen by pushing its front wall forward into an exterior front atrium. They eliminated interior pantries and closets and incorporated a former servant's porch as well. Now they had a spacious eat-in kitchen with wall-to-wall windows facing the view. For the cabinetry, Jane chose black wood with a visible grain. Black may seem like an odd choice in a gleaming new kitchen, but Jane found that the matte black cabinetry receded, allowing her ever-changing

TRADE TIP

THE OPEN AND EXPOSED GRAIN OF THE ADLINS' KITCHEN CABINETS MAKES THE BLACK STAIN, ALWAYS SUBJECT TO FINGERPRINTING AND SPOTTING, MORE FORGIVING AND EASIER TO MAINTAIN. PATTERN—THE GRAIN, IN THIS CASE—IS A CONCEALER.

display of artwork on the walls to take center stage. The Adlins went from a galley kitchen to a gallery kitchen.

The dining room was now partially open to the kitchen. Why not keep going? The Adlins decided to open the once narrow dining room to the front hall, too. The front hall had been sealed off from the rest of the house. The architect suggested they put in pocket doors, giving them the option to close off the space when they wanted a little more intimacy during a dinner party. In addition, they replaced a closet in the entry with a window seat beneath a new picture window. Upon entry, guests are now greeted with a front-to-back view of the Adlins' beautiful property.

The living room was the next space to be reviewed and reconfigured. It was accessible only through single closed doors from the entry and the dining room. The prior owners clearly liked to close off their spaces. Not so the Adlins, who enlarged both door openings and removed the built-in

[**ABOVE**] ADDING FLOOR-TO-CEILING WINDOWS GAVE THE DINING ROOM A SOARING SENSE OF SPACE AND AN UNENDING SOURCE OF LIGHT. SIMPLE FURNISHINGS REITERATE THE CLEAN LINES OF THE ARCHITECTURE. [**BELOW**] TO MAKE A COMFORTABLE EATING AREA, THE ADLINS ENLARGED THE ORIGINAL CRAMPED KITCHEN BY INCORPORATING SPACE FROM AN ADJACENT ATRIUM AND A BUTLER'S PANTRY (NOW SANS BUTLER).

[**RIGHT**] *BEFORE:* A FOREBODING-LOOKING FIREPLACE PUT A DAMPER ON THE LIVING ROOM. [**ABOVE**] *AFTER:* SOME SIMPLE REPOINTING OF THE STONE, POWERWASHING OF THE CEMENT MANTEL, AND PAINTING OF THE WINDOW FRAMES HELPED LIGHTEN THE OVERALL EFFECT OF THE FRANK LLOYD WRIGHT–INSPIRED STONE FIREPLACE AND FLANKING WALL, WHICH THE ADLINS DECIDED TO LEAVE INTACT. THE FURNITURE ARRANGEMENT FELT AWKWARD, GIVEN THE LIMITED FLOOR SPACE; THEY RESOLVED THIS WITH A CANTILEVERED BENCH, OBVIATING THE NEED FOR A SOFA.

bookcases that hemmed in the windows. On the rear wall they replaced the old and cloudy glass doors with streamlined new ones. Rather than sliding, the doors recede into the floor via a complicated and expensive system that the previous owners had installed and the Adlins chose to keep. The wall's massive stacked-stone fireplace simply needed minor restoration and repointing. It burned a beautiful fire.

The room had other quirks as well. A funky seventies-style built-in conversation pit with a round banquette framed by a book balcony, accessible from the living room via odd, narrow, wall-hugging steps, was the next casualty. First, the Adlins brought forward the elevated floor of the book balcony. The conversation pit but a memory, the Adlins lined the walls of their new library/reading room with handsome mahogany bookcases and furnished it with a pair of leather chairs. They knew those awkward stairs to the new area had to be relocated but were on the fence about whether to move them to the left, right, or center. Finally, they decided to have them span the entire width of the room, giving the room a sense of breadth and fresh air.

With the main rooms redone, it was time to move on to the auxiliary ones. The Adlins built themselves two home offices, a decision Arnold said has worked out extremely well. Jane's office, down a flight of stairs near the bedroom, is colorful and loaded with eccentric art, memorabilia, and keepsakes. Arnold's office has a more intellectual tone and is filled with reams of reading material.

Next to Arnold's new office was the old master bedroom and bath, which contained another seventies

[BELOW] *BEFORE:* A RETRO LEFTOVER— A SO-CALLED CONVERSATION PIT—CREATED TRAFFIC FLOW PROBLEMS. [**ABOVE**] *AFTER:* THE EXISTING STEPS WERE EXPANDED TO THE FULL WIDTH OF THE ROOM, CREATING BETTER ACCESS AND A WELCOMING AND MORE SOCIABLE SCENARIO. A COAT OF SOFT GRAY LIGHTENED UP THE HEAVY WOOD BEAMS.

To emphatically link one space to another several steps below or above, the stairs can span the length or breadth of the rooms' openings. The stairs make wonderful overflow seating when you have a crowd.

SOFTENING THE HARD EDGE OF MODERN: ORIGINAL FIELDSTONE FLOORS, A STACKED STONE FIREPLACE, AND STREAMLINED FURNITURE WERE ARTFULLY JUXTAPOSED AGAINST A WALL-TO-WALL LIBRARY FULL OF BOOKS AND THE GREENERY OF PLANTS.

[**BELOW**] *BEFORE:* FORMICA COUNTERS, VINYL TILES, OLD-FASHIONED DRESSING-ROOM LIGHTS, AND DITSY WALLPAPER MADE THE BATHROOM FEEL DREARY AND OUT-OF-DATE.
[**RIGHT**] *AFTER:* A COUNTER OF 2-INCH-THICK HONED VENETIAN MARBLE, AN OVERSIZED MIRROR, AND AN ALL-GLASS SHOWER STALL CREATE A SYBARITE'S DELIGHT. AS THE BEFORE AND AFTER FLOOR PLANS ON PAGE 22 SHOW, THE SIZE OF THE BATH-ROOM STAYED THE SAME, BUT THE SHAPE WAS RECONFIGURED FROM AN ODDLY CURVED AND ANGLED SPACE WITH CONFLICT-ING GEOMETRY INTO A CLEAN RECTANGLE.

anachronism. You could say the house shared an, uh, original feature with the Playboy mansion: a large indoor hot tub in a louvered cupola featuring a water channel to an outdoor pool, so one could swim from inside to outside. That wasn't going to work for the Adlins. They redesigned the bathroom with a striking custom bowed-front vanity. In the bedroom, the Adlins replaced the old windows with a pair of doors that lead directly out to the backyard and a newly redone pool.

Finally, to create a guest suite for their elderly parents, who visited often, the Adlins transformed the former staff dining

THE MASTER BEDROOM, WITH DOORS OUT TO THE POOL AND GROUNDS, BEGAN LIFE WITH MORE PLANES THAN AN AIRPORT. AS A 14-SIDED ROOM, IT WAS A VERITABLE JIGSAW PUZZLE. SCRAPING OUT ALL OF THE PLANES AND ANGLES AND USING ONLY CLEAN-LINED FURNISHINGS TRANSFORMED A HODGE-PODGE INTO A TRANQUIL REPOSE.

hall and part of the staff porch off the kitchen into a ground-floor bed-sitting room and separate bath. With its own door from the back, guests now had real privacy from the rest of the house and family.

Once the house was, indeed, finally *fini,* the Adlins admitted to a few coulda-woulda-shoulda moments, such as paving the driveway instead of using stones, said Jane, who likes the look of the gravel but finds it to be rough during snowy winters. Jane also fought for limestone in the kitchen (Arnold favored marble), and while she pre-vailed, the limestone has proved easy to scratch and hard to maintain.

So would they do it all again? No, said Arnold, not if they'd known how much renovation was needed. Then he equivocated. Of course, having seen the value of modern homes rise in their neighborhood, they know their invest-ment can be recouped if and when they sell. Most important, at the end of the day, they're living in the most beautiful house they've ever owned.

From Gloomy to Glamorous

[the program] Accomplished in eleven months

- Hollow out a two-story entryway
- Reconfigure a staircase
- Enlarge the family room and bump out the kitchen and the dining room
- Relocate the master bedroom
- Install new arched windows throughout the house
- Add a well-detailed three-story deck

BARBARA AND JACK QUINLAN HAD BEEN LOOKING AT HOUSES for three years before they put in an offer on a Mediterranean in a coastal town on the eastern seaboard, close to where Jack grew up. Dark and gloomy, it was known in the neighborhood as the haunted house. More than fifty prospective buyers had walked through the old house, circa 1924, and subsequently walked right out. But the Quinlans wanted a value investment—that is, the worst house on a good block. This was not only the worst on the block but the worst they'd ever seen.

The Quinlans knew they could afford the house but questioned whether they could afford the renovation. Absolutely everything needed to be done. The day they saw the house, the Quinlans came back with a friend, an electrician, who was familiar with remodeling, and based on his encouraging guesstimate decided to take the plunge.

Barbara's first call was to Christopher Powell, an architect whose work she had admired at a neighboring home. Before he even stepped foot inside, his design mind started working. The rear of the house, four full above-ground levels, was flat and featureless—like an Italian tenement building, said Barbara. But it hadn't always been that way. In researching the house, Chris discovered it had been built by

THE QUINLANS RESTORED THE BEAUTY OF THEIR 1920S HOME, WHICH WAS MASKED BY DECADES OF NEGLECT AND YEARS OF OVERGROWTH, AND HAD ONCE BEEN DUBBED THE DOG ON DOGWOOD STREET. A FRONT DOOR WITH RIBBED GLASS BROUGHT LIGHT TO THE DOWNSTAIRS ENTRANCE HALL WITHOUT SACRIFICING PRIVACY.

one of the Ringling Brothers for his son and daughter-in-law and was originally a nice-looking Mediterranean with detail and life on its façade. But, as is done with many older homes, more interior space was created at the expense of three-dimensional elements. Porches and other exterior features were closed in, stripping away the home's detail.

The overarching strategy for the house was to make the rooms work for the Quinlans and their two small sons while adding as little square footage as possible. At the same

TRADE TIP

YOU CAN PAY TO HAVE FILL TAKEN AWAY, AND YOU CAN PAY TO HAVE FILL ADDED. IF YOU CAN COMBINE THE TWO, YOU'VE GOT IT MADE. WHEN BUILDING FOUNDATION WALLS TO LEVEL THE YARD, THE QUINLANS FOUND AN EXCAVATOR WHO MIXED THE ROCKS TAKEN FROM THE PROPERTY WITH BROKEN-UP OLD CEMENT SIDEWALKS FROM AN AREA UPSTATE. THE 13-FOOT WALL IS STRONG ENOUGH TO TAKE A MORTAR, CAME IN UNDER BUDGET, AND IS COMPLETELY CONCEALED BY WOODLAND.

time, the Quinlans sought to restore dimension and interest by bumping out exterior walls and breaking down interior ones, relocating rooms, and building a three-story deck at the back of the house.

The renovation started off with a bang with the demolition. The Quinlans were eager to get started and reasoned that they could manage the demolition process themselves. They figured that by opening up the walls before getting a contractor's bid they would face fewer surprises, fewer of those oh-no moments when the contractor informs you that your electrical system is antiquated and your plumbing

[ABOVE] THE GLOOMY FORMER BREAKFAST ROOM WAS INCORPORATED INTO THE NOW LIGHT-FLOODED DINING ROOM. [FAR LEFT] A TASTE OF TUSCANY . . . ON THE SHORES OF NEW YORK. OLD PHOTOS PROVIDED CLUES AS TO HOW TO ARTFULLY RESTORE THIS FORMERLY ROMANTIC AND GRAND MEDITERRANEAN HOME. [LEFT] THE FIRST- (I.E., GROUND-) FLOOR ENTRANCE IS UNUSUAL AT BEST. THIS LOWER LEVEL IS HOME TO A BILLIARD ROOM, A GUEST ROOM, AND JACK'S OFFICE. A CIRCULAR STAIR LEADS TO THE SECOND-FLOOR LIVING, DINING, KITCHEN, AND FAMILY ROOMS. WANTING TO LINK THE TWO LEVELS, THE QUINLANS HAD THE GENIUS IDEA TO CUT A HOLE, LITERALLY, IN THE LIVING ROOM FLOOR. THE CUTOUT WAS A TWOFOLD SUCCESS. LIGHT FLOODED THE GROUND-LEVEL ENTRY, AND THE PARENTS CAN WATCH THE YOUNG BOYS AS THEY RATTLE AND ROLL ON THE STONE FLOOR BELOW.

corroded. That's just what happened with the Quinlans, who realized they would need to install all new heating, air-conditioning, and plumbing systems. When it came to the electrical system, the architect advised them to not just replace the existing system (which blew out when a hairdryer and a dishwasher were on at the same time) but to upgrade it—to install two 100-amp units in case they added a swimming pool in the future.

The Quinlans also discovered that the roof was leaky—really leaky. Barbara and Jack came to the site one rainy day and found water sluicing through all four floors of the house. With the demolition crew on site and the walls exposed, the Quinlans could also see evidence of termites. All the wood framing on one side of the house had rotted away, and the house was being supported only by the stucco and wire lathe. A bit unnerved, Jack called in a structural engineer, who went through the house with a fine-toothed comb. This time there was good news. The house was built on a cement slab and anchored in natural rock. It had a solid foundation that would last forever.

TRADE TIP

WINDOWS AND DOORWAYS DO MORE THAN LET IN LIGHT AND ALLOW FOR PASSAGE. DEPENDING ON WHERE THEY'RE PLACED, THEY CAN CREATE VISUAL RELATIONSHIPS BETWEEN ROOMS, WHICH IN TURN CREATE A SUBTLE BUT STRONG OVERALL SENSE OF BALANCE AND HARMONY WITHIN THE HOUSE. DOORS CAN LINE UP SO THAT YOU LOOK FROM ONE THROUGH ANOTHER AND EVEN THROUGH ANOTHER.

[**OPPOSITE**] THE HOME'S POSITIVES WERE EMPHASIZED, AGGRANDIZED EVEN. ARCHED WINDOWS WERE SUPERSIZED THROUGHOUT—UNIMAGINABLE WHEN THE HOUSE WAS BUILT IN THE 1920S BEFORE INSULATED GLASS. [**ABOVE**] THE KITCHEN, FORMERLY DARK AND CLOSED-IN [**BELOW**], WAS OPENED UP ON ALL SIDES TO CAPTURE VIEWS OF THE INTERIOR ROOMS AND THE WATER BEYOND. THE ROOM IS NOW SO INVITING, IT HAS BECOME HANGOUT-CENTRAL FOR THE FAMILY. [**RIGHT**] MID-RENOVATION, THE QUINLANS DECIDED TO ADD A PASS-THROUGH BETWEEN THE KITCHEN AND LIVING ROOM TO CATCH A NEWFOUND VIEW OF THE WATER (ONCE THE AUTUMN LEAVES FELL, THEY GOT A CLEAR SHOT OF THE BAY).

from gloomy to glamorous | 37

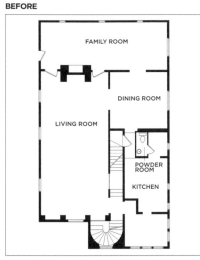

FAMILY ROOM

DINING ROOM

LIVING ROOM

POWDER ROOM

KITCHEN

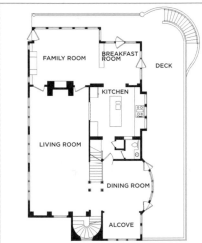

FAMILY ROOM

BREAKFAST ROOM

DECK

KITCHEN

LIVING ROOM

DINING ROOM

ALCOVE

While the demolition crew continued to pound away for six weeks, Barbara and Chris fine-tuned the designs, submitted paperwork to the town architectural review board, and got estimates from several contractors. The bids were, not surprisingly, all over the map, and Barbara hired the low-price guy. At their first meeting, however, he started listing all the extras. The relationship ended there. The contractor they ultimately used, Raul Monges, assured the Quinlans that he would keep add-ons to a minimum, and he held true to his word.

The renovation began on the ground floor, which, oddly, was one level below the main floor yet included the front door. Faced with an entrance that made the Quinlans feel like they were in a catacomb, the architect briefly considered building an exterior stone staircase before dismissing the idea as too costly and,

with all the wet weather, too hazardous. Instead, he chose to make the existing entrance work with some modifications—scraping out the spacious entrance hall and removing a surfeit of small closets and adding light and detail in their place. He also installed a floor-to-ceiling arched window in the ground-floor foyer and a pair of French doors that led to what became the billiard room.

Barbara then came up with an unorthodox and dramatic idea: Why not cut a square into the ceiling of the entry and floor of the living room directly above to make a kind of giant interior skylight, albeit one without glass? The generously sized living room ran the length of the house and could easily withstand a 9 by 7-foot cutout. Surrounded by a clean-lined iron railing, the opening suffused the entry below with light and air, turning it into an interior courtyard of sorts. A

[LEFT] THE TV/FAMILY DINING ROOM WAS ORIGINALLY CONCEIVED AS ONE CONTIGUOUS SPACE, BUT AS THE WALLS WERE FRAMED, THE ROOM LOOKED RUN-ON AND ILL DEFINED. A HALF-WALL SOLVED THE PROBLEM, PLUS IT CREATED AN ANCHOR FOR THE SEATING ARRANGEMENT. [OPPOSITE, ABOVE] ONLY SLIGHT CHANGES WERE MADE TO THE FOOTPRINT OF THE HOUSE VIA SMALL BUMP-OUTS THAT REQUIRED NO FOUNDATIONAL UNDERPINNINGS. IN THE FAMILY ROOM, ONE SUCH BUMP-OUT YIELDED A RECESS FOR THE COUCH. [OPPOSITE, BELOW] MOVING-IN DAY, THE BEST REWARD OF RENOVATION.

grand chandelier was suspended through the space. When the sun hits, every one of its prismatic crystals shatters a rainbow of light into the entry. The railing elegantly frames the space, and when guests arrive, inevitably one of the Quinlans hangs over the railing, welcoming and inviting them up.

The makeover of the main floor presented another challenge. A staircase with a series of landings hemmed in by narrow walls, like a tunnel, closed off the living room on one side from the dining room on the other. The Quinlans decided to eliminate the landings, thus shortening the run of the stairs, and to knock down the walls to expose the staircase. But solving one problem revealed another. With the walls down, the Quinlans realized they needed some definition to keep all the public rooms from running together. The architect suggested a trio of arches leading

from the staircase to the living room.

With walls down and arches up, it was time to focus on the function of the rooms. The kitchen was at one end of the house, the family room directly at the other—and the Quinlans wanted them side by side. Flipping the kitchen

SINCE THE FRONT OF THE HOUSE WAS ACCESSIBLE ONLY THROUGH A LOWER
LEVEL FRONT DOOR, THE QUINLANS DECIDED (AT THE ELEVENTH HOUR!) TO ADD
A SMALL DOOR TO THE FAMILY ROOM BUMP-OUT. IN ONE FELL SWOOP, THE NEW
DOOR CREATED ACCESS TO AN UPPER TERRACE WITH WATER VIEWS AND
ADDED DETAIL TO THE FORTRESS-LIKE FEELING OF THE FRONT FAÇADE.

TRADE TIP

IT'S NATURAL TO ASSUME THAT EVERY ADDITION IS BUILT
ON A SOLID FOUNDATION, BUT THAT'S NOT ALWAYS THE
CASE—OR ALWAYS NECESSARY. WHEN CREATING SMALL
NEW SPACES OR ENLARGING EXISTING ONES BY BUMPING
OUT ONLY A FEW FEET OR SO, LIKE IN THE QUINLAN'S
DINING ROOM BAY, THE RATIO IS 1:3—THAT IS, IF LESS
THAN ONE-THIRD OF THE ORIGINAL ROOM'S DEPTH IS
BEING ADDED ON, THE ADDITION MAY BE ABLE TO BE
CANTILEVERED OR SIMPLY SIT ON AN EXISTING TERRACE
OR PORCH.

and the dining room, which was at the center of the house, was the obvious move to make. Once switched into the rectangular dining room, though, the kitchen felt just a little too narrow for the big island Barbara had in mind. It was clear they had to add—but only a few feet. Luckily, they didn't have to pour a new foundation because, as the architect pointed out, they could bump out and simply build the addition on the surface of the new deck.

The layout in the new kitchen was determined by Barbara's strong desire to cook with a view. She wanted to be able to stand at the stove and look out through a window at the pretty backyard and wetlands beyond. And she liked the idea of working at the sink in the island and being able to see her guests in the living room. At first Barbara thought she would just open up the kitchen to the living room with a wide walk-through. In planning the new kitchen, however, Barbara realized she didn't want to give up a whole wall where she could place a message center with phone and computer. Instead, she struck a compromise: a wide window-height opening, countertop to ceiling, framed to allow the rooms to feel visually connected.

The family room needed a little extra space, too, so the room was bumped out 3½ feet to create a recess for a sofa. Once again, there was no need to pour a foundation for such a small amount of footage. Finally, the Quinlans added a glass door to the long bank of windows in the room leading out to a terrace, with a view of the water beyond.

On the third floor, a couple of rooms exchanged identity and purpose. The master bedroom was relocated to the opposite end in a new space created by combining two small bedrooms. The former master became a new children's room for the two toddlers. Meanwhile, both the master and children's baths were completely gutted and redone. One of the key considerations in the master was a large shower, a request from Jack—and quite a reasonable one, as he's 6 foot 3 and needs plenty of elbow room. Another was to make room for a washer-dryer upstairs. The architect was able to fit stacking units into a closet near the master

HOUSE RULES

EXPLORE YOUR OPTIONS. Shocked by the initial cost of new windows, the Quinlans asked the architect to find another supplier. He discovered the Canadian-based Norco. When the cost for the oversized triple arches in the living room came in exorbitantly high, the Quinlans decided to make them nonoperable, which reduced their cost drastically by doing away with the need for hardware and custom screens. The look is cleaner and less cluttered.

BUYER, BE AWARE. The Quinlans purchased directly from large home improvement stores wherever they could, armed with a list from the contractor for particular plumbing fixtures, electrical needs, and cabinets. Sheetrock and lumber were about the only items supplied by the contractor.

DON'T BE HOODWINKED BY THE FANCY STUFF. When prices for the pro-style oven hood came in high, the Quinlans decided on a greatly simplified version by an old-time manufacturer: Vent-a-Hood. As it turned out, the spare hood design is one of their favorite kitchen features.

BUILD TO SCALE. The size of columns that could be used on the interior was restricted by the depth of the wall, so the architect used 6-inch columns as opposed to 8- or 10-inch. To keep them from looking like toothpicks, Chris used pairs to add substance, two on each side of the arch.

ONE PERSON'S TRASH . . . Barbara took a valuable chandelier she didn't like to an antique lighting store and traded it in for two she adores. These now hang over the kitchen counter.

TAKE THE LOW-MAINTENANCE ROUTE. When choosing whether to paint the exterior, which would have required constant maintenance and upkeep, or to use colored stucco, the Quinlans chose the latter. The stucco turns darker when it is wet and lighter when it dries out. They like it both ways. Aside from the deck and trim, they never have to repaint.

SOMETIMES A LONG, NARROW ROOM IS EASIER TO FURNISH THAN A BIG SQUARE ONE. THE MASTER BEDROOM DIVIDED LOGICALLY INTO TWO ZONES, SEPARATED BY THE ENTRY DOOR—SLEEPING ON ONE SIDE AND TV AND LOUNGING ON THE OTHER. THOUGH THE ROOM IS SHORT ON FURNISHINGS, THE HIGH-CONTRAST BLACK-AND-WHITE COLOR SCHEME PUNCHES IT UP A NOTCH.

where they could, patched where they couldn't, and stained all the boards a uniform deep shade to even out textural differences. However, most of the old windows had to go. The house was too closed in, with a lot of little windows punched randomly about the back. The Quinlans put in new, larger windows, many of them arched, except on the bedroom floor, where they retained a few of the original leaded Hobst windows. To let in more light, they relocated and enlarged other window openings. All this did wonders for the continuity of the home, particularly with respect to the oversized triple-arched windows in the living room. Arches, in fact, are a signature in the house. There's one place at the bottom of the stairs where the Quinlans can stand and see twenty-three arches.

The Quinlans moved into their newly refreshed house less than eleven months from closing, not bad in the world of renovation. What's more, the project was on budget, with the exception of the deck, which turned out to be elaborate and expensive. Still, the Quinlans are thrilled, and the house has been drawing attention from passersby. Commercial agents and location scouts often stop by and knock on their door, looking to shoot there. Friends come over and never want to leave, finding the Quinlans' house no longer haunted but happy, light-filled, and welcoming.

bedroom, and that has turned out to be quite convenient. The Quinlans' big bed is a handy place to fold and sort laundry.

Throughout the house, the Quinlans left the original wood floors intact

THE QUINLANS FORGED THE NARROW DINING ROOM OUT OF WHAT WAS ONCE
THE KITCHEN. TO ADD ENOUGH WIDTH TO COMFORTABLY PASS BY THE TABLE,
THEY INSTALLED A BAY WITH DOORS LEADING TO THE SECOND-FLOOR TERRACE.
THEY ALSO OPENED UP AN ADJACENT PANTRY TO ALLOW FOR A SECOND SMALL
DINING TABLE—PERFECT FOR BOTH *DINERS À DEUX* AND A KIDS-ONLY TABLE.

The Realists

[the program] Accomplished in eighteen months

- Colonize the basement to incorporate a home theater and wine cellar
- Enlarge a greenhouse and install a true conservatory
- Supercharge the heat, air, audio, and video systems
- Subdivide a colossal flat-roofed 1970s Florida room with sliding doors into a paneled family room and gentleman's game room
- Reconfigure a dark, dungeon-like master bath into a chic "en suite"
- Create a bedroom loft for a teen daughter with a spiral staircase to her personal atelier

BELIEVING, AS ALL TEXANS DO, THAT ANYTHING WESTERN IS better, Nancy and John Tomasso imported an all-star western building team lock, stock, and barrel to renovate their home—a 1930s brick house in New York State. The Tomassos knew and trusted this particular crew; the architect, the contractor, and the workers had renovated their ski home in Jackson, Wyoming. Between phone, fax, and computer, the Tomassos could keep in daily touch with the architect. As for the contractors, they were planning to pack their tool bags and move right in.

The job was going to be a big one. The scope of the project would touch every room of the house, from major construction endeavors, such as turning the basement and the attic into usable spaces, to the smallest and finest of decorative details.

The Tomassos went into the renovation process assuming, wisely, that it was going to "cost twice as much and take twice as long" as estimated (hey, they had renovated before!). They wanted to do things right and were savvy enough to know that there are no real shortcuts to quality. So, being realistic by nature, and having previously worked with their assembled team, the Tomassos didn't agonize over the budget or submit their plans for multiple bids. Of course, additions and changes inevitably crept in, but they expected those and took them in stride.

THE FRONT OF THE HOUSE, THANKFULLY, REQUIRED LITTLE RENOVATION. THE ORIGINAL DETAILING AND EXTRAORDINARY DOOR SURROUND WERE ALL INTACT AND NEEDED ONLY RESTORATION; EXISTING LANTERNS AND WINDOW GRILLES WERE REFURBISHED TO THEIR EARLY GRANDEUR.

Because the house was already big enough for the Tomassos and their preteen daughter, Jenny, little was added to the actual footprint. Still, they needed to file for the requisite number of permits to authorize changes. Even though Nancy declared the multitude of codes and regulations a "pain," she knew it was best to dot her *i*'s and cross her *t*'s. As it turned out, the municipal zoning boards were receptive and cooperative. Here, for a change, was a family who wanted to restore a home without increasing square footage. Their plans were quickly approved.

The Tomassos began the process by upgrading the home's inner workings. They decided to "supercharge" the house. They installed monster cables to power all the systems: electrical, security, intercom, audio, and video. They supplemented an intricate heating system, comprising a Hydronic heated floor system that brought heat to all of the bathrooms and many of the rooms, by a network of HydroAir ducts.

Next, they decided to plumb the depths and develop the basement. The goal was to dramatically transform a dank and meaningless space to a series of new rooms, including a home theater, a climate-controlled 1,500-bottle wine cellar, a bath and a half, a laundry room, and an exercise area. John used his Trojan House (pun intended) strategy for the home theater. Nancy did not want a TV in every room, and she did not want the family room to be dominated by a supersized TV, either. John suggested a media room in the basement, and the project snowballed from there. A home theater company out of Palm Beach installed a front projection system. The twelve-seat theater and stage, complete with electronically operated velvet

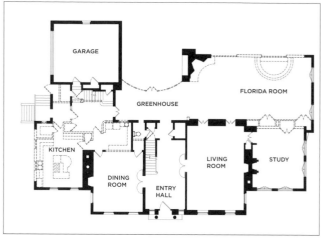

BEFORE

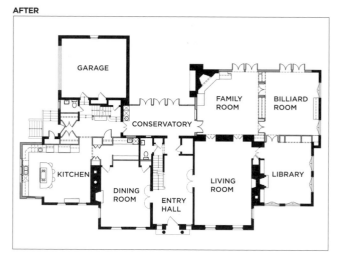

AFTER

[**ABOVE**] THE HOUSE WAS BIG ENOUGH, PLENTY BIG, BUT THERE WASN'T ROOM WHERE THE TOMASSOS NEEDED IT. THEY HAD THE KITCHEN/SITTING ROOM INCREASED BY 8 FEET AND THE CAVERNOUS FAMILY ROOM DIVIDED IN HALF. [**LEFT**] WHEN THE TOMASSOS COLONIZED THE BASEMENT THEY TREATED THE WALLS WITH A STUCCO-LIKE FINISH AND THE STEPS WITH TERRA-COTTA TILES AND HANDMADE INSERTS. [**OPPOSITE, ABOVE**] THE MILLWORK AND THE DETAILING IN THE ENTRY HALL WERE EXTRAVAGANT—BUT A SPANKING NEW SHINY MARBLE FLOOR (BETTER SUITED TO A HOTEL BATH THAN A GRAND RECEPTION HALL) HAD TO GO. THE TOMASSOS ORDERED CUSTOM OVERSIZED HONED MARBLE FROM ITALY. THE 28 BY 28-INCH STONES WERE NOT AS ONEROUSLY EXPENSIVE AS YOU MIGHT EXPECT—BUT THEY REQUIRED A LOOOOONG LEAD TIME. [**OPPOSITE, BELOW**] SIX DISCRETE WINDOW PANELS IN A CUSTOM-DESIGNED FRONT DOOR KEEP THE ENTRY BATHED IN LIGHT.

TRADE TIP

TRYING TO CONCEAL AWKWARD
CENTRAL HEATING OR AIR-
CONDITIONING UNITS IS LIKE
DEALING WITH AN ELEPHANT IN
THE ROOM. ONE WAY TO ARTFULLY
CAMOUFLAGE THEM IS WITH
ATTRACTIVE AND AUTHENTIC WIRE
GRILLES IN PATTERNS RANGING
FROM FRENCH COUNTRY CHICKEN
WIRES TO GREEK KEY GRIDS,
AVAILABLE FROM HOME RENOVA-
TOR CATALOGUES. STANDARD-
ISSUE MOLDING AND TRIM PIECES
TURN AN ELEPHANT ELEGANT.

[ABOVE AND RIGHT] AN UNORTHODOX BUT INGEN-IOUS IDEA FOR THE DINING ROOM: TWO SMALLER TABLES RATHER THAN ONE LARGER ONE. AS A FAM-ILY OF JUST THREE, THE TOMASSOS DIDN'T WANT TO FEEL LONELY AROUND A LARGE DINING TABLE. THE PAIR OF WALNUT DINING TABLES WORK INDI-VIDUALLY, BANQUET STYLE, OR AS AN OVERSIZED SQUARE.

curtains, has already been the venue for countless singing and dancing per-formances by Jenny and her young friends. Terra-cotta tiles with hand-painted Mexicana accents and stucco walls add old-world Hollywood glamour.

Back on the main floor, the entrance hall was due for a redo, but just a few cosmetic touch-ups made a big differ-ence. The entry had a shiny (too shiny) marble floor when the Tomassos bought the house. Nancy envisioned a matte marble floor in large 3-foot squares. She found a supplier in Italy and had the tiles shipped. Almost any-thing is possible if you allow yourself enough lead time (and budget).

The living room, with its exquisite moldings, elegant details, and generous proportions, was, fortunately, simply in need of a few restorative touches. The only problem involved the new heat/air systems, which stood 30 inches high on the beautiful plaster walls. How to conceal these very visible units? One of the painters volunteered to make a plaster mold, creating a unique and appropriate cover. Not only are the units (here and in the entry hall as well) virtually invisible, but they're actually quite artful.

In the dining room, Nancy, always realistic but rarely routine in her approach, decided she'd like to have *two* identical tables to give her the most flexibility for dinner parties. The custom-made tables could be combined end to end as one long banquet table or used separately for smaller, more intimate dinner gatherings. This seating solution, however, created spatial problems. When she measured out the tables and the sideboard, the room felt a bit crowded. Serendipitously, the existing laundry room, backing on the dining room, was wider than necessary. Nancy co-opted a good 2 feet for the dining room and reverted the rest of the space to its original function as a pantry.

The powder room, just down the hall from the dining room, was well located for guests but not so well designed. The toilet sat front and center when the door was open. Fortunately, on the other side of the wall was a too-deep dining room china closet. Shrinking the closet by 2 feet allowed space to tuck the toilet out of sight and put an elegant chrome-legged pedestal sink front and center in its stead.

Meanwhile, the whole back of the house needed major attention. It had sustained an unfortunate seventies-era Florida-room addition complete with an oversized built-in bar. The room, nearly 40 feet long and half as wide, was simply unworkable. In an unorthodox move, Nancy and John decided to reduce the size of the room, subdividing it into two spaces: a TV/family room and a game room. Their New York decorator helped articulate and enunciate the great divide with walls of built-in bookcases. For mood, they installed a dark coffered wood ceiling inspired by a certain London hotel lobby that John had always admired. Then they augmented the room's glass apertures. To the original Palladian glass doors they added French doors opening to the garden.

The house suffered from another seventies eyesore—a

IN THE CONSERVATORY, PREVIOUSLY A SORRY SUNROOM, FRESHLY PAINTED EXTERIOR BRICK FOSTERS AN INSIDE/OUTSIDE CONNECTION.

TRADE TIP

BY PIRATING 2 FEET HERE AND ADDING 2 FEET THERE, LAURIE WAS ABLE TO ENLARGE OR SHRINK SPACES WITHOUT ALL NEW FRAMING HEADERS AND MOLDINGS. SHE RECESSED HER DINING ALCOVE AND UPSTAIRS HALL LANDING NICHE WITH DROPPED HEADERS, ALLOWING HER TO KEEP THE ELABORATE MOLDINGS INTACT.

[ABOVE] AN AUDITORIUM-LIKE FAMILY ROOM HAD BEEN ADDED ON IN THE 1970S—COMPLETE WITH A BUILT-IN TIKI BAR AND MISMATCHED WINDOWS. TO MAKE THE SPACE MORE USABLE, IT WAS GRACIOUSLY SUBDIVIDED INTO A TV/BILLIARD ROOM VIA A WALL OF BOOKCASES. THE SHEETROCK CEILING WAS PANELED AND COFFERED AFTER THE TOMASSOS SAW SOMETHING SIMILAR ON A TRIP ABROAD. THE POSITION OF THE ROOFTOP CHIMNEY MADE THE ANGLED FIREPLACE FAR TOO BIG A DEAL TO CHANGE, ESPECIALLY WHEN THE TOMASSOS WANTED TO PRESERVE THE TERRA-COTTA ROOF TILE. [BELOW] THE FORMER SUNROOM ALSO SERVED AS THE LINK BETWEEN THE KITCHEN, BACK STAIRS, THE FAMILY ENTRY, AND THE FAMILY ROOM. DATED AND LEAKY, IT NEEDED TO BE REPLACED. WHEN THE TOMASSOS HAD THE CONSERVATORY ENLARGED BY A MERE 2 FEET, IT BECAME FAR MORE THAN A HALLWAY. A SMALL KITCHENETTE CONCEALED BEHIND A SKIRTED COUNTER SERVICES THE EXPANSIVE TERRACES AND POOL.

leaky sunroom that happened to be the main artery of the family area at the rear of the house, a nondescript viaduct linking the kitchen and back stairs to the family room. Looking out over the wide terrace, pool, and beautiful yard, Nancy thought it would be nice to make this the spot for taking afternoon tea and catching up on school activities with Jenny. The architect suggested they put up a real conservatory. They had one shipped up from a southern supplier, then extended it an additional 3 feet, allowing for a walkway and a small seating area of bamboo furnishings. Because the conservatory was close to the pool, terrace, and outdoor entertaining, the Tomassos installed a kitchenette inside, concealed in a curtained cabinet (an idea Nancy poached from a European magazine). Now, rather than traipsing through to the kitchen, they can grab a snack or a beverage right inside the conservatory door.

The existing study, situated at the opposite end of the house from the kitchen and accessible only through the living room, needed rethinking. The Tomassos wanted a second entrance to the room, and they needed more file and document storage—in other words, a proper office that wasn't a dead end. The original study, underheated and tired, got a complete gut job, leaving only the fireplace and four sets of original Palladian French doors. A heated floor and all new cabi-

[ABOVE] TERRACE FLOORS WERE RESURFACED WITH PERDIDO, A CHARMING AND INEXPENSIVE STONE USED FOR MOST OF THE EARLY ROADS IN EUROPE AND FOR COMMERCIAL BUILDING WORLDWIDE. [BELOW] PALLADIAN WINDOWS AND THE FAMILY'S PRIZED POOL TABLE OUTFIT THE OTHER HALF OF THE FORMERLY GARGANTUAN FAMILY ROOM.

netry and paneling were installed. Nancy found an antique French marble mantel and fitted her cabinetry around it. She then covered the Palladian-style French doors with faux bois to make them read as part and parcel of the paneled walls. Finally, reasoning that the billiard/game room was not a hotbed of activity, the Tomassos cut a double door between the two rooms, providing a much-needed second access to the study.

When the Tomassos turned their attention to the kitchen, with its old Formica cabinets and graphic 1960s wallpaper, they realized they were facing another gut job. Nancy had hoped to stay within the original footprint, but it wasn't feasible—not if she wanted a separate family

TRADE TIP

OFTEN A KITCHEN WITH A LOT OF COUNTER SPACE CAN HANDLE MORE THAN ONE MATERIAL OR COLOR. DON'T FEEL OBLIGED TO TIE THEM ALTOGETHER. IN FACT, DIFFERENT SURFACES—SOLID SURFACES (CORIAN), BUTCHER BLOCK, STONE, AND STAINLESS STEEL—CAN SERVE DIFFERENT FUNCTIONS: MARBLE FOR ROLLING DOUGH, STAINLESS STEEL FOR HEAT RESISTANCE, BUTCHER BLOCK FOR FOOD PREP, AND SO ON.

breakfast table and seating area and the oversized island John likes to cook at. They got a design for a single-story addition measuring 8 by 15 feet, and they started from scratch.

With stone floors now gracing the entry and running through the back hall, conservatory, family room, and billiard room, Nancy felt she had quite enough stone floors, thank you. Wood, she thought, was the way to warm up the kitchen, a room of hard surfaces. Rather than trying to match the existing wood floors in the living and dining rooms, Nancy once again took an eclectic approach, installing wide 5-inch quarter-sawn oak, finished in a lighter stain. She was aware that, historically, older homes used different floor woods for the kitchen.

Nancy did opt for stone in a couple of places in the kitchen. The painted cabinets are topped by two different stone counters: a Crema Delicata, honed and color-enhanced for the perimeter counters, and a honed charcoal-colored Bursting Stone from England for the island. Not a fan of tiled backsplashes—or anything slick, for that matter—Nancy specified an 8-inch marble slab between counter and cabinet.

Upstairs, the Tomassos faced a labyrinth of little rooms. Except for the master suite, which consisted of a bedroom and a sitting room, plus his-and-hers baths, the bedrooms were quite small. The first move was to combine two tiny former maid's rooms into one generous guest room. That left three other smallish rooms, two of which the Tomassos left intact, and the third, their daughter's room, which they wrestled with. Jenny's room was itty-bitty, with virtually no closet space. Another niggling glitch in the upstairs plan was the hall landing, which was too narrow for any furniture whatsoever.

The designer, the architect, and the contractor batted around questions and solutions. Could they remove the attic stairs, leaving space for a furniture niche in the upstairs hall landing? Was the only way to expand Jenny's room to go up into the attic space? Wouldn't a single bathroom be fine for John and Nancy to share?

BEFORE

SITTING ROOM

MASTER BATH

BEDROOM

BATH

MASTER BEDROOM

MASTER BATH

AFTER

READING ROOM

TOILET

DRESSING ROOM

MASTER BATH

CLOSET

BATH

MASTER BEDROOM

BEDROOM

[BELOW] *BEFORE:* THE TEENAGE DAUGHTER'S ROOM—LACKLUSTER AND LIGHT-DEPRIVED. [ABOVE] *AFTER:* TO CREATE A NEW PIED-A-TERRE FOR THEIR DARLING DAUGHTER—COMPLETE WITH SPIRAL STAIRCASE AND SLEEPING LOFT—THE TOMASSOS ELIMINATED THE ATTIC STAIRS (A SMALLER ATTIC SPACE CAN BE ACCESSED THROUGH THE BACK OF THE LOFT).

THE EXISTING MASTER BEDROOM WAS SIM-
PLY NOT BIG ENOUGH AND THE ADJOINING
BATH WAS POSITIVELY TOMB-LIKE. THE SOLU-
TION [ABOVE AND RIGHT], WAS TO OPEN UP
THE MASTER TO THE ADJACENT BEDROOM
VIA A POCKET-DOOR DOUBLE-WIDTH OPEN-
ING. WHEN THE TOMASSOS PUNCHED OUT
THE PLASTER, THEY DISCOVERED THAT
THE ROOMS HAD ORIGINALLY BEEN LINKED
IN JUST THE SAME WAY. [OPPOSITE] IN
THE NEWLY FORMED MASTER BATH, THEY
INSTALLED A DORMER—HIGH ENOUGH THAT
NO WINDOW TREATMENT WAS NECESSARY—
OVER THE TUB.

The answers were yes. Jenny's room became a loft-like suite with a spiral stair between the original space and part of the attic converted for her use, featuring a built-in desk, ballet barre, and dance mirror. Because the attic was now accessible via the spiral stair and since they had ample basement storage, the Tomassos did away with the attic stairs. The cramped hallway now had room for a linen closet with curtained glass doors and a console, a mirror, and a pair of lamps.

John and Nancy then chose to double the width of the door between their bedroom and sitting room, the idea being to visually enlarge the bedroom. They did, however, put in pocket doors, so that if their wake-up times differed they wouldn't disrupt each other. They also wrapped the sitting room with closets: one side for Nancy, one side for John, with a TV concealed within. Only the space directly across from the bed remained closet free, providing a spot for a sofa.

John and Nancy outfitted the bathroom with his-and-hers vanities, a freestanding soaking tub, an ample shower, and a separate room for the toilet. The vanity drawer banks held interior electrical outlets so appliances never littered the countertops. They put in heated flooring and mounted towel bars. And, lest we forget the "art" in a state-of-the-art bathroom, they installed an audio system in the shower and recessed a mini flat-screen TV in an eave. Nancy mixed styles and tones in the décor: a black velvet slipper chair, an antique semanier, and original art. Because all the windows were high up, window treatments were unnecessary. Still, the bathroom suffered a shortage of light and air until they replaced the rear dormer with an atelier-like triple window. The result: very Left Bank.

HOUSE RULES

HAVE A CAPTIVE AUDIENCE. Although using an out-of-town architect sometimes made decision making difficult, having captive contractors, who literally moved into the house during construction, proved a bonus. Working on only the Tomassos' job meant no other projects clamoring for the construction crew's attention. What's more, the workers were motivated to get the job done because they were getting homesick—workdays were extended, weekends ignored.

HOTFOOT IT. The Tomassos love their heated floors, which are quiet, efficient, and uniform. They do caution, however, that you have to know where the coils are laid. When installing a floor-mounted doorstop, their contractor punctured a coil. The pressurized water spouted quite a gusher.

STAY CALM UNDER PRESSURE. When the Tomassos turned on the water in their amenity-laden master shower, they got merely a trickle. They were surprised, as they had already increased the diameter of the water pipes from ½ inch to ¾ inch. A booster pump had to be added to accommodate all the spray sources.

DO HOLD BACK. Even though the Tomassos knew their western team and trusted them, they also knew it was good business to retain a percentage of each invoice. They believe a 5 percent holdback on the contractor's profit and overhead until the job is done is fair. It's enough to be meaningful without being crippling.

CODES AND REGS. Your local zoning and building board is not out to get you. The members are just doing their job. But that doesn't mean some calls aren't subjective and you shouldn't try to work the system. Word of advice: Don't go with attitude. Try not to be defensive or arrogant. Pretend you've got a traffic ticket and be suppliant, never strident.

Back Home
to Sweet Alabama

[the program] Accomplished in eighteen months

- Relocate the ground-level stairs to improve the kitchen layout and overall flow of the house
- Turn a roomy boudoir bath into a home office
- Create two master baths from a single existing bath
- Restore a family room to grandeur
- Pirate space from the garage to construct a mudroom
- Enclose outdoor space underneath a dining room terrace to make a home gym

AFTER TWENTY YEARS UP NORTH, MAE AND WEBB Robertson—musicians, fund-raisers, art collectors, and Birmingham natives—were ready to return to their southern roots. Their parents were aging and their children were growing (they had a teenage daughter and a son in college). So when the Robertsons went down to Birmingham on one of their frequent visits and Webb received several job offers, they figured it was now or never. He took the best one, and they never looked back.

Decamping from a circa 1895 mansion in the suburbs of New York City, rich in history and moldings, the Robertsons thought they would surely reside in a like-minded old home, somewhere within the Birmingham city limits. Thus,

they were taken by surprise when they fell for a new-for-them 1965 brick manse on 11 rolling acres in nearby Mountain Brook. Coincidentally, the house was designed by the same prominent Birmingham firm (Sprott Long) that designed Mae's childhood home.

From the outside, the house had a distinct French flavor, with its ivy-covered walls, gabled slate roof, and antique double front door, purchased when a neighboring old mansion was torn down. Inside, however, there were no old details to speak of, not even window mullions. The lovely, private

THE IVY WAS ENCOURAGED TO GROW, CONCEALING SOME OF THE "NEWNESS" OF—FOR THE ROBERTSONS—A VERY YOUNG HOUSE. THE HERRINGBONED BRICK WALK PROVIDES EASY ACCESS FROM A CENTRAL PARKING COURT—A NICE CHANGE FROM THEIR PREVIOUS HOME, A TURN-OF-THE-CENTURY BEAUTY ACCESSIBLE ONLY VIA TEN TORTUROUS STEPS.

setting, however, ultimately proved irresistible. Tucked away from the street with no neighbors in sight, the house was nevertheless just fifteen minutes from everything.

The Robertsons had been down the renovation road before. Each time they had used a new architect and contractor, but they always found themselves consulting long-distance with their high school friend Phillip Woods, now a prominent Birmingham contractor. When the Robertsons moved "home" and bought their brick house, Phillip undoubtedly was the man for the job.

The Robertsons, who are educated in architecture and have a strong aesthetic sense, decided to live in the home while the work was going on so they could be on-site to make decisions. But the Robertsons were not naive. They understood the inefficiencies and additional costs associated with a family in residence (Phillip estimates the project would have taken a third less time—twelve months rather than eighteen—if the house had been unoccupied).

The renovation included three phases: downstairs, upstairs, and, finally, the kitchen. During phase one, the Robertsons moved themselves upstairs and started reworking their first-floor master bedroom. The bedroom was large, but for all its floor space had very little wall space. A fireplace flanked by a pair of windows filled one wall. There were doors galore—to the entrance, the bath, and

TRADE TIP

DON'T SABOTAGE THE JOB BY NOT HIRING A FRIEND IF HE OR SHE HAPPENS TO BE THE BEST IN TOWN. CHANCES ARE IF THE CONTRACTOR OR ARCHITECT IS REALLY A PROFESSIONAL, YOU'LL STILL BE FRIENDS AT THE END OF THE JOB.

the so-called boudoir, plus French doors leading to a secret garden. There was barely an inch of free wallspace on which to put any furniture. There wasn't even space for bedside tables or a TV.

In an unorthodox move, the Robertsons removed the fireplace (this is the South, after all) and created a perfect spot for an antique French armoire to hold a TV. They found room for bedside tables by removing the door to the boudoir. They then reconfigured the single dressing/bathroom into his-and-hers master baths linked by a common dressing room.

[LEFT] THE MASTER SUITE WAS AN ANACHRONISM MADE FOR A LADY OF LEISURE. A BOUDOIR, A FIREPLACE (IN ALABAMA? IN THE BEDROOM?), A STEPDOWN CARPETED "TOILET ROOM," AND NO REAL CLOSETS TO SPEAK OF. [ABOVE] THE MASTER BATHROOM, PUT RIGHT: HIS-AND-HERS BATHROOMS WERE CARVED OUT OF THE FORMER BATH AND CLOSET. THE SOAKING TUB SITS BY A WINDOW FACING A WALLED GARDEN.

[LEFT] THE LIVING ROOM, ENTERED VIA A STEP-DOWN FROM THE ENTRY, WAS A GRAND AND GRACIOUS ROOM. DESPITE ITS GRANDEUR IT WAS EGREGIOUSLY LACKING IN ONE AREA—THE CEILING. UPON ENTERING THE ROOM FROM AN ELEVATION OF TWO STEPS, ONE WAS CONFRONTED WITH WHAT SEEMED LIKE AN ACRE OF FLAT WHITE SHEETROCKED CEILING. A SIMPLE SOLUTION WAS TO ADD BEAMS ALONG THE LENGTH OF THE ROOM. [BELOW] A TWENTIETH-CENTURY BOUDOIR FOR MADAME IS NOW A TWENTY-FIRST-CENTURY OFFICE FOR MAE ROBERTSON, A SINGER/SONGWRITER/ENTREPRENEUR. WE'VE COME A LONG WAY, BABY!

TRADE TIP

IN LIEU OF UPHOLSTERED WALLS—EXPENSIVE AND HARD TO CLEAN—WALLPAPER YOUR WALLS WITH A SUBTLE TONE-ON-TONE DAMASK PATTERN LIKE THE ONE ABOVE. IT ADDS RICHNESS AND DEPTH TO A ROOM WITH A LOT OF UNARTICULATED WHITE WALL.

The living room holds three sofas, a grand piano, multiple chairs, several seating areas, a bar, a desk, and much more—plenty of room for musicales, soirees, and entertaining.

THE BEST LIVING ROOMS ARE ALL ABOUT SEAT-
ING. AFTER ALL, THEY'RE MOST OFTEN USED
WHEN THERE IS A CROWD, OFTEN MULTIGENERA-
TIONAL. THE ROBERTSONS DESIGNED THE ROOM
WITH A VARIETY OF SEATING OPTIONS: UPRIGHT
CHAIRS (GRANDPA'S WING CHAIR), OTTOMANS
(FOR THE LITTLE CHILDREN), AND LOVESEATS
(FOR THE COZY COUPLES). A PIANO PROVIDES
AN OPPORTUNITY FOR ENTERTAINMENT.

[**ABOVE**] TO GIVE THE RATHER
UNADORNED FAMILY ROOM MORE
DRAMA, THE FORMERLY FLAT CEIL-
ING WAS OPENED UP TO THE
RAFTERS AND CLAD WITH PECKY
CYPRESS. MAE CAME HOME ONE DAY
TO FIND THE CARPENTER NAILING
UP THE PECKY CYPRESS PANELING
ON THE FAMILY ROOM CEILING,
USING ONLY PERFECT BOARDS. HE
HAD CREATED A REJECT PILE OF THE
HOLEY ONES. "HEY," MAE SAID, "I
PAID A LOT FOR THOSE HOLES! I
WANT TO SEE THEM!"

Next on the agenda was an office for Mae, a singer and songwriter who often works from home. A logical candidate: the large boudoir bathroom. The Roberstons sealed off the connecting door from the master bedroom and replaced the bath fittings with walls of built-in cabinetry, which gave Mae a private office within easy access of the front hall, complete with French doors and a Provençal flair.

The living and dining room renovations, also part of this phase, received purely cosmetic alterations. The living room had a vast and flat banquet hall–like Sheetrock ceiling. And because the living room was two steps down from the entrance hall, the expanse of plain white Sheetrocked ceiling was quite visible. Its height of 9½ feet allowed for the addition of ceiling features. When boxed beams and a central chandelier were installed, the space took on the air of a salon. For more character, iron cross details were added to existing transom windows over the rear French doors, echoing existing ones in the antique entrance hall doors. Throughout the house, all the many plain windows were given mullions to make them period appropriate.

The Robertsons greatly improved the dining room by restoring its original integrity—specifically, stripping the columns of their fake fluting. In a bohemian decorative step, the Robertsons put up a bold floral paper, which provided an intriguing contrast for their collection of colorful outsider art. They expanded the eclectic mix with an oriental rug, a crystal chandelier, and ruby-red drapes.

The last piece of the living/dining room renovation involved a shallow two-step drop between the spaces. The Robertsons had barely moved in before a visitor took a nasty tumble down the awkward steps. To make the steps both less treacherous and more gracious, the Robertsons had them rebuilt deeper and less steep.

Six months later, they entered phase two with the renovation of the library/family room. The Robertsons had to rip out the tray ceiling to remove asbestos. In the process they uncovered a wonderful surprise: a cathedral ceiling. In an effort to duplicate the look of the ceiling of the famed Spanish Lounge at the Cloisters resort in Sea Island, Georgia, Webb and his contractor/friend Phillip went way out into the woods of Northern Alabama to salvage rough-hewn timbers. The beams they brought back were installed trestle-style. Between the beams they specified boards of Pecky Cypress, a prized local wood with an old worm-hole appeal.

HOUSE RULES

SOMETIMES GOOD IS GOOD ENOUGH. The Robertsons thought about replacing the kitchen, but with everything in good working order, they had to ask themselves why. It would be shiny and new, but would it be better? Unlike other renovators, who come in with a Disneyesque fantasy of everything eye-poppingly new, the Robertsons simply changed the tile and island and gave the rest a fresh coat of paint. They discovered their money and creative juices were better spent in other areas of the renovation.

KNOW THE SUBSTITUTES. Just after the job was complete, Hurricane Ivan paid the Robertsons a visit. The roof leaked, and Mac didn't have the roofer's number. She wished she'd complied a list of everyone's individual contact information—and at that point, she did. Now she knows how to reach the plumber, the painter, and the cabinetmaker down the road without having to pester the contractor.

DIVIDE AND CONQUER. Mae and Webb worked well together because they each knew their own strengths. While Mae was involved in reviewing blueprints (as a former multiple storeowner, storage and space planning is one of her strong suits), Webb, the art collector, dealt more with color, fabrics, and design details.

THIS ISN'T THE TIME TO THINK LIGHT. If you're moving out of a bedroom during a renovation, clean sweep your closets. The construction, the sanding, the painting makes the air thick with dust—and the last thing you want to do is venture into a dusty construction site to retrieve a pair of heels. Take everything, even out-of-season things (they can be put into storage bags in a basement or designated space). Sounds extreme, but it's absolutely worth it.

At this point, Mae and Webb moved back downstairs into their master bedroom, and their thirteen-year-old daughter, Cally, camped out in a guest room while her own room and bath got a makeover. Both Cally's bath and a guest bath were carved from one supersized hallway bathroom shared by the previous owner's three daughters. The guest bath got a sophisticated look with paneling painted tobacco brown, while Cally's bath, with its blue glass sink, was half Little Mermaid and half grown-up spa.

Saving the toughest for last, phase three started with the kitchen. Expecting that essential room to be out of commission for three months, Phillip refurbished an existing kitchenette in the basement (using it meant lots of walking up and down stairs, but at least they had a fridge, a sink, and an oven). The Robertsons' approach to the kitchen renovation was pragmatic—to do what works. Mae and

Webb could not care less about trends, fads, or someone else's idea of a dream kitchen. Webb, the chef in the family, needed more counter space, so that's where they began. They replaced the rather small island with a much larger one, giving Webb a really wonderful prep surface and a restaurant-grade cooktop. This put Webb in the center of the room and made him the center of the action while cooking. He helped design new under-island base cabinets with lots of storage specifically for his most-used pots and pans.

As for hanging storage, the Robertsons decided to keep many of the wood wall cabinets, which had been installed in the mid-nineties, and repainted them a faded sage. They also retained the sink, dishwasher, and Sub Zero refrigerator (updated with a new stainless-steel panel). They kept a Corian countertop but replaced a matching backsplash with glazed handmade tiles in a warm white, laid with an extra-wide grout margin, which added character to the overall effect.

One of the cleverest changes the Robertsons made to the kitchen was the redirected traffic flow. As it was, too many doors opened from the kitchen and led to too many areas— dining room, hallway, outside, family room, basement. All the doors had to stay, except for the entrance to the basement, which they determined could be easily relocated to a cleaning closet off the foyer; flipping the stairs and reversing the direction, not a difficult project, made this possible. With the former basement door closed up, the Robertsons captured a corner in the kitchen, providing a home for an oversized French armoire that holds platters and serving pieces.

TRADE TIP

WHEN SPACE IS TIGHT, LOOK TO SEE IF IT'S POSSIBLE TO BORROW JUST A BIT—A FOOT OR TWO—FROM A CLOSET OR A PANTRY IN A NEIGHBORING ROOM. OFTEN, ESPECIALLY IN OLDER HOMES, CLOSETS WERE MADE UNUSUALLY DEEP, AND COOPTING THE SPACE ON THE OTHER SIDE OF THE WALL IS AN EASY AND INEXPENSIVE WAY TO ENLARGE AN AREA.

[OPPOSITE] THE EXISTING BACK HALL PANTRY WAS SKIMPY ON STORAGE. FOR-
TUNATELY, IT BACKED ON TO A CLOSET IN THE GARAGE. BY OPENING THE CLOSET
UP TO THE PANTRY, THE ROBERTSONS FASHIONED ENOUGH SPACE FOR A WON-
DERFUL PANTRY, A FLOWER-ARRANGING SINK, AND A DOGGIE BEDROOM. THE
WALLS WERE CLAD IN 5-INCH V GROOVE, THE FLOORS COVERED IN CHECKER-
BOARD VINYL SQUARES. A DUTCH DOOR HELPS THE ROBERTSONS KEEP AN EYE
ON THE DOGGIES. [ABOVE] THE RENOVATED KITCHEN. THE ROBERTSONS LIKED
THE GALLEY LAYOUT AND THE SIMPLE WOODEN CABINETS OF THE FORMER
KITCHEN. TO GIVE THE SPACE AN UPDATED LOOK AND FUNCTION, THEY PAINTED
THE CUPBOARDS, PUT UP A NEW COTTAGEY BACKSPLASH, AND INSTALLED
STAINLESS-STEEL APPLIANCES. THE ISLAND WAS ALSO REWORKED: ENLARGED
SLIGHTLY, TOPPED WITH HANDSOME GEORGIA MARBLE, AND FITTED WITH A
PROFESSIONAL COOKTOP AND HOOD. [LEFT] THE ROBERTSONS' DAUGHTER
WEIGHED IN ON THE DESIGN OF HER BATH, CHOOSING A GLASS "VESSEL" SINK
AND A MIRROR-MOUNTED "FALLING WATER" FAUCET. PLENTY OF STORAGE IS
NEVER ENOUGH FOR A TEENAGE GIRL.

The mudroom, once no more than a walk-through back hall, grew into a more substantial and stylish space by recessing closets and cabinets into a large former storage closet in the adjacent garage. Closets were clad in wide V-groove boards and painted slate blue, as was simple new cabinetry. A copper farmhouse sink and wooden counter, handy for both dog grooming and flower arranging, reinforced the vintage look of old-fashioned vinyl checkerboard floors. And a hinged half-height doggie door keeps the two pooches in sight but out of the kitchen.

The postscript to the project was the new home gym. Webb was in the midst of a high-pressure period at work, and he was missing his workouts at the local gym. The Robertsons dug around and unearthed a viable solution. Underneath the dining room terrace was a lattice-covered space—dank and creepy. Could it be made dry enough to use as an indoor space? It just so happened the Robertsons needed to repair the dining room terrace above this found area, as it leaked badly. They installed a waterproof mem-

brane and surfaced the terrace with local crab orchard stone. Like the rest of their creative solutions for tweaking the house, the gym gained them space without adding square footage. Now with the house, and the whole family, in great shape, the Robertsons feel they are truly home to stay.

TRADE TIP

WHEN RENOVATING, BE SENSITIVE TO HOW YOU TRAVEL THROUGH THE HOUSE—BOTH FROM ROOM TO ROOM AND FROM INSIDE TO OUTSIDE. EASE OF MOVEMENT IS A KEY PART OF RENOVATION. THE MORE AMENABLE THE ACCESS, THE MORE LIKELY YOU ARE TO ACTUALLY USE THE SPACE. WIDE DOORS ARE MORE INVITING THAN NARROW. GRAD-UAL, DEEPER STEPS ARE NOT ONLY MORE INVITING BUT SAFER AND MORE VISIBLE THAN SHORT, SHALLOW STEPS.

A Grande Dame's Face-Lift

[the program] ## Accomplished in two and a half years

- Restore a classic seaside Shingle-style house, inside and out
- Design an inviting new entrance
- Pickle and patch the floors and walls
- Refurbish moldings and mantels in the living room, dining room, and family room
- Recess a convenient kitchenette within interior walls and then closet it in an antique armoire
- Relocate doors and rearrange dressing rooms in the master bedroom and bath
- Rebuild a commodious back porch

RALPH AND JOAN AMMIRATI SPENT SEVEN YEARS LOOKING for a house in Southampton, on the shores of Long Island, New York, to share with their three children as a weekend escape. They were living in a town house in the city and wanted a family seat, a place where their extended families could convene year-round for holidays and vacations.

It was a case of good things coming to those who wait. The 1904 home they eventually found, on a beautiful and level piece of property, had great bones. Of course it also had fundamental design and structure flaws, thanks to several ill-conceived prior renovations. In recent years the house had been used as a summer rental. The previous owner's maintenance style could be called deferred maintenance or benign neglect.

The Ammiratis had the means and, more importantly, the patience to do right by the grande dame, so there was never pressure to compromise on quality in either materials or design. The couple also had a vision. Joan and Ralph, who owns a legendary advertising agency, share a penchant for the clean and chic. That aesthetic guided them through the restoration plan, which included everything from the micro (refinishing moldings) to the macro (rebuilding the front face of the house, completely reshingling and reroofing, and building a three-car garage).

OUT WITH THE ASPHALT AND VINYL, IN WITH THE CEDAR SHINGLES, AS BEFITS A CEDAR SHAKE HOUSE CIRCA 1904. TO MAKE SENSE OF A SERIES OF AWKWARD AWNINGS AND OVERHANGS, THE AMMIRATIS RESITUATED THE ENTRY, PULLING IT FORWARD AND FINISHING IT WITH FRENCH DOORS.

The Ammiratis also knew that good taste is based on a good foundation, so they started off the renovation process, wisely, with an engineer. Unfortunately, he declared the house a train wreck. The old house was truly a dinosaur in terms of systems—plumbing, electrical, and heating. (Since it had been built as a summer house, there was almost no heating system at all.) To update these systems, the Ammiratis excavated a basement and installed all new wiring and pipes. The result was seven heating zones and five air-conditioning zones to service the home's thirty rooms.

Moving outside, the Ammiratis found the exterior awkward and irrational. It was broken by a plethora of rooflines (nine on the front of the house alone). There were planes and angles and contradictions in the extreme. To top things off, the main chimney hugged the house until the second story. The third story sat back about 15 feet, which left the top third of the chimney sticking up like a feather out of a cap. The clever solution was to build out the third floor of the house, moving it forward to align with the lower two floors and carry the chimney. The additional third-floor space became attic storage—something this substantial home was surprisingly short on. A graceful Palladian window was installed in the new eave, echoing existing windows on the back of the house.

Structure aside, the skin of the house needed attention as well. Somewhere in its century-old life, it had taken on vinyl siding and an asphalt tile roof. The Ammiratis stripped the house of the offending materials, replacing the siding with simple cedar shingles and installing a wood tile roof. (While they were at it, they took the opportunity to add insulation to the walls to prepare the home for the off season.) As the cedar shakes went up, Joan decided *not* to paint the house white, the color it had been for years. Many beautiful details, like the original window casings, fascias, and sof-

fits, were concealed by the overall coat of white. The shakes, however, were likely to age unevenly (darker on the ocean side and lighter on the drier sides), given the house's proximity to the ocean and its humid, salty air. To get them to weather uniformly, the Ammiratis had the entire house hosed with water at regular intervals throughout the first summer.

Inside, the house retained almost all of its original detail and woodwork and was in good structural shape—but in dire need of freshening and lightening. Starting from the ground up, the Ammiratis decided to lighten and unify the old floors both downstairs and upstairs. They took up miles of wall-to-wall shag carpeting, patched the floors where needed, and then pickled, or whitewashed, them all. The pickling liquid, a semi-opaque stain, helped mask dings and scrapes and made patching less obvious. Next, the Ammiratis addressed the walls, many of which were papered or painted in garish colors. They stripped the walls throughout the house and started from scratch, skim-coating with new plaster for a smooth, even, elegant surface. They went with an all-white palette—an ideal choice where natural light is plentiful, as was the case throughout this many-windowed house—and plenty of texture, as with the prevalent

TRADE TIP

PICKLING—A WHITEWASHING PROCESS SIMILAR TO, THOUGH LESS DAMAGING THAN, BLEACHING (WHICH TENDS TO WEAKEN THE WOOD)—HAS DEGREES OF OPACITY. THE DEGREE OF OPACITY (AMOUNT OF PAINT IN THE MIX) DETERMINES HOW MUCH OR HOW LITTLE OF THE GRAIN OF THE WOOD IS REVEALED. TEST DIFFERENT PROPORTIONS ON YOUR FLOOR TO DETERMINE WHAT'S RIGHT. ADD THE PAINT LITTLE BY LITTLE. YOU CAN ALWAYS ADD MORE TO THE MIX, BUT IT'S HARD TO SUBTRACT.

[ABOVE] *BEFORE:* THE EXISTING FRONT HALL WAS A CACOPHONY OF FLOCKED WALLPAPER AND WALL-TO-WALL CARPET. [TOP] *AFTER:* LESS IS DEFINITELY MORE. STRIPPING AWAY THE CARPET AND THE PAPER AND BEAM-MASKING THE SHEETROCK REVEALED A SPARE AND SPACIOUS FOYER.

[ABOVE] THE LIVING ROOM, ONE OF THE DARKEST ROOMS IN THE HOUSE THANKS TO THE OVERHANG OF A NEIGHBORING COVERED LOGGIA, WAS LIGHTENED VIA PICKLED FLOORS—THE INSPIRATION BEHIND THE PICKLING SCHEME FOR ALL ROOMS. [LEFT] WHEN BEVERAGES ARE SERVED FROM THE CHARMING CONCEALED KITCHENETTE, THE FAMILY ROOM'S LUNCHEON TABLE, WHICH SOMETIMES DOUBLES AS A GAME TABLE, OFFERS A COOL RESPITE FROM THE POOLSIDE SUN.

woodwork in the form of ceiling beams and richly detailed wainscoting. In the process of painting, the Ammiratis took the opportunity to restore much of the woodwork in the old house, from the main stairs, which got a new newel post and railing, to windows, which needed new sashes, to mantels, which they stripped and restored to the original pine finish (in the living room) or repainted white.

With the house looking brighter and better already, the Ammiratis thought about how best to fine-tune the layout to fit their casual lifestyle. They managed to enlarge the kitchen, small but serviceable, by pushing out one of the exterior walls by a few feet. Still, there wasn't enough room for an eat-in space. Fortunately, the family room, on the opposite end of the house, with its easy access to the porch and the pool, looked like the ideal spot for casual family meals. As it's a l-o-n-g walk from one end of the house to the other, however, the Ammiratis decided to install a full kitchenette right in the family room, cunningly tucked into a generously proportioned armoire. Designed to house a microwave, a refrigerator, and an ice maker, it was partially recessed into the thick walls between the living room and the family room. Outside, the armoire reads antique, while the all-white inside looks crisp and efficient.

For the family's regular sit-down meals, the Ammiratis looked to the

[ABOVE] BECAUSE THE FAMILY DOES NOT HAVE AN EAT-IN KITCHEN, THE DINING ROOM HAD TO BE COMFORTABLE AND EASY TO USE. NO VENEERS OR HIGH POLISH FINISHES. A TABLE THAT'S MAINTAINED WITH PASTE WAX PAIRED WITH INDOOR/ OUTDOOR FRENCH BISTRO CHAIRS GUARANTEED THAT THE DINING ROOM WOULD BE OVER- RATHER THAN UNDERUSED.

[LEFT] AS WITH MOST GRAND TURN-OF-THE-CENTURY HOMES, THE KITCHEN WAS FAR REMOVED FROM THE LIVING AND FAMILY ROOMS. THE AMMIRATIS CO-OPTED DEAD SPACE BETWEEN THE LIVING ROOM AND FAMILY ROOM WALLS TO CREATE A MINI-KITCHEN JUST STEPS FROM THE POOL. A BISECTED AND RETROFITTED FRENCH ARMOIRE CONCEALS THE FRONT OF THE KITCHENETTE. CLEVER AND SO CONVENIENT.

[**ABOVE**] THE AMMIRATIS SHIFTED THE ENTRY DOOR IN THE MASTER BEDROOM FROM THE CENTER OF THE ROOM TO THE FAR LEFT, CREATING A GRACIOUS DIVISION BETWEEN SLEEPING AND SITTING. [**LEFT**] WITH THE ADDITION OF A SOFA TABLE, A "HALLWAY" DIRECTS TRAFFIC PAST THE SEATING AREA TO BED, BATH, AND BEYOND. [**BELOW**] PRISTINE AND PERFECT WAS THE DECORATING MANTRA. PRIMITIVE AMERICAN AND SWEDISH ANTIQUES SAVED IT FROM PRECIOUSNESS. [**OPPOSITE**] TILES DON'T HAVE TO BE FUSSY OR FANCY TO BE ELEGANT. THE SIMPLEST OF TILES—IN A CLASSIC BLACK-AND-WHITE PATTERN—PAIR WITH A SHAKER CUPBOARD-CUM-MEDICINE CABINET FOR A TIMELESS BATHROOM.

house's traditional dining room. With the kitchen tight on table space, the inviting, comfortable dining room would be truly used—quite a marvel these days. A long, well-loved country table, originally from a university refectory in England, dominated the room. It easily seated twenty, with every chair an armchair, the better to recline and dine in. To retain the relaxed mood of the room, the Ammiratis chose to keep the lighting soft and low. Instead of an overhead light—the room is so long it would require a cavalcade of chandeliers for proper proportion—they added sconces all around the perimeter of the room, and they use candles liberally.

Upstairs, much of the renovation work was cosmetic. The bedrooms were already graciously proportioned, and each had its own bathroom (which the Ammiratis upgraded as needed). The master bedroom required a little more reworking. The door to the room was right at the top of the main staircase, where the pitter-patter of little (and big) feet running up and down the steps interrupted the peace and quiet. The Ammiratis moved the door down the hall, which also changed the interior layout for the better. The original entrance at the middle of the room bisected it into a left and a right side and made furniture placement difficult. When the entrance was moved to the far side, the Ammiratis gained a reading area facing the fireplace. The décor was kept to a crisp black-and-white scheme with simple yet comfortable furnishings.

In the master bath, the credo was likewise to keep things simple. The Ammiratis achieved a timeless look by lining the walls with classic white tiles and two running black borders, one at the base molding, the other at chair-rail height. They replaced the decrepit original sink with a graceful pedestal fixture with vintage detailing. (This was actually the only sink the Ammiratis replaced. In the other upstairs baths, all the plumbing fixtures, including the deep old tubs, were retained.) They hung a

TRADE TIP

PEOPLE DON'T THINK OF USING FURNITURE IN A BATHROOM, THEY JUST WANT VANITIES. BUT IF YOU HAVE THE SPACE, REAL FURNITURE, LIKE A CUPBOARD, A BENCH, OR EVEN A CHAIR, ADDS CHARACTER AND CACHET. FURTHER, IT PROVIDES YOU WITH EITHER STORAGE OR SEATING.

[ABOVE] THE PLANK PORCH FLOORS, PAINTED WITH BOAT PAINT FOR A LONG-LASTING FINISH, WERE LAID WIDTHWISE ALONG THE LENGTH OF THE PORCH AND FRAMED WITH A BORDER OF THE SAME WOOD. UNFORTUNATELY, WATER DRAINED INTO THE SEAM BETWEEN THE PLANKS AND THE BORDER, CAUSING IT TO ROT. IT WOULD HAVE BEEN BETTER TO ELIMINATE THE BORDER AND HAVE THE PLANKS RUN ALL THE WAY TO THE EDGE OF THE PORCH. [RIGHT AND OPPOSITE] THE AMMIRATIS RETAINED AND RESTORED THE ORIGINAL FRENCH DOORS THROUGHOUT THE HOUSE, COMPLETE WITH ORIGINAL HARDWARE AND GLASS.

small antique wooden mirror over the sink; small suffices when you have a nearby dressing room with a full-length mirror. Finally, they chose a museum-quality Shaker cabinet from the 1800s as a storage piece for everything from towels to shampoo. If you have the floor space, furniture is always a nice way to make a bathroom feel like a real room.

The following spring, with the inside in good shape, the Ammiratis stepped outside again. It was time to tackle that quintessential summerhouse sta-

ple, the back porch, which needed rebuilding. They traded the old columns, which were rotting, with newer versions in the same style; they replaced ceiling and floor boards; and they painted the wood floors with glossy porch paint. At that point, the Ammiratis also rebuilt the pool and enclosed it with a white wooden fence in a classic grid pattern.

As the renovation of the house wound down, the Ammiratis geared up for their biggest piece of construction on the property. They built a three-car garage (the small existing garage was converted into a laundry room, mudroom, and back hall) that would connect to the expanded kitchen and house Ralph's vintage car collection. The new garage was designed to keep with the style and sensibility of the house itself.

From beginning to end, the detailed restoration took more than two years. As any contractor or client who has been through it can tell you, restoration takes more effort and time than building anew—but it is usually worth it. That's certainly true for the Ammiratis, who now have themselves a gem of a house with great bones, great amenities, and plenty of great rooms for their kids, and now grandkids, to visit and stay . . . and stay.

HOUSE RULES

TALK TO ME. Because the Ammiratis were off-site during the week (this was a weekend house, after all), they learned that they needed to catch up in person. They made a regular meeting time with the contractor—every Saturday morning—to go over what had happened the previous week and what was planned for the following week. They also realized that if they missed a meeting, they'd miss two weeks' worth of communication and decision making. They made a commitment to themselves to be out every Saturday, rain or shine.

CONTENT COUNTS. When the Ammiratis added new cabinetwork to the house, they kept the lines ultra-simple. Even extremely simple cabinets have a lot of decorative impact. It all depends on the contents. Bookshelves can display not only books but also collectibles—in the Ammiratis' case, unusual doorstops.

DON'T BE AFRAID TO DECORATE AGAINST TYPE. Just because a house is a century old doesn't mean the décor needs to be of the same vintage. The Ammiratis wanted nothing heavy, dark, or overfurnished. They wanted the house to feel breezy and easy, to look like it could be swept clean with a broom or a summer breeze. Going with all-white walls has the advantage of providing a noncompeting backdrop for arresting or unusual furniture —here, painstakingly chosen antique pieces with pristine lines and simple silhouettes.

KEEP IT LOW MAINTENANCE. Painted porch floors look great. But with years of experience and hindsight, the Ammiratis admit that painted oak floors in a beach area require a bit too much maintenance—a dedication to repainting the porch every three to four years. A harder wood like cedar or mahogany, treated with a semitransparent stain, would have been more durable, though perhaps not quite as consistent and sleek.

Cleaning Out the Stable

[the program] Accomplished in three six-month stages over three years

- Reconfigure an awkwardly shaped master bedroom
- Create a new master bath and dressing room
- Upgrade and update the fireplaces
- Square off the former stable, now the living room, by demolishing an old stablehands' bathroom
- Remove a dinged wood ceiling and relocate a door
- Convert the sunporch into a dining room
- Design a new entry and dress up the staircase

FRIENDS OF TENA AND HAYES KAVANAUGH AND THEIR THREE children suggested this chapter be titled "Confessions of the Old House Junkies." Indeed, the Kavanaughs' latest renovation, of a hundred-year-old former stable, follows the remodeling of several mews houses, a hotel-turned-home, a rambling Victorian, and a cluster of summer beach shacks. The common thread: The homes were all calling out for remodeling and reinvention.

The stable in upstate New York, built in the late nineteenth century for the grand house next door, consisted of a large central space with a small adjacent tack room and sunporch. The second floor housed a chauffeur's apartment with two bedrooms and a bath. Twenty years ago, the previous owners converted the stable into a home and built a peculiar two-story addition along the back. The result was a floor plan that was too open below and too divided above.

The Kavanaughs zeroed in on their renovation goal: to create a comfortably individual environment without adding square footage. Next, they set their priorities in terms of which rooms needed the most rejigging and refinishing: the master bedroom and bath, living/great room, family room, dining room, and entrance (or lack thereof, as there was neither a dining room nor an entrance hall).

TO MAKE ROOM FOR THE BED IN THE COZY MASTER BEDROOM, THE KAVANAUGHS TOOK AN INNOVATIVE APPROACH, CREATING A NICHE FOR THE HEADBOARD RECESSED INTO THEIR DRESSING ROOM.

[BELOW] THE STABLE THROUGH THE AGES: THE ADDITION OFF THE BACK OF THE ORIGINAL STRUCTURE HAS TAKEN MANY FORMS—FROM A GREENHOUSE TO A SUNROOM TO ITS PRESENT-DAY INCARNATION AS A LIGHT-SUFFUSED DINING ROOM/ENTRY. [RIGHT] EVERY NICHE COUNTS: IN THE MASTER BATH, 39-INCH-HIGH VANITIES AND RECESSED WALL-TO-WALL MEDICINE CABINETS MAKE THE MOST OF A TIGHT SPACE. THE KAVANAUGHS POSITIONED THE SOAKING TUB IN A WINDOWED ALCOVE. [OPPOSITE, ABOVE] IN THE FAMILY ROOM, STORAGE ARMOIRES REPLACED THE CLAUSTROPHOBIA-INDUCING CLOSETS. RAISING THE HEARTH—A CONTROVERSIAL DECISION—ALLOWED THE FIREPLACE TO BE GLIMPSED FROM THE ADJACENT STUDY. [OPPOSITE, BELOW] TO ADD GRACE AND SPACE TO AN UPSTAIRS HALLWAY, THE KAVANAUGHS REMOVED A TINY CLOSET, ADDED A SKYLIGHT, AND CHARMED UP THE WALLS WITH TIFFANY CROSS MOLDING.

TRADE TIP

HALLS, UNLESS THEY TAKE YOU FROM HERE TO THERE, CAN BE SPACE WASTERS. THINK ABOUT MOVING A BEDROOM DOOR FORWARD TO TRUNCATE A LONG HALL AND ADD AN INTERIOR ENTRANCE TO THE BEDROOM.

The work started upstairs. The master bedroom was a quirky space with many jigs and jogs. Two-thirds of the room was under a peaked ceiling, the result of the 1970s addition/renovation. The remaining (original) third was under a flat ceiling. Tena decided they should run a wall down the seam between the flat and peaked ceiling, creating, in one stroke, a dressing room that quadrupled the couple's closet space. The new bedroom, though, was not quite large enough to accommodate the couple's king-size bed. Tena improvised. An alcove 15 inches deep was notched into the new wall, forming a sort of ceremonial second headboard and a cozy bedrest.

To make the upstairs baths more functional, Tena cobbled together space from unnecessary hallways. The master bath now adjoins the dressing room instead of being accessed by the redundant hallway (hardly private). A formerly awkward space, there's now room for a double-sink vanity, claw-footed tub, and commodious shower stall. Tena chose timeless Carerra marble to clad the shower, vanity, and floor. The hall bath was made big enough to comfort-

TRADE TIP

IN A SMALL SPACE, IT PAYS TO EXAGGERATE OR OVERPLAY
THE DETAILS. TENA'S CRISP WHITE "TIFFANY X" POLYMER
MOLDINGS AND SHARP CHARTREUSE PAINT IN HER TINY
UPSTAIRS HALL GIVE IT DEPTH, DIMENSION, AND DARING.

ably serve all three upstairs bedrooms and features a charming shallow cupboard-like linen closet where once was a secondary door.

At the top of the stairs lay a minute, dark, undistinguished hall and landing. Tena stole a few square feet by cutting into an under-the-eaves closet, which helped a bit. But it was a skylight, installed at the crux of the space, that really amplified the illusion of space in the form of light and air. As a final touch for the walls, Tena applied picture molding with a Tiffany cross—an unusual choice, but one

TRADE TIP

EVERY ROOM NEEDS A FOCAL POINT FOR THE FUR-NITURE PLAN. USUALLY IT IS THE LARGEST VERTICAL ELEMENT IN A ROOM. IT COULD BE A FIREPLACE, A ROW OF FRENCH DOORS, OR, LACKING ANY SIGNIFI-CANT ARCHITECTURAL FEATURE, AN ELABORATE WINDOW TREATMENT OR EVEN A KING-SIZE BED AND HEADBOARD IN A MASTER SUITE.

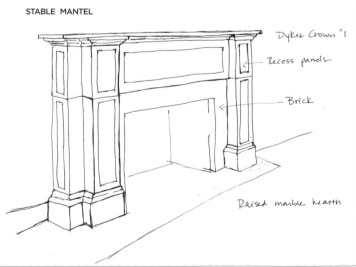

STABLE MANTEL

Dykes Crown "1

Recess panels

Brick

Raised marble hearth

she serendipitously stumbled across at a lumberyard. It wasn't what she looking for, but she loved it. And it worked.

With the upstairs now designed, the Kavanaughs turned their attention to the first floor. The family room, though spacious, felt claustrophobic due to wall-to-wall cabinets. The adjoining study opened directly into it, and it lacked definition. The Kavanaughs stripped the family room of the built-ins, replacing them with two antique pine armoires—not a perfect match but certainly a pleasing pair. Next, they moved the fireplace onto a raised hearth for better distribution of heat. Why shouldn't a fire warm your whole body instead of your shins? The Kavanaughs then defined the *L*-shaped study with the addition of partial walls, or wing walls, and pocket doors, leaving the study open enough for Hayes to see the family room's real hearth as well as the new electronic hearth, the oversized plasma TV, while seated at his desk.

The living room, nearly the same size, had great charm but an unappealing view of an exposed bathtub in the corner. Although good for a few laughs, the tub joke wore thin. The Kavanaughs removed the shoved-in-a-corner bath, replacing it with a more decorous, if tiny, powder room down the hall. Even with the awkward bath gone, the room felt askew. The challenge was to make it more symmetrical. The brick firebox was technically centered on the wall, but a log bin on the left side made it feel off-kilter. Tena was bothered by the asymmetry (out went the log bin) and by the brick (too sixties New York City). She designed a proper mantel, using one of her many historical reference books as a guide.

As the room came together, Tena assessed its walls and ceiling, both covered in the original beadboard. She eyed

the ceiling more closely and thought, why not take all the beadboard down. It was showing its warts, gashes, and spreading seams anyway. On the bare ceiling she added broad pine beams for heft and definition. As for the discarded boards, they had another life to live. They could be recycled, Tena realized, to patch the walls as needed. To make the patched areas work seamlessly with the rest of the walls, Tena had a restorer sand the boards and faux-grain the mismatched pieces to resemble the rest. The finished effect, the total picture of the beadboard and beams, was wonderfully warm and woody. The room now had the presence of a barn with the warmth of a home.

The house had no dining room; the former owners had a table in a corner of the living room. Tena cast her eye about, looking for a space to appropriate. The existing sunporch was a likely candidate. The porch was situated on the house's south façade, where it was flooded with light. It was

[OPPOSITE] THE NATURAL WAINSCOTED LIVING ROOM, THE HEART OF THE FORMER STABLE, WAS THE ONE EXTRAVAGANTLY SIZED ROOM IN THE HOUSE. IT HAD BEEN DOCTORED, LIKE MUCH ELSE, IN THE SEVENTIES. THE KAVANAUGHS RECENTERED THE FIREPLACE AND TENA DESIGNED A NEW MANTEL. THE COUPLE'S ENGLISH FURNISHINGS STAND IN ARTFUL JUXTAPOSITION TO THE RUSTICITY OF THE REST OF THE ROOM. [RIGHT] THE SMALL STUDY, ONCE TOTALLY OPEN TO THE ADJACENT FAMILY ROOM, WAS DEFINED WITH A FRAMED DOORWAY AND "WING" (OR PARTIAL) WALLS TO GIVE IT A SENSE OF ENCLOSURE.

[ABOVE] THE KAVANAUGHS RESQUARED THE LIVING ROOM BY REMOVING A FULL BATH AND A SMALL HALL. THE BAVARIAN ARMOIRE SITS WHERE A BATHTUB ONCE DID. [BELOW] THE ROOF WAS RAISED IN THE NARROW DINING ROOM. CEILING TILES WERE REMOVED FROM THIS FORMER GREENHOUSE, ALLOWING THE CEILING TO REACH TO ITS FULL SHED-ROOFED HEIGHT. [OPPOSITE] THE LARGE INTERIOR WINDOW IN THE LIVING ROOM, ALSO VISIBLE IN THE CURRENT DINING ROOM, WAS ORIGINALLY AN EXTERIOR WINDOW. RATHER THAN REMOVE IT WHEN THEY ADDED THE GREENHOUSE/SUNROOM/DINING ROOM, THE KAVANAUGHS DECIDED TO LEAVE IT TO SHARE LIGHT WITH THE LIVING ROOM.

also, occasionally, flooded with water; the room had leaky sliding doors and slimy ceiling tiles. To make the space suitable for dining, the tiles came down and the roof, newly Sheetrocked, was raised all the way to the rafters, shed roof style. Out came the old sliding doors and in went new sliding French doors. Tena said she had a philosophical objection to sliders, but, since space was tight and there simply was no place for a door to swing, she changed her mind. The converted space made a perfect segue to its new life. Yes, the room was long and narrow—but so was her dining room table.

The final challenge of the house remained: how to enter it in the first place. At the time of renovation, there was no entrance hall. In fact, one had to enter through the sunporch. As soon as the porch was slated to become the new dining room, it was clear the entrance would have to be moved. Tena had the bright idea of borrowing a few feet from one end of the porch/dining room to create a tiny foyer, just big enough to fit an antique Chinese-painted cabinet stocked with various and vintage bar accoutrements. With the new foyer creating a more interesting entrance to the house, Tena knew she had to address the stairs, which were torturously tight and claustrophobic. Staircases, whether large or tiny, are among the strongest architectural features in a home and often benefit from being highlighted. Tena

AS THERE WAS NO PROPER ENTRY, THE KAVANAUGHS DRESSED UP THE NOOK BY THE STAIRS TO ACT AS A GREETING SPOT, COMPLETE WITH CHINOISERIE BAR, BRASS STAIR RODS, AND FAUX-LEOPARD TRIM ON THE STAIR RUNNER. TINY DOESN'T NEED TO MEAN UNDECORATED.

TRADE TIP

TINY POWDER ROOMS CAN BE FULL OF CHARACTER AND DRAMA. MAKE THE SINK VISIBLE FROM THE HALLWAY AND PLAY IT UP BY SETTING IT IN AN ANTIQUE CABINET OR DRESSING UP THE COUNTERTOP. TUCK THE TOILET BEHIND THE DOOR AND OUT OF SIGHT. A HOOK BEHIND THE DOOR PROVIDES A SPOT TO HANG A PURSE OR A JACKET.

HOUSE RULES

GATHER YOUR RESOURCES. When it came time to design both the stair spindles and the new mantels, Tena consulted extensive references. Armed with historical precedent, she then took liberties with her interpretation of the facts, borrowing an element from here, an influence from there.

GO FAUX IT. The Kavanaughs lived for a time in Bavaria, a region famed for the art of faux finishes. Tena found the effect not only decorative but also useful. If a piece of furniture is undistinguished, faux it; if a wall is dinged and damaged, glaze it. With all the beadboard in the Kavanaugh's house faux-grained, it's hard to tell where it was patched—the right side of the fireplace or the left? Her suggestion: Look for a painter who knows how to fake it with finesse.

FILL IN THE BLANKS. When a room is small, even the littlest change can make a big difference. Take one of the Kavanaughs' tiny upstairs bedrooms, which didn't even have enough wall space for a pair of twin beds. As soon as Tena eliminated a secondary door connecting one bedroom to the next, she gained a new stretch of wall that graciously accommodated the beds.

KEEP YOUR EYE ON THE VIEW. When renovating, Tena kept sight lines in mind, emphasizing the good (a fireplace) and hiding the not-so-good (an existing, much-used side door behind a new partial wall). This means considering the possibility of moving doors, adding half-walls, opening up a stair wall, or stealing a hall's floor space.

decided to open up the stairs by taking down one of the walls and installing new spindles and railings in its place. A sisal stair runner bordered with leopard print added an off-beat touch—a mix of rustic and luxe. The stairwell had breathing space, no small feat in such a small house. Like the entire former stable, it now had the feeling, if not the footprint, of a new space.

The Art of Simplicity

[the program] Accomplished in eleven months

- Build a two-story wing with a garage below and a master suite above
- Combine a small kitchen, pantry, and laundry room into one gracious, multicook kitchen with state-of-the-art storage systems
- Convert the old garage into a dream laundry room and mudroom
- Convert the existing screened porch into a den
- Construct a new back porch with fireplace
- Create a new master bath with his-and-hers dressing rooms
- Retrofit existing baths in the children's wing

TWO AND A HALF YEARS AGO, INTERIOR ARCHITECT AND furniture designer Laura Lee Samford and her husband, John, purchased their first home together. They'd been living in John's bachelor-pad house in Birmingham, Alabama, since they got married nine years earlier and were ready for more space and a more "grown-up" residence. They told their Realtor to look for something that sat back from the road and that needed work. They were willing to wait as long as it took.

As it turns out, it wasn't much of a wait. The Realtor called about a tempting prospect in their very own neighborhood—a white house on 11 acres that had been unoccupied for several years and was just about to go on the market. Their Realtor—like any good Realtor—finagled an early look.

The large house with a graceful hipped roof had been built in 1950, but it was not a typical fifties house. Rather, it was a mix of styles—or, as Laura Lee put it, an American house with traces of many influences. The triple-hung windows, extending from floor to ceiling, were Jeffersonian, reminiscent of those at Monticello, and the entry, with its arched over-door window and leaded glass sidelights, was in the Georgian genre. To Laura Lee, the lack of architectural pedigree was actually an advantage. It would allow her to keep the elements she liked, jettison those she didn't, and come up with a look of her own. She and her husband made

THE RIGHT EYE AND THE RIGHT PERSPECTIVE—ALONG WITH NEW ROOF TILES, LANDSCAPING, AND A COAT OF PAINT—TURNED A SOUTHERN HOUSE FROM UNDISTINGUISHED TO SUPERB.

TRADE TIP

DO FIRSTHAND RESEARCH ON YOUR HOME'S STYLE. IF
YOU KNOW SOMETHING'S WRONG, LIKE THE JALOUSIED
WINDOWS BELOW, BUT DON'T KNOW HOW TO FIX IT, DRIVE
THROUGH NEIGHBORING AREAS IN SEARCH OF A SOLU-
TION. BOOKS ON HOUSE STYLES WILL SHOW YOU WHAT
YOUR OPTIONS ARE AND OFFER POTENTIAL RESOLUTIONS.
YOU DON'T HAVE TO REINVENT THE WHEEL EVERY TIME. IF
IT WORKED ONCE, IT WILL WORK AGAIN.

a preemptive offer on the spot, without even looking at another house.

Laura Lee was brimming with design ideas about the renovation. Her overall approach, however, was straightforward: to keep as much of the existing structure as possible while adding square footage in a few key places. For one thing, she and John knew they wanted a new, proper master bedroom, set apart from the other bedrooms in the house. At the time, there were three bedrooms in the same wing, one of which Laura Lee planned to turn into an office for herself (where she could close the door and close off the mess), the second into a guest room, and the third and largest —the former master—into an elegant crash pad for John's daughters from an earlier marriage, when they came to stay. Also high on the to-do agenda was the kitchen, which was inefficient and cramped. Laura Lee envisioned a sleek, spacious eat-in space, gracious enough for entertaining.

To determine where they could most easily find and finesse the space they wanted, Laura Lee sized up the exterior—a simple single-story rectangle, built on a concrete slab, with an attached garage in the front. Right away, Laura decided to incorporate

THE SAMFORDS KNEW THE HOUSE WAS SALVAGE-
ABLE. WHILE THEY DIDN'T LIKE THE WAY IT LOOKED,
THEY KNEW THEY WOULD LOVE THE WAY IT LIVED.

the existing garage into the interior of the house and locate the new garage in the lower portion of a new two-story addition behind the old garage. This addition would consist of the garage, storage, and wine cellar below and a master suite above. The house would now total 6,000 square feet.

With the footprint of the addition set, Laura Lee sat down to draw the interior plans for the master bedroom, incorporating as much of their personal wish list as possible. John and Laura Lee had always wanted his-and-hers dressing areas. As Laura Lee pointed out, a dressing room means you don't have to dress in the bathroom, and it keeps the bedroom free of clothes draped on a chair or shopping bags dropped in a corner. She also liked the idea of placing a bench in the dressing room, for packing and unpacking her suitcase for the frequent trips she and her husband take. For the décor, she selected white-painted walls and cabinetry, except for her ebony-stained dressing table, and infused the room with light. She went in a different direction in John's dressing room, which he affectionately calls his padded cell, with its tobacco-colored wool-sateen upholstered walls and dark stained woodwork.

For the master bathroom itself, Laura Lee's instinct was to keep it spacious and basic. Her notion of luxury is

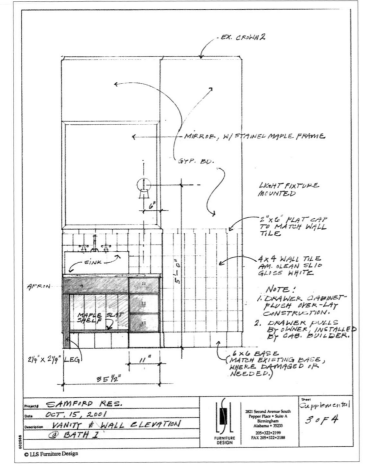

THE MASTER BATH WAS CONCEIVED AS A SPACIOUS, UNDERFURNISHED DRESSING ROOM. THE LUXURY COMES FROM THE SPACE AND GOOD-QUALITY MATERIALS, NOT ORNATE TILE OR FINISHES. THE FREE-STANDING BENCH WAS DESIGNED BY THE OWNER, WHO HAS HER OWN FURNITURE DESIGN COMPANY.

TRADE TIP

WHEN MARRYING FLOORING SURFACES—TILE TO CARPET, WOOD TO TILE OR STONE—THERE MAY BE A HEIGHT/LEVEL DISCREPANCY. TO KEEP FRIENDS AND FAMILY FROM TRIPPING, GET A REDUCER SADDLE MADE FOR THE THRESHOLD. HIGHER ON ONE SIDE, A REDUCER SADDLE SLOPES DOWN TO MEET THE LOWER FLOORING SURFACE, MAKING THE TRANSITION LESS HAZARDOUS.

[**ABOVE**] THE SAMFORDS INSTALLED SLABS OF MARBLE, INDIGENOUS TO ALABAMA, UP TO DADO HEIGHT IN THE MASTER BATH TO SET OFF A FREESTANDING SOAKING TUB. [**RIGHT**] IN HIS DRESSING ROOM, THE APPROACH WAS ENTIRELY DIFFERENT: EXTENSIVE BUILT-IN CABINETRY AND TOBACCO-COLORED WALLS—WHAT THE HUSBAND AFFECTIONATELY CALLS "HIS PADDED CELL."

TRADE TIP

TODAY'S TILE STORES ARE LIKE A CANDY STORE: LINED WITH EVERY COLOR AND TRIM PIECE UNDER THE SUN. BUT REMEMBER, FANCY TRIMMINGS DON'T ALWAYS MAKE FOR A SOPHISTICATED DÉCOR. SOMETIMES, IN FACT, THEY'RE JUST MOLD COLLECTORS. QUALITY COMES FROM THE MATERIAL ITSELF, AND STYLE COMES FROM BEING SELECTIVE, NOT OVERINDULGING.

inspired by memories of the grand homes of the Carnegies she visited on family vacations to Cumberland Island off Georgia. The bathrooms in those homes, she said, were like rooms, in contrast to the little closets of most modern-day homes. And they were never overwrought: a freestanding tub, a pedestal sink and a water closet, and maybe a piece or two of real furniture. Laura Lee didn't want to overdecorate her own master bathroom with tile inlays and inserts and fancy fixtures. Instead, she chose the simplicity of a marble wainscot around her bath. This minimalist aesthetic, along with an awareness of history, gives Laura Lee's designs their uniquely elegant and streamlined stamp.

The next space the couple targeted was the woefully undersized kitchen. The solution was clear: Knock down the walls to the two flanking spaces, a butler's pantry and laundry room, then raise the roof from 9 to 10 feet, adding significant visual and cubic space. Laura Lee had new windows installed throughout—including a wide, pretty bumped-out bay over a pair of farmhouse sinks—to bathe the kitchen in light. She put in gleaming stainless appliances, which contrasted strikingly with the rough-sawn cedar support beams framing the door openings. Finally, for flooring, she laid down a Mexican limestone in a mottled beige, earthy and practical. You simply can't see the dirt—and in a house with visit-

ing kids and two large Labradors, that's a plus.

With the shell of the kitchen established, it was time for Laura Lee to nail down the style of cabinetry. She originally intended to have custom cabinets built in her own woodworking shop, but ultimately she opted to

A SUCCESSION OF RUSTIC CEDAR BEAMS FRAMES A SERIES OF SPACES— PANTRY, KITCHEN, AND BREAKFAST ROOM. THE ROUGH-HEWN BEAMS PLAY OFF THE POLISHED FURNISHINGS—EXPECTED, IT'S NOT.

have a local kitchen cabinet fabricator make them. Why reinvent the wheel over something so basic? she asked herself. She selected a recessed door profile and had the cabinets painted a subtle putty color. Laura Lee also decided to keep the number of wall cabinets to a minimum to maintain a clean, uncluttered look. Of course, that meant she had to be smart about storage, which she wanted out of sight but still within reach. One clever solution was to house small appliances in a cabinet built to sit on the counter, with covert outlets on the inside. The mixer and blender stay plugged in, behind closed doors, ready to be pulled out and used right on the counter. Another smart storage move: Laura Lee had the cabinet company install slotted dividers in a pullout cabinet that allow her to line up her pots and pans vertically and separately; this way they're not stacked in an awkward jumble on a shelf.

Now to the dramatic centerpiece of the kitchen renovation. Laura Lee designed an island that was not only unusually large—10 feet by 5½ feet— but unusually shaped: a sculptural marble-topped oval, with chairs at one

WHERE DOES STORAGE FIT INTO A KITCHEN FREE OF MOST UPPER CAB-INETS? AS AN INTERIOR ARCHITECT, LAURA LEE INCORPORATED ANY AND EVERY MEANINGFUL STORAGE AMENITY SHE HAD ENCOUNTERED. [BELOW] BAKING PANS AND COOKIE TRAYS GET STORED UP-RIGHT IN A PULL-OUT DRAWER. A TRAY CABINET WAS DIVIDED VERTI-CALLY, AS IS CUSTOMARY, AS WELL AS HORIZONTALLY. [BELOW, RIGHT] A SUPER-SUSAN, THE MODERN-DAY LAZY SUSAN, PULLS FORWARD AND SWIVELS ALL THE WAY TO MAKE USE OF WHAT WERE FORMERLY AWK-WARD CORNER CABINETS.

TRADE TIP

IF YOUR ISLAND (OR ANY PIECE OF FURNITURE) IS OVERSIZED, A ROUNDED OR OVAL PERIMETER, AT LEAST ON ONE SIDE, SOFTENS THE BULK, MINIMIZING THE MASS.

end and a bar/prep sink at the other. Because the island is so big, Laura Lee can cook on the stove side and reserve the other for serving informal meals. Over the island she hung a pair of white globe Italian lights—a sleek modern touch.

The old garage was rebuilt as a util-ity wing consisting of a laundry room, mudroom, pantry, and back hall. The laundry room got its own luxurious treatment. Once again, for Laura Lee, that meant space. By any laundry room standard, this one is vast, with room for drying racks, linen closets, a fold-

ing island, and even an extra refrigerator. Laura Lee designed double-wide doorways to line up symmetrically with a matching opening from the kitchen, a maneuver that makes the two rooms feel connected. She retained the charming, unusual sink from the original laundry room. Laura Lee completely gutted and re-outfitted the room, installing cabinetry to match the kitchen, open shelving for supplies, and—to satisfy her own idiosyncratic desires—a pet supply drawer, a cleaning rag drawer, and a closet dedicated solely to hanging tablecloths and linens. Never the predictable designer, Laura Lee brought in a touch of the Old World with large antique champagne grape-collecting

THE KITCHEN ALSO SERVES AS PASSAGEWAY TO THE LAUNDRY ROOM, THE MUD-ROOM, AND THE GARAGE. THE OVERSIZED AND SLEEK TORPEDO-SHAPED OVAL, CHIPPED FROM A SINGLE GIANT SLAB OF INDIGENOUS ALABAMA MARBLE, EASED TRAFFIC THROUGH THE ROOM.

baskets made of wicker. She uses them as laundry baskets.

Moving on to the old bedroom wing, the next renovation task was converting the former master bedroom suite—two nondescript spaces separated by flimsy folding doors—into the new kids' room. Laura Lee removed the doors and made one large double bedroom with a pair of queen-size beds. She wanted John's daughters to have a full-fledged bathroom to go with their grand new room. All she had to

TRADE TIP

WE SPEND MORE TIME THAN WE REALIZE DOING LAUNDRY, INCLUDING WASHING, DRYING, IRONING, AND HAND-WASHING. WHY NOT MAKE THE ROOM FEEL CRISP AND CLEAN—EVEN REFINED? IT'S JUST A MATTER OF MAKING THE ROOM BRIGHT AND OUTFITTING IT WITH NICE SHELVING, A PIECE OF FURNITURE, GOOD LIGHTING, AND A SOUND SYSTEM OR LITTLE TV. IF THE ROOM IS BIG ENOUGH—THINK BEYOND THE WASH—THE LAUNDRY CAN DOUBLE AS A PLACE TO WRAP PRESENTS AND BATHE THE DOG.

[ABOVE] A LAUNDRY ROOM TO INSPIRE ENVY. FROM DOG FOOD TO DRYING RACK, THE SAMFORDS THOUGHT THROUGH EVERY DETAIL. THE VINTAGE UTILITY SINK WAS ALREADY THERE; THEY BUILT UPPER CABINETS WITHOUT DOORS TO KEEP SUPPLIES AT REACH. [LEFT] THE FAMILY'S PRIMARY ENTRANCE WAS ADJACENT TO A CAPACIOUS PANTRY AND CLOSET. OVERSIZED HARNESS HOOKS WERE MOLLY-BOLTED INTO THE WALLS TO SUPPORT PLENTY OF WEIGHT. THE MUDROOM IS TWO STEPS DOWN, LENDING IT A DEGREE OF SEPARATION AND VISUAL PRIVACY.

do to bring the adjacent one up to par was add a tub. The other bathrooms—one off the second guest room, used by John's son, plus the powder room—were simply treated to handsome new vanities made of dark-stained alder wood.

With the major construction work behind them, Laura Lee began the final phase of unifying the new wing with the old. She started with the floors. Luckily, the decision of which material to use was easy. Laura Lee happened to have acquired and kept in storage for just such a day 2,000 square feet of foot-wide heart pine (a material close to her heart, since it was used in the house her great-great-grandfather built when he returned home from the Civil War). She laid the pine throughout the newer portions of the house. In the entry hall, which rested on a cement slab, her choices were limited to tile. She chose the same Mexican limestone she used in the kitchen, laid in a simple pattern without border detail. Fortunately, the floors in the bedrooms, original thick parquet wood from the days when craftsmen assembled the parquet on-site, were in good shape and could be left as they were.

The other great unifier was paint. Laura Lee used only two colors for the entire house, albeit in different combinations and intensities: Benjamin Moore's Simply White and a warm putty color she lightened slightly with white. She painted both the walls and the trim in the entry hall and all the public spaces the Simply White. In the living room, however, she gave the crown and the base a wash of white but painted the walls the softer putty. The luster of the paint varied, too: Laura Lee specified high gloss for the moldings and door frames while the walls were given an eggshell finish even where there were wood dados and paneling—not a common approach.

The next phase of the renovation focused on furniture. For the dining room, Laura Lee designed a pair of contemporary china cabinets lit from within. Contrary to her usual minimalist instincts, she then hung a crystal chandelier, inherited from John's mother, over a round table from her line of sleek furniture—a juxtaposition of historical and hip

HOUSE RULES

HAVE A HIDDEN AGENDA. You can't be organized without a place to put things away. Hide electrical outlets behind cabinet doors or beneath hatches set into a dressing tabletop, to keep ungainly appliances out of sight but close at hand.

DON'T NEGLECT THE FINISHING TOUCHES. Using a combination of paint finishes—gloss for shine and visibility, eggshell for quiet—creates depth and dimension with a limited color palette of understated shades.

GAIN AXIS. Whenever doors and window openings are on a direct axis with each other, you gain symmetry and balance. This is one of the oldest but surest tricks in a designer's book.

STAY OFF BALANCE. Rather than laying out a kitchen, predictably, with upper and lower cabinets framing the room, try putting all your storage on two walls with full-length cabinets and letting the other walls breathe.

ANY PAINT CAN BE DOCTORED. If you're torn between two shades of a color, one darker than the other, choose the darker shade. It's far easier to lighten a color than it is to darken it. To lighten, dribble the white into your can little by little. You can always add more, but it is impossible to subtract. Later, paint two coats of your new home-made color on a portable flat surface. Whenever you need more paint, take the sample to the paint store, where their computer will read it and create a new formula.

that reminded Laura Lee of photos she'd seen in European design magazines showing stark contemporary furniture in a crumbling villa.

For the upholstered pieces in their bedroom and den, Laura Lee indulged in a few sumptuous yet understated fabrics: one a muted pale green velvet, the other a tobacco-brown wool sateen. It was only later that she realized, with nostalgia, that this was the very color scheme of her grandmother's house. The richness clicks in a house that's all about low-key luxe.

[ABOVE] THE MASTER BEDROOM SUITE, A COMPLETELY NEW ADDITION, WAS BUILT WITH 9-FOOT CEILINGS, SEVEN TRIPLE-HUNG WINDOWS (CONFORMING TO THOSE EXISTING ON THE FRONT OF THE HOUSE), AND A BOUNTY OF FLOOR SPACE. [RIGHT] IN THE CHILDREN'S BATH, THE SAMFORDS LEFT THE TUB, TILE, AND TOILET ALONE BUT BROUGHT IN AN EXOTIC WOOD VANITY TOPPED WITH COOL GRAY MARBLE, ADDING A UNIQUE TWIST ON BOTH FARMHOUSE AND VESSEL SINK.

THE SAMFORDS CONSIDERED THE DINING ROOM A BIT OF AN ANACHRONISM, BUT HAVE ENDED UP USING IT MORE THAN THEY EXPECTED. THE CHANDELIER, A FAMILY PIECE, HANGS IN CONTRAST TO A MODERN TABLE OF LAURA LEE'S OWN DESIGN. EXTENSIVE BUILT-IN CABINETRY ON EITHER SIDE OF THE ROOM'S ENTRANCE ELIMINATES THE NEED FOR ADDITIONAL FURNITURE.

All-in-the-Family Style

[the program] Accomplished in three years

- Turn a fusty attic into a rustic skylit kids' retreat
- Add a new family/media room
- Enlarge and remodel the kitchen
- Refinish the basement, adding a mudroom, laundry room, and wine cellar
- Attach a pretty pergola to the back of the house

WHILE ON WALKS THROUGH THEIR SUBURBAN NEIGH-borhood, the Caglieros—Veronica, Bob, and their two school-aged kids—had always admired a certain stone colonial for its good bones and gracious presence. When it went on the market and the couple finally got a chance to look inside, however, they were a tad disenchanted. The house was dark, overdecorated, and overpriced. The colonial stayed on the market for a year before the Caglieros decided its charms outweighed its drawbacks. They made a lowball offer, which was accepted.

The couple—he a TV producer, she an art director—knew they faced significant renovations to make the house work for their family. They bought it knowing that, ulti-mately, they wanted a state-of-the-art media/family room (there was only a formal living room) and a new expansive kitchen (the obsolete and cramped kitchen was definitely not going to make the cut), plus a cool playroom and a bona fide wine cellar. Even though they had plans, the Caglieros wanted to start slow. They figured they'd simply paint inside and out and refinish the floors, and then live in the house for a time before beginning a radical renovation.

Well, you know what they say about the best-laid plans. While an official inspection gave the house a clean bill of health, a sharp-eyed painter, on-site for an estimate a week

CHOOSING TO PRESERVE THE HISTORIC CHARACTER OF THEIR HOME, THE CAGLIEROS LEFT THE DESIGN OF THE FRONT OF THE HOUSE UNCHANGED AND UNTOUCHED—WITH THE EXCEPTION OF THE WINDOWS (WHICH NOW OPEN) AND THE ROOF (WHICH NO LONGER LEAKS).

before closing, pointed out the third-floor dormer in the attic was dangerously bowed. Rot, it turned out, had compromised the main beam of the house, which was also sagging.

The Caglieros had sold their existing home and were nearly packed, but Veronica refused to close on the new house until the price could be dropped to reflect the extensive repair work needed. The couple hired an architect to give a dollar value to the necessary repairs, then hired an attorney to renegotiate the purchase price. Eventually the owners relented, and the Caglieros recouped the cost of jacking up the roof and replacing the rear dormer. Had they already closed on the house, they would have had no recourse.

To make the immediate improvements to the roof, the

TRADE TIP

KEEP STYLE FILES OF COLORS, FIXTURES, AND CABINET PULLS FROM A MULTITUDE OF MAGAZINES. THIS IS WHAT I CALL TAKING THE TEARSHEET TEST—DON'T THINK IT, JUST FEEL IT. ONCE YOU'VE COLLECTED REAMS OF MATERIAL, PASTE THE TEARSHEETS, SWATCHES, AND REFERENCES ONTO A DESIGN BOARD SO YOU CAN "LOOK" AT EACH ROOM AND CONTEMPLATE.

Caglieros took a proactive approach, getting estimates, checking references, and gathering a team of subcontractors. Control freaks in the best sense, they kept job and spec sheets for everyone from the roofer to the floor refinisher, including contact information, referral notes, the date of the appointment, and the estimate. They interviewed a host of contractors, many of whom had dramatic and wild solutions to save the doomed dormer: whole new roof, whole new wall, whole new house! The contractor they ended up choosing had a resourceful and much more reasonable plan, using jacks to pull up the main beam of the house and cable wires to pull and hold the wall in place permanently.

Once that work was done, the Caglieros saw an opportunity in the newly saved attic: a playroom. With the addition of a few skylights, some simple pine paneling on the walls and ceiling, and the installation of wires for Internet access, the formerly dank space became a cool retreat for their kids and their friends. The Caglieros furnished the room with a pair of log beds and put some of the family's favorite collectibles on display—railroad lanterns, old globes, and guitars both vintage and new.

Painting the house was the next project on the list—and a messy one at that. What should have been an easy exterior job became more complicated when the painters did not properly seal the windows. While they were sanding, dust settled like a light snow throughout the house. (The Caglieros' son Bobby, then seven, suffered his first asthma attack in three years.) Inside, the painting went more smoothly. The interior plaster walls, many with hairline cracks, were scraped, patched, and repainted.

The Caglieros were ready to move on to the floors, which needed sanding and restaining. They decided to move out during that phase. After the dusty disaster of the exterior painting, they thought it wise to live with Bob's mother for a few weeks. Relocating, even for a short time, created unbudgeted expenses, including coverage on cell phone minutes while they lived without a designated land line,

THE LEAKY DORMER, CAUSE OF MUCH CONSTERNATION, WAS REPAIRED WHILE RETAINING ITS ORIGINAL FIFTIES CHARM. ADDING SKYLIGHTS, SCHOOLHOUSE PENDANTS, AND INTERNET ACCESS TRANSFORMED THE ONCE GLOOMY ATTIC-LIKE SPACE INTO A PLAYFUL SLEEPING LOFT–CUM-LODGE.

TRADE TIP

TO KEEP THE PROJECT ON SCHEDULE AND ON BUDGET, IT'S BEST TO AGREE ON A PAYMENT SCHEDULE LINKED TO PHASE COMPLETION RATHER THAN A FIXED REGULAR SCHEDULE. THIS WAY THE BUILDER HAS AN ADDED INCENTIVE TO STAY ON TRACK, COMPLETE A PHASE, AND RECEIVE A PAYMENT. TOWARD THE END, WORK ON THIS PROJECT SLOWED CONSIDERABLY WHEN FIXED REGULAR PAYMENTS GOT TOO FAR AHEAD OF THE COMPLETED WORK. ALSO CONSIDER DRAWING UP A CONTRACT SPECIFYING THAT ANY TIME CHANGES ARE MADE, THE WORK CHANGE ORDER IS SIGNED BY BOTH PARTIES. IT'S EASY TO LOSE TRACK OF NEW EXPENSES INCURRED. ON A LONG PROJECT, WORK CHANGE ORDERS CAN ADD UP TO A STAGGERING SUM.

[**LEFT AND ABOVE**] THE ALL-NEW FAMILY ROOM WAS ADDED
ON BEHIND THE LIVING ROOM. IT REPLACED AN EXISTING, BUT
CERTAINLY NOT ORIGINAL, BAY WINDOW WITH FRENCH DOORS
LINKING THE TWO ROOMS. BECAUSE THE FAMILY ROOM CON-
NECTS TO THE EXPANDED KITCHEN, THE CAGLIEROS NOW HAVE
A 360-DEGREE FLOW. WHILE THE ROOM WAS BEING FRAMED,
THE CAGLIEROS DECIDED TO ADD WAINSCOT PANELING TO
WHAT WAS DEEMED A TOO-MUCH-SHEETROCK CEILING. AS PRI-
VACY WAS NOT AN ISSUE, THEY LEFT THE WINDOWS AND
DOORS EXPOSED AND UNENCUMBERED.

TRADE TIP

CONTRACTORS INSIST THAT HAVING HOME-
OWNERS ON-SITE CAUSES COSTS TO ESCA-
LATE. WHEN A FAMILY IS IN RESIDENCE, AS
MANY AS TWO OF A CONTRACTOR'S EIGHT
HOURS MAY BE DEVOTED TO CLEANING,
SWEEPING, MOVING TRUCKS FROM DRIVE-
WAYS, AND SECURING STAIRWAYS.

[RIGHT AND FAR RIGHT] *BEFORE:* THE KITCHEN AND TRULY TINY BREAKFAST ROOM WERE CUTE AND KITSCHY—BUT NOT EXACTLY FUNCTIONAL. [ABOVE] *AFTER:* WITH AN OPEN PLAN, THE KITCHEN AND EATING AREA ARE MADE FOR COOKING AND ENTERTAINING. A GREAT DEBATE ENSUED OVER THE BREAKFAST BAY: WOULD IT BE JUST A WINDOW OR GO TO THE FLOOR? TURNED OUT THE CAGLIEROS NEEDED THE SPACE TO HOUSE THE BREAKFAST TABLE AND HOMEWORK DESK AT THE END OF THE KITCHEN. THE WAINSCOT-CLAD ISLAND ECHOES THE ADJACENT FAMILY ROOM CEILING.

storing Bob's vintage car, eating many meals out, and renting a tent, table, and chairs for Bobby's birthday party, which was to have been at their home.

By the time the floors were finished, the Caglieros were happy to move back home to begin planning phase two of the renovation. They took their time, ruminating about what they wanted and what the house needed. A year later, they embarked on the process of selecting a contractor to build a new family/media room and redo the kitchen.

The Caglieros knew that, unlike the dormer renovation, this phase of the job was too much to manage themselves. They decided to go with a design-and-build firm, a relatively new category of company that provides everything from architectural services and permit filing to construction and carpentry with in-house staff. They found the firm in the best possible way —through a neighbor's word-of-mouth referral—and double-checked all references with the town's local building board. Next, they had a face-to-face meeting with the head contractor, whom they immediately liked. Life is a lot easier when you feel comfortable with the professionals who will be an intimate part of your household for months, even years.

Together with the design firm, the Caglieros came up with a plan to build a new family room—an 18-foot addition on the back of the house. To make

the most of the 10-foot ceilings, they had them wainscoted and detailed with beams. They put in two sets of French doors—an exterior pair with sidelights to provide access to a new terrace facing their wooded lot, and an interior pair to link the family room to the existing living room. They placed transom windows high on what would become the TV wall—a nice detail and a smart way to cut down on glare to the

[BELOW] COMMERCIAL QUALITY—BUT NOT OVERSCALE APPLIANCES MADE THE MOST OF LIMITED SPACE. A TELEVISION, SITUATED OVER THE MICROWAVE, WAS A CLEVER CHOICE— VISIBLE YET OUT OF THE WAY. COUNTERTOPS WERE FABRICATED FROM A SLAB OF VERDI MARBLE.

screen. The Caglieros then hung white wood shutters (in the same vernacular as the wainscoting) on windows facing a neighbor for privacy. The final stroke: a strong dose of red paint, which made the white wainscoted ceiling and the room come alive.

[**RIGHT**] AS VIEWED FROM THE DRIVEWAY SIDE OF THE HOUSE, A SERIES OF SMALL TRANSOM WINDOWS PERFORATED THE FAMILY-ROOM ADDITION TO CONTROL GLARE FOR THE STATE-OF-THE-ART ELECTRONICS. GREAT FOR THE INTERIOR—BUT SEVERE ON THE EXTERIOR. TO SOFTEN THE SIDING, THE CAGLIEROS ERECTED A PERGOLA TO TURN THE NEGATIVE INTO A DISTINCTIVE AND CHARMING POSITIVE. [**OPPOSITE**] BIGGER IS NOT ALWAYS BETTER. BOB, A TRUE OENOPHILE, TUCKED HIS EFFICIENT AND ACCESSIBLE CELLAR UNDER THE STAIRS.

TRADE TIP

THE IMPACT OF THE RENOVATION ON THE FAMILY WAS ENORMOUS, AND THE NEIGHBORHOOD WAS AFFECTED AS WELL. THINK OF IT: YOU ARE NOT ONLY INVADING YOUR NEIGHBOR'S AIRSPACE AND SIGHT LINES BUT THEIR VERY LIVES. THE STREET HAS A NEW POPULATION BASE—EXCAVATORS, ROOFERS, CARPENTERS, AND CEMENT TRUCK DRIVERS—NOT TO MENTION THE NOISE. IF YOU PLAN A RENOVATION CLOSE TO YOUR NEIGHBORS, IT'S A GOOD IDEA TO TALK TO THEM, TO ANSWER QUESTIONS, AND ASK FOR PATIENCE.

During the planning process, it didn't take long to realize that the kitchen, too, should be enlarged. Veronica, a serious cook, wanted a kitchen that worked not only for the family but also for a party of adults, since the couple frequently entertains. A 6-foot bump with a bay window was designed to link the new kitchen to the new family room and accommodate a breakfast table. Veronica went with clean-lined white cabinets and restaurant-grade appliances. A Verdi green marble countertop and yellow walls warm the white cabinets.

For the basement renovation, the design-and-build firm gave the Caglieros several options—from modest cubbies to a fully loaded package with wine cellar, bath, and a kid hangout space. Thinking ahead to their children's teenage years, the couple took the entire package. This included additional excavation, during which they discovered rock— another unexpected expense. The wine cellar was tucked under the basement steps, with terra-cotta tiles on the floor, plaster troweled on the walls, and a marble bistro table set in the center, creating a café ambiance. The cool temperature of the wine cellar meant the Caglieros could also use the space as a pre-party holding area for platters of food or bunches of flowers.

Outside, on the back of the house, the Caglieros realized they now needed some detail to break up the driveway side mass of the new addition, which was clad in white clapboard. A pergola, running alongside the exterior wall, was the perfect solution. When the flowering clematis climbs and covers the framework, the pergola will provide color, texture, and romance.

Originally, the Caglieros expected the remodel to take a year, inclusive of the initial must-do repairs and the subsequent wish list. Instead, it took three years to complete. Unexpected cold caused ice to collect on the open roof; pipes froze, and endless mud was tracked through the house. Heavy equipment throughout the freeze/thaw/ freeze winter cracked and damaged the driveway; new macadam was an unbudgeted expense. Demolition killed shrubs and trees they had planned to retain. Leaking chemicals from a portable toilet perched at curbside killed a section of lawn (the area was reseeded and eventually grew grass again). The Caglieros got through this rough patch, like the others, with patience, perspective, and a healthy sense of humor.

HOUSE RULES

TAKE ATTENDANCE. Too often you return home at the end of the day and wonder: Was the plumber here? Did the electrician show up? Veronica left a notebook on a table in the foyer as a way to communicate. She'd jot down a question and they'd jot down an answer. The log cut down on the inevitable miscommunications—and everything was in writing.

DOCUMENT DIGITALLY. Once Veronica made design choices, she went into showrooms and took digital pictures of all of her selections, from tiles to appliances, to give herself a record of what she'd ordered. These pictures came in handy when the marble countertop arrived with a large flaw in the center. It was not the slab she had selected. Restitution was made.

BE FOREWARRANTED. The warranty for your appliances is activated when they are installed, not when they are purchased. More often than not, the refrigerator, dishwasher, oven, and so on are bought and delivered to the job site long before the installation date— in the Caglieros' case, six months before. Since Murphy's Law states that your dishwasher will break the moment the warranty expires, it's nice to know you can have your contractor write a letter for your files stating the installation date, thereby giving yourself the longest legitimate warranty time.

CHOOSE YOUR BATTLES. In every renovation, something is bound to go awry. At the very end of the Cagliero project, when workers moved the refrigerator into place, they gouged the just-refinished floor. Veronica briefly considered dismantling her newly functional kitchen before deciding it was smarter to barter additional carpentry work for the repair.

Shades of White

[the program] ## Accomplished one project at a time over two decades

- Convert the attic into two bedrooms and a bath
- Turn a former garage into a gleaming, light-filled kitchen
- Modify the front to create a more gracious entry
- Co-opt a courtyard for a sitting room
- Enclose and enlarge a rear deck to form a screened-in porch and music room
- Add on a rocking-chair front porch
- Redo the master bedroom and bathroom with clean, classic touches

WHEN DESIGNER KRISTIINA RATIA FIRST LAID EYES ON A charming old caretaker's cottage in the Connecticut countryside twenty-five years ago, she was drawn to the sun streaming through countless oversized windows. Having grown up in Finland, where the days are notoriously short, she had a lust for light. Kristiina was also attracted to the private setting of the two-story clapboard house, which sits far back from the road on an open plateau overlooking a large pond.

At first glance, the house looked to be in good shape. The walls were freshly painted, and the floors were buffed to a shine. Kristiina, young and idealistic, wanted to move right in. Of course, she and her husband realized the house had certain problems—an unfinished second floor, an inade-

quate kitchen situated, oddly enough, in the entry, and an ancient bathroom—but believed they could resolve them over time. They also had foresight. They saw that they could create space for additional bedrooms, a larger kitchen, a music room, and a sitting room.

The first transformations took place in the raw attic. In short order, the Ratias framed in two new bedrooms, a walk-in closet, and a large bath with a platform tub. At the same time, Kristiina sized up the former garage, which had been turned it into a laundry room and cold storage area.

THE DINING ROOM OF A CONNECTICUT COTTAGE MIXES THE MODEST AND THE MAJOR. KRISTIINA ATTACHED A SERIES OF IKEA CHESTS OF DRAWERS—TWO HIGH, THREE ACROSS—AND PAINTED THEM BLACK TO CREATE A BUREAU OF STORAGE. AN EXTRAVAGANT RUSSIAN CANDELABRA TOPS A SIMPLE WALNUT REFECTORY TABLE, SURROUNDED BY LINEN-COVERED CHAIRS.

island, served as the growing family's daily dining spot, where wonderful meals seemed to appear spontaneously.

Kristiina painted the kitchen her favorite hue, Benjamin Moore China White (it became the home's signature color). In keeping with the white theme, all the countertops, the floor, and even the sides of the large center island were covered in gleaming tiles. True to her Scandanavian spirit, Kristiina had conjured up a winter-white fairyland warmed with Finnish antiques.

BEFORE

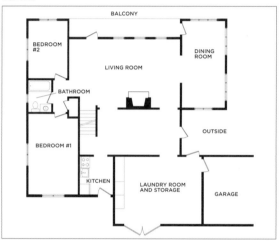

She envisioned the space, with its generous proportions and unusually high ceilings, as the kitchen she'd always wanted—big enough to cook for family and friends.

Kristiina's colleague, the late designer Michael Haskins, drew up plans for the new kitchen, and construction began. Kristiina was working out of her house at this point, designing children's clothing and bedding for Marimekko, the Finnish fabric house started by her husband's family. In true European fashion, Kristiina served a daily hot lunch to Marimekko associates and construction crew alike, endearing herself to all.

And, indeed, the former garage turned out to be the perfect kitchen—pristinely white, warmed by touches of wood. Skylights were punched into the raised roof, sending shafts of welcome light into the formerly windowless space. Structural rafters, now needed to support the weight of the skylights, add an architectural element. The swinging wood double garage doors were left intact; Kristiina found them charmingly appropriate. Pine kitchen cabinets were built to Kristiina's specifications: the upper ones designed as open shelves and the lower ones as drawers (it's easier to pull out cooking pots than to lean down and dig inside a cupboard). A butcher-block table, placed perpendicular to the center

AFTER

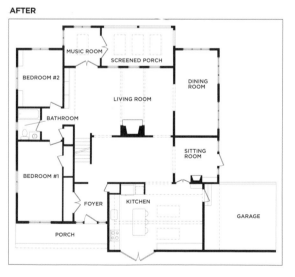

[ABOVE, LEFT] THE KITCHEN STARTED LIFE AS A GARAGE. HERE, IN ITS FIRST INCARNATION AS A KITCHEN, THE ROOM WAS ALL-WHITE TILE WITH FINNISH COUNTRY CHARM. [ABOVE] FLOOR PLANS, *BEFORE* AND *AFTER:* THE HOUSE GREW INCREMENTALLY—A ROOM HERE, A SKYLIGHT THERE.

TRADE TIP

ONE WOULD THINK THAT LIGHT COLORS WORK BEST IN DARK SPACES. NOT SO—THEY SIMPLY DISAPPEAR. STRONG CONTRAST, FROM LIGHT TO DARK, IS WHAT WE SEE BEST. IN THIS CASE, THE ORIGINAL KITCHEN WAS REFASHIONED INTO AN ENTRY HALL. A BLACK SISAL CARPET (PAINTED BY AN ART-MAJOR DAUGHTER) COVERED MUCH OF THE ENTRY'S WHITE TILED FLOOR. A DUTCH DOOR WITH CRISP CHROME HARDWARE, BLACK GRASSCLOTH WALLCOVERING, CLEAN WHITE TRIM, AND OVERSIZED ACCESSORIES MADE WHAT COULD HAVE BEEN A MUNDANE SPACE QUITE STUNNING.

The door was now just as Kristiina wanted it, but not so the entry inside, which was a dark little nook with the merest hint of afternoon light. To give the entryway presence, she papered the walls in black grasscloth, which contrasted sharply with the bright white moldings and doors. As much as she loves white rooms, Kristiina, who by then had her own interior design business, believed that in a dark space, white looks dingy and feels gloomy. She also learned that oversized furnishings can give a small space greater impact. With that in mind, she furnished the entry with a large zinc-topped bistro table and an oversized English walnut mirror. As Kristiina says, seeing furniture as soon as you open the door makes you feel you are coming into someone's home, not just a hall.

The third renovation go-round for the family took place a few years later, in the living room. To house her countless design and reference books, Kristiina built wall-to-wall

A couple of years later, Kristiina was ready to tackle the home's entrance. The front door was awkwardly jammed into the corner between the converted kitchen and the main living space without any adornment, ornament, or grace. First, Kristiina decided to move the doorway out of the corner to the center of the small entry hall and flank it with double-hung casement windows. It wasn't long before she replaced the door itself with an old-fashioned Dutch door, which she painted glossy black.

[ABOVE] KRISTIINA ADDED A MUSIC ROOM WHEN HER THREE DAUGHTERS WERE DEEP IN PIANO LESSONS. FLOORS, ONCE NATURAL, RECEIVED A HIGH-GLOSS MIX OF EBONY WITH A BIT OF WALNUT. THE ADDED BONUS: THE MUSIC ROOM LINKS TO A WONDERFUL, NOW ROOFED AND SCREENED, POND-SIDE PORCH. [RIGHT] *BEFORE,* THE LIVING ROOM FELT TRUNCATED. IT HAD FRENCH DOORS THAT LED TO A PORCH BUT MOSQUITOES FROM THE POND MADE ALFRESCO DINING DIFFICULT.

ground for use when referencing books in the "stacks."

Next, Kristiina cast her creative eye around the living room, searching for a way to incorporate a piano for her three musically inclined young daughters. There was no way. So she zeroed in on the living room's pond-side rear wall, outside of which ran a balcony, too narrow to accommodate any real function. By doubling the width of the balcony, Kristiina got two new spaces in one fell swoop: She turned two-thirds of the enlarged space into a screened-in porch and enclosed the remaining third to create an interior piano room. To let in the light, Kristiina added banks of windows —and set her mercury glass collection asparkle on the piano top's glossy black lacquer surface. Kristiina also installed a few well-spaced skylights in the new shed roof spanning the porch and the piano room to keep the adjacent living room from being overshadowed.

In Kristiina's world, a house is never

bookcases on one side of the room. The shelves were made of simple 1 by 12 planks of stock lumber; later, the fronts were embellished with fluting to dress them up a bit. In a Finnish twist, Kristiina placed a modern Formica table—in black, of course, the only alternative to white—in the fore-

TRADE TIP

PAINT CHANGES IN VARYING LIGHT AND AS IT AGES. IDEALLY, STUDY A COLOR OVER THE COURSE OF A DAY (AND NIGHT) OR TWO BEFORE YOU COMMIT. BECAUSE IT'S PARTICULARLY HARD TO IMAGINE HOW ANY COLOR WILL LOOK FROM EVERY ANGLE, ASK THE PAINT STORE FOR MULTIPLE PAINT CHIPS AND POSITION ONE ON EACH WALL. BETTER YET, BUY A QUART AND PAINT A LARGE SAMPLE— ABOUT 2 FEET SQUARE—ON WALLS WITH TWO DIFFERENT EXPOSURES.

[**LEFT**] FINDING THE SPACE FOR A FIREPLACE (IMPORTANT TO A SCANDINAVIAN) IN THE NEWLY CREATED FAMILY ROOM NECESSITATED SOME CLEVER ENGINEERING, AS IT BACKED ONTO THE KITCHEN. [**BELOW**] THE PITCH OF THE OVERHANGING ROOF WOULD ALLOW ONLY A VERY NARROW FRONT PORCH. STILL, THE PORCH WAS JUST DEEP ENOUGH FOR A TRIO OF KENNEDY ROCKERS, PAINTED BLACK, AND DECKED OUT IN TEXTILES FROM RATIA'S OWN FABRIC LINE FOR MOTIF DESIGNS.

done, and so she circled back to face the front of the house again. The entrance still lacked a portico or overhang. A front porch was the solution. Because of the gentle pitch of the roofline (which meant not a lot of headroom), Kristiina had to keep this porch on the slender side—just wide enough for a lineup of classic country rockers. As it turned out, the porch not only dressed up the entrance but also served as the perfect vantage point from which to watch the sunset—and her son (both spectacular), who liked to shoot hoops in the front drive.

The renovations didn't end there. As the kids grew, Kristiina felt she needed her own grown-up sitting room. Rather than usurp an existing room, she decided to enclose the small interior courtyard sandwiched between the kitchen and the dining room. By building a fourth wall and roofing the space, Kristiina was able to fashion a tiny but engaging study; it even had a fireplace, a feature she had her heart set on. For such a snug room, with openings on all sides but one, she needed to search for a small-scale fire-

[**ABOVE**] THE KITCHEN TODAY: MARBLE TOPS HAVE REPLACED TILES. THE ISLAND WAS CLAD IN WAINSCOTING AND A WALL-TO-WALL BUILT-IN CABINET HOUSES KRISTIINA'S EXTENSIVE COLLECTION OF—WHAT ELSE?—WHITE CHINA AND TABLE TOPPINGS. THE ONCE NATURAL BUTCHER BLOCK TABLE WAS NARROWED WHEN IT SHIFTED FROM ISLAND APPENDAGE TO FREE-FLOATING TABLE.

[**RIGHT**] WHEN FIRST CONSTRUCTED, THE UPPER CABINETS WERE RAW PINE. NOW THREE GENERATIONS LATER KRISTIINA ADDED DOORS PAINTED A FRESH GLOSSY CHINA WHITE.

and painted all the cabinets, woodwork, and beams glossy white. The result was crisp, fresh, revitalized. As for the old swinging garage doors, they now seemed cumbersome for letting active children in and out, and they obscured the view of Kristiina's new front garden. Her bright idea—literally—was to replace them with mullioned French doors, which let even more light, and now a view, into her kitchen.

Fast-forward another decade, and Kristiina once again renewed the kitchen. The twenty-year-old white tiled countertops were pitted and chipped. She replaced the tiles with slabs of honed white Carerra marble, in keeping with her white aesthetic but softer and more refined, and traded her old stainless sink for a marble one of her design. She loves the sink even though it was the first one the marble fabricator had ever attempted, and, truth be told, it is not quite pitched to perfection (she knows because water pools in the corners). The island was resided in wainscoting and topped in the same Carerra marble, with a generous 12-inch

overhang to tuck chairs beneath. Suddenly the standing island was a sitting island—an ideal perch for homework and meals on the run.

To create a place for a proper sit-down meal, the old

place. Undeterred, Kristiina did her homework and located a manufacturer who offered a parlor-size premade firebox. To accommodate the fireplace's depth, Kristiina had to intrude into the kitchen, where she cleverly concealed the back of the fireplace with a wainscot-backed bookcase.

The family had been ensconced in their home a good dozen years by now, and major structural changes, roof raisings, and additions were complete. It was time, however, to revisit the original renovations. The all-white kitchen was showing wear and tear—like shoes, Kristiina said, things get worn—and she didn't blame the contractor. After all, moldings separate, paint flakes, and floorboards spread with time, age, and humidity. Factor in the kids—in Kristiina's case, four—and her shelves and drawers were plenty dinged and scratched. This time around she closed in the open shelving

butcher-block table was scooted over to the side of the kitchen. Kristiina brought its function and form up to date by having it cut narrower and lacquer-sprayed a glossy white in an auto body shop. Kristiina also installed a new wainscot-backed display case for her dishes. Though sleeker, the kitchen is still familiar and friendly, with warm touches of Finland, including the same antique pine hanging cabinets.

Upstairs, the bath, of the same original renovation era as the kitchen, was also in need of freshening up. There was nothing wrong with the layout, just the look, which was tired and dated. Kristiina gutted the space but left the fixtures in the same location, which helped enormously to cut down on costs. The tiled platform tub, which proved more than once to be slippery when wet, was replaced with a freestanding deep, or soaking, tub. In lieu of the standard sink, Kristiina installed a vintage pedestal harvested from one of her customers' renovations. She removed the tiles from the floor, revealing the underlying wood planks, which she then lacquered white. To tie the whole space together, both the walls and the sloped skylit ceiling were clad in wainscoting. To Kristiina, wainscoting was the great concealer, masking walls that are a bit crooked or out of plumb.

Her latest oeuvre: the master bedroom. It was two decades before Kristiina decided it was time to renovate a space purely for her. The bedroom, she says, was nothing special to start with—a basic box, albeit with lovely light. In keeping with the origins of the house, she turned to wainscoting to add character and texture. Kristiina ran the beadboard three-

HOUSE RULES

BE SMART ABOUT MARBLE. Kristiina was warned against using white marble, notorious for staining, in her kitchen. She stuck to her guns but did listen to sage advice from a marble yard: If you're going to use the stone in a kitchen filled with the staining and scratching potential of red wine, lemons, or any other acidic ingredient, you are best off honing the surface—which means removing the polish. A matte stone shows less wear and tear.

GO DOOR TO DOOR. One of the easiest transformations to make to a room is through the door, whether it's leading inside to out or from one space to another. Kristiina changed exterior doors in the front and the back of the house from single to double, from solid to Dutch. Switching a pair of wood doors for a pair of French doors brought the outside into her kitchen. Replacing a solid wood door between the kitchen and the sitting room with a pair of slender glass sidelights, hinged like doors, eliminated door swing problems and dressed up the doorway.

KEEP SKYLIGHTS OUT OF SIGHT. Because skylights aren't the most graceful of additions, try to confine them to the back of the house, where they aren't noticeable as you approach. And be aware that they don't last forever; fifteen years is the average lifespan. As skylights age, they tend to leak and must be replaced. That said, the quality and amount of light you get from a window to the sky is transforming.

LIVING WITH WHITE IS NOT EASY. There's the obvious: It needs frequent touchups for smudges and fingerprints. And you need to be disciplined, which goes beyond being neat and tidy. A white home lends itself to a spare and well-edited aesthetic. The less clutter, the better it works.

quarters of the way up the walls and added a narrow display ledge on which to mount a gallery of black-and-white photographs. She also flanked the window with bookcases the height of the wainscoting.

The ceiling got the wainscot treatment, too. Kristiina loves lying in bed and looking up at this pretty wood—so much more interesting than a plain Sheetrock view. She can also appreciate the new ceiling fan—a romantic detail and a nice source of circulating air, as she's never liked air-conditioning.

Through the years of renovating—twenty-five in all—

Kristiina fine-tuned the house and remodeled in small increments to adapt to her changing life, needs, and design desires. No matter the variations on her white theme (tile, marble, wainscoting), Kristiina always strove to keep the look and feel of the house in its original style even as it reflected her own innate preferences. For brief periods she flirted with color and pattern—saddle-colored sponged walls, faded English florals, and kilim and tribal rugs. But these were short-lived love affairs because they weren't true for her. When they were over, Kristiina found her way home—not surprisingly, right back to her Finnish roots.

TRADE TIP

WAINSCOTING, EITHER THE REAL DEAL—INDIVIDUAL STRIPS—OR IN 4 BY 8-FOOT SHEETS, ADDS INSTANT ARCHITECTURE TO A ROOM WITHOUT BEING GRANDIOSE. IT IS BEST SUITED TO SIMPLE TRIMMINGS, SO KEEP CAPPING PIECES AND OTHER MOLDINGS SPARE. WAINSCOT ADDS DEPTH AND DIMENSION TO AN OTHERWISE PLAIN SHEETROCKED ROOM. TRADITIONAL WAINSCOTING IS A NATURAL WOOD IN COLOR; TODAY WE PAINT IT WHITE MORE OFTEN THAN NOT. BUT WAINSCOTING NEED NOT BE EITHER WOOD OR WHITE.

[RIGHT] *BEFORE:* THE MASTER BATHROOM, IN A PREVIOUS LIFE.
[ABOVE] *AFTER:* THE SIZE AND THE SHAPE OF THE SECOND-FLOOR BATH DIDN'T CHANGE BUT EVERYTHING ELSE DID. A SOAKING TUB AND PEDESTAL SINK REPLACED THE PLATFORM TUB AND TILE-TOPPED VANITY. KRISTIINA ADDED A PARTIAL WALL TO CONCEAL THE TOILET AND SLIPCOVERED CHAIR. THE NEW SMALL CASEMENT WINDOW CAN BE CRANKED OPEN FOR VENTILATION.

[ABOVE] THE LIGHT-FILLED, HIGH-CEILINGED LIVING ROOM WAS WHAT ATTRACTED KRISTIINA TO THE HOUSE ALL THOSE YEARS AGO. IT IS THE ONE ROOM THAT REMAINED UNCHANGED STRUCTURALLY. THE MANTEL AND OVERDOOR DETAILS ARE ALL ORIGINAL.

[LEFT] IN THE BEDROOM, A SIX-SIDED BOX WITH "PRETTY WINDOWS," WAINSCOTING PANELING AND BUILT-IN BOOKCASES WERE ADDED TO PROVIDE DETAIL AND DECORATIVE WARMTH.

Country in the City

[the program] ## Accomplished in three years

- Enlarge the kitchen by 300 square feet to accommodate a breakfast table
- Rebuild the front and back entrances and cobblestone the courtyards and terraces
- Custom build a kitchen island and cabinetry
- Tame a double-height family room
- Add a back staircase and detail it with artistry
- Turn a run-down pool cabana into a full-fledged guesthouse

WHEN OLIVIA AND TED MATTHEWS MADE THE MOVE from a city they loved, Chicago, to a city they didn't yet know, Atlanta, they looked on the bright side: a warmer clime, year-round greenery, and the notion that they could have a country house within city limits. The couple soon found what they were after: a gracious southern Georgian 1940s brick home perched on 9 acres overlooking a wide meadow and only ten minutes from downtown. The house had enough space to put up their parents, visiting kids, hoped-for grandkids, and family friends, most of whom lived plane rides away. It's the "if-you-build-it-they-will-come" approach. Only in this case, the situation was "if you renovate, they will come." And they will stay.

With the house in hand, the goal was to renovate to suit their lives—and guests. At the top of the agenda for the Matthewses, who both have demanding careers (he as a CEO, she as an advocate for juvenile diabetes research), was reworking the kitchen and the family room and building proper guest quarters, all while infusing the whole house with an easy elegance.

The Matthewses set about assembling a top-quality team, starting with the interior decorator, Atlanta-based Jackye Lanham. At their first meeting Olivia intuitively knew that the match was right, without even seeing Jackye's portfolio.

HOW CAN A HOUSE AND PROPERTY LIKE THIS BE SO CLOSE TO THE DOWNTOWN OF A MAJOR METROPOLITAN CITY? A NEW ENTRANCE AND A COBBLESTONE DRIVEWAY WERE THE ONLY CHANGES MADE TO THE FRONT FAÇADE OF THIS CIRCA 1940S HOME.

There was a certain simpatico—maybe because they're both natural blondes, Olivia joked. They struck a deal the old southern way—with a handshake. The designer, in turn, called on well-respected architect Norman Askins and contractor Nick Britting (who, coincidentally, had worked on the house before).

Too often in the zeal for renovation, said Jackye, homeowners think in

grandiose terms: creating soaring ceilings and huge additions not true to the integrity of the house and impossible to warm up and furnish. The Matthewses had a different approach: a desire to stay within the home's vernacular. In the kitchen, for example, they demol-

ished the eating area, an awkward and fussy glass conservatory space grafted onto the back of the house, and replaced it with a more appropriate rectangular eating area meant to look like a former summer porch now enclosed. They designed simple kitchen cabinets and kept upper cabinets to a minimum. The generous island and a roomy, open-shelved walk-in pantry made up the difference, storage-wise, housing all cookware and plates.

They kept the kitchen color scheme to a whisper. Understated grays and taupes, based on traditional English drabs, repeated on cabinets, moldings, and wicker chairs, came off anything but drab. The hues worked naturally with the various finishes in the room, from stainless-steel appliances to nickel faucets to Olivia's collection of antique pewter platters displayed on the wall. Even the range hood, which seemed too shiny-new in the space, got a toning down; it was rubbed with paste wax, which lent it a warm and worn patina. The Matthewses chose lighting to reflect a variety of intensities, from the utilitarian recessed lighting at the perimeter of the room to the softer glow cast by three institutional-size perforated tin hanging pendants over the island and an antique black chandelier suspended over the break-fast table. The one break from the muted sensibility was the choice of a glass-front Traulsen refrigerator, which

[ABOVE] A 1970S GREENHOUSE ADDITION WAS INCORPORATED INTO THE KITCHEN BREAKFAST AREA. THE MISSION STATEMENT WAS THAT IT SHOULD SEEM LIKE AN OLD SUMMER PORCH THAT HAD BEEN ENCLOSED AND WINTERIZED. A STAINLESS-STEEL OVEN HOOD WAS HAND-WAXED TO GIVE IT A ONE-OF-A-KIND PEWTER FINISH. CRAB ORCHARD STONE SEEMED IDEAL FOR THE KITCHEN WHEN THE FIRST CHOICE WAS DEEMED TOO "SLICK." [FAR LEFT] INSTEAD OF A TRADITIONAL TILE OR STONE BACK FOR THIS SECONDARY SINK, A SMALL STONE SPLASH WAS CAPPED WITH SIMPLE 4-INCH WIDE V-GROOVE BOARDS, A LOOK INSPIRED BY AN OLD POTTING TABLE. [LEFT] WITH WALL CABINETS AT A MINIMUM, MANY DISHES AND FOODSTUFFS WOULD BE STOWED IN A SPACIOUS PANTRY, COMPLETE WITH MICROWAVE, MINI FRIDGE, AND DISHWASHER.

Olivia insisted upon. She couldn't resist seeing all the produce, all the colors, at a glance. Like going to the market, she said.

As in any renovation project, the Matthewses had their share of miscalculations. Olivia, who is tall, wanted the kitchen island built several inches higher than standard. However, once the marble countertop—a stone quarried north of Atlanta—was installed, the island was so large and so white it looked like a beached whale. After much discussion, she agreed to lowering the island a few inches, an easy (and not too costly) mistake to undo.

The Matthewses discovered that certain decisions could and should be reversed. Nothing's set in stone, even when it's a stone floor—though a misstep of this scale was both trickier and more expensive to fix. The Matthewses had ordered limestone tiles for the kitchen floor. The tile installer was halfway through the job when Olivia realized the tile choice was dead wrong—too slick, too polished for her "drab" kitchen. Instead of waiting and hoping the look would grow on her, she bit the bullet and had the stone pulled up. For a new flooring idea, their contractor suggested they look no farther than their own backyard, to the terrace made of crab orchard stone. That particular stone, indigenous to the area, had the muted tone and rustic quality Olivia wanted. To differentiate the indoors from the outdoors, the interior stones were laid on the diagonal, sanded, and sealed several times over. The sanding process not only made the stones less rough but actually altered the color from a cool gray to a warmer gray.

The Matthewses brought the same warm country-house sensibility to the family room, which was too large, too cold, and had a double-height ceiling with a curious loft-balcony space—so very eighties—at one end. A simple plan emerged: to pull the ceiling all the way across the room, allowing for a more intimate room below and a much-needed guest suite above to replace the retro loft. The walls of the downstairs space were paneled with V-groove boards, specified in an extra-wide width for a more country feel and

[OPPOSITE] THE OVERSIZED STONE FLOORING WAS BANDED AS IT STEPPED DOWN INTO THE ADJOINING FAMILY ROOM. THE MATTHEWSES INTENDED FOR THE FURNISHINGS IN THE FAMILY ROOM TO DIVIDE IT INTO TWO DISTINCT SEATING AREAS; BAMBOO SEATING FOR CONVERSATION; UPHOLSTERED PIECES FOR TELEVISION VIEWING. [ABOVE] IN THE POOL HOUSE A TINY STAIRWELL IS A STUDY IN BLACK AND WHITE: BLACK WINDOW MULLIONS, A SHAKER-STYLE RUG, AND ROMANTIC MIRROR AND LIGHT FIXTURES.

TRADE TIP

HOW TRUE DOES A RENOVATION NEED TO BE TO THE ARCHITECTURAL ROOTS OF A HOUSE? IT DEPENDS. IF THE RENOVATION IS SMALL AND TAKES PLACE WITHIN THE EXISTING SPACE, IT'S PROBABLY BEST TO USE THE SAME DECORATIVE LANGUAGE IN THE NEW AREA AS THE ORIGINAL (FOR EXAMPLE, AN ULTRA-MODERN APPLIANCE CAN SEEM JARRING IN AN OTHERWISE PERIOD-APPROPRIATE SPACE). HOWEVER, IF YOU'RE ADDING TO THE BACK OF THE HOUSE, YOU CAN EASILY DEVIATE FROM THE DESIGN DISCIPLINE AND IF YOU'RE LUCKY ENOUGH TO BE BUILDING A WHOLE SEPARATE STRUCTURE, LIKE THE MATTHEWS' GUESTHOUSE, YOU CAN REALLY REINVENT THE GENRE AND BE YOUR FANTASY SELF.

painted a rich ivory. The final construction element was a staircase connecting the two spaces. The stairs, narrower at the top and wider at the bottom, created a spindle problem. If the spindles were to descend directly from the narrower upper portion of the staircase, the wider bottom stairs would be truncated, leaving a good portion of the stair tread awkwardly outside the spindles. The architect came up with a clever solution in the form of serpentine-shaped stair spindles, which gave the staircase character. The spindles ballooned out at the base. The handrail descended directly, creating alignment, and the serpentine shape ballooned to encompass the wider treads. The couple loved the unexpected and artful twist.

The Matthewses clearly weren't afraid to inject their personality into the house, even in the smallest of ways. They converted an exterior porch to an interior doggie dining room next to the family room to accommodate their two lovable dogs. They built glass display shelves in the nearby

butler's pantry to house a collection of face jugs, popular southern collectibles. At the front of the house, they expanded the exterior entrance and added limestone pavers. In the foyer, they replaced the solid wood rear doors with custom doors inset with glass, the better to glimpse the greenery. Moving through the house, they added a basement gym and game room, renovated the bathrooms, and reworked a sunroom as a home office.

The couple lived in the house throughout the entire two-year renovation. For one year of it, they went underground (albeit with plenty of provisions and style) to the basement. By the time the family's first southern Thanksgiving rolled around, they were able to move into the kitchen, though it was still rough. Planks of wood, laid across sawhorses, held food prepared by a caterer and white roses in a crystal bowl.

Amazingly, not counting change orders, the couple stayed within 3 percent of their original estimate until the very end. When the main house was finished, the Matthewses, inspired and energized by their successful project, turned to the ramshackle pool cabana. That, too, could be renovated, they thought, into a gracious guesthouse. Of course, this would take them substantially over their original budget, but they considered the extra expense well worth it. Working with their team had been a pleasure, and this time they wouldn't even have to live in the basement.

The two-story guesthouse, as a separate entity, gave the Matthewses a chance to indulge a little decorating wanderlust. They went on a British colonial bender: sea grass mattings for carpets, crisp linen canvases on couches, breezy curtains to draw against the afternoon sun, and ceiling fans in the bedrooms. They considered *everything*. For example, they painted the concrete floors black and sanded them for a more rustic look and to camouflage wear; the resulting surface was cool underfoot and easy to care for. A compact kitchen housed junior-size state-of-the-art appliances.

IN THE POOL-HOUSE KITCHENETTE, THERE WAS NO COMPROMISING ON STYLE. A COPPER FARMHOUSE SINK, WHITE-PAINTED CABINETS, AND EUROPEAN APPLIANCES DON'T STINT ON LUXURY.

TRADE TIP

CONSISTENCY OF COLOR CAN CREATE CALM THROUGH A HOUSE AND A SENSE OF FLOW BETWEEN ROOMS. THAT'S NOT TO SAY, HOWEVER, THAT YOU NEED TO USE ONLY ONE COLOR, OR ONLY ONE SHADE OF THE COLOR. VARIATIONS OF GRAY, TAUPE, OR SAGE, FOR EXAMPLE, MAKE FOR SUBTLE CHANGES THAT YOU SENSE, EVEN IF YOU DON'T ALWAYS SEE THEM. COLOR IS TRANSIENT. A TAUPE IS WARM ON THE SOUTH SIDE OF THE HOUSE AND COOL ON THE NORTH SIDE. TO GET THE SAME COLOR, YOU NEED TO CHANGE IT TO REFLECT LIGHT AND EXPOSURE.

THE MAIN ROOM OF THE POOL HOUSE WAS DE-SIGNED TO STAND UP TO USE BY MANY GUESTS. THE MATTHEWSES PAIRED CHIC LINEN SLIPCOVERS, PRIM-ITIVE WOODS, WICKER, AND BAMBOO WITH EXTE-RIOR LANTERNS. UNDER THE SEA GRASS RUG LAYS A CEMENT FLOOR—PAINTED BLACK AND THEN ROUGH SANDED TO PROVIDE FUTURE CAMOUFLAGE FOR YEARS OF WEAR.

[**ABOVE**] IN A GUEST BATH, A SURPRISING LIGHTING SOURCE—A PAIR OF GOTHIC LANTERNS—PLAYS OFF AN OVERSIZED OVAL MIRROR. [**RIGHT**] IN A SMALL GUEST ROOM, A GRACEFUL GOTHIC PALLADIAN WINDOW MAKES THE ATTICLIKE SPACE ALL THE MORE MAGICAL. CLOSETS WERE CONCEALED ON EITHER SIDE AS YOU ENTER THE ROOM.

Upstairs, in an enfilade of guest rooms, the decorating scheme continued: grasscloth headboards, cotton matting on the floor, white matelasse fabrics and black-painted window mullions. The completed guesthouse turned out to be the perfect country companion to the Matthewses' main house, which was already a great oasis in the city.

HOUSE RULES

PROBLEM = SOLUTION. Sometimes great design comes from limitations. The serpentine spindles on the back stairs were designed to span the differential between the narrower upper portion of the treads and the more expansive lower portion.

WATCH THE SCALE. When Olivia was unsure about oversized spaces and soaring ceiling heights, the architect, Norman Askins, literally drew on the walls so she could see the relationship between the new proposed space and their furnishings.

GO FOR A PERFECT PATINA. Sometimes high shine isn't what's called for, even when that's the way the appliance arrives. Olivia found out from her decorator that it's not hard to tone down the brilliance of stainless steel. With several coats of standard-issue clear paste wax from the hardware store, applied with a steel wool pad to rough up the surface and then buffed with a cloth, the oven hood had a low-gleam sheen and a completely original look.

STAKE OUT YOUR TERRITORY. If you're going to live in the house through a long-term renovation, ask your contractor to construct a temporary kitchen using a portion of your old kitchen cabinets. More than a microwave or hot plate and minifridge, a functioning sink is a must-have.

SAND SURFACES. The terrace stone that was brought inside to surface the kitchen floor was deemed too rough. Each piece was subsequently machine sanded at the job site to smooth its rough edges. The sanding process manipulated the inherent color of the stone, leaving it with more warm tones and less cool grays.

The Little House That Grew and Grew

[the program] Accomplished in bits and pieces over twenty-five years

- Construct a two-story great room with attached atrium
- Dress up the main entrance to make it more gracious
- Add walls of books so a dining room does double duty
- Build an addition for a home office and later a guest room
- Renovate the kitchen and add a bay to house a breakfast table
- Convert an old farm structure into a home gym
- Gut and enlarge the master and hall baths

THIRTY YEARS AGO, HILLARY AND JACK LOVE, NEWLYWEDS with a baby, bought their first home, a former servant's cottage on Warren Farm in New Jersey. They've never left. The house, a red clapboard dating from 1859, had been added to over the years, most recently in the 1920s. When the Loves bought the house, it was an overgrown mess and still quite small; there wasn't even a coat closet, let alone a first-floor bath. But there was just something about it that Hillary loved. With its low ceilings and cozy spaces, it reminded her of a cottage out of *The Secret Garden*.

She and Jack bought the charming little farmhouse, knowing they would have to make changes to make it work for them. With a family to raise and a graduate degree

(hers) under way, the house, as it was, didn't fit their needs. So began a rolling process of renovation—and one that may not be over yet.

The Loves' first architectural move was their most substantial, both in terms of changes made and square feet gained. They added a two-story great room with a steeply pitched roof, giving the space the feeling of a barn, and attached a glass atrium on the side. At 17 by 20 feet, the great room is actually not so great a room as to be grand, Hillary is quick to point out, though it does feel bigger than it measures because of its double-height ceiling and the atrium. The Loves and their architect took a good long look

THE FRONT OF THE 1800S FARMHOUSE IS A STUDY IN PERFECT SYMMETRY. WHILE DIFFERENT OWNERS HAD DONE MUCH TO THE HOUSE IN ITS 150 YEARS, NONE HAD, THANKFULLY, TOUCHED THE ORIGINAL FAÇADE.

up at that ceiling, and they made a bold decision. They would erect a balcony outside the master bedroom, projecting into the space and overlooking the great room below. Once built, however, the Loves found the little gallery wasn't practical; the loss of privacy in their bedroom, open to below, was ridiculous. Years later they reinvented the balcony by enclosing it, cutting it off from the great room, and turning it into a small but much-needed walk-in closet for the bedroom.

On the heels of this major renovation, the Loves built a small but significant addition—a new "front" doorway and entry hall—in what was actually the back of the house. They created a bona fide entrance with a white-columned overhang where the naked entrance and plain door, without a portico, had been. Off the new entry hall inside they were able to fit in a full first-floor bath.

Once built, the new additions—the entry (with bath) and the great room—were tied together with the same flooring material: warm, rich terra-cotta tiles. Jack and Hillary, both hands-on types, did the work themselves, laying the tiles in a straightforward pattern well suited to their do-it-yourself skills.

A few years later, the Loves, who now had two kids running around, were feeling squeezed for space—particularly Hillary, who was in the thick of finishing up her thesis and needed a private space in which to write. She craved a home office. It was time for another addition, only this one was a

simple box, cantilevered off the back of the master bedroom on the second story. This type of structure is known in architect lingo as a flying box. The plans for the box looked great on paper—a nice-size office with windows on two sides and even a few extra feet they could graft onto the master bedroom.

The Loves, who took a lengthy trip to the Far East during the construction, were looking forward to seeing the finished project. But Jack and Hillary dropped their suitcases and their jaws when they saw the finished box, which jutted out awkwardly from the house. It looked like a transplant or some sort of unattractive growth. Short of taking a sledgehammer to the addition, what could they do? Hire a new architect who could find a way to make the addition look decent from the outside, that's what. The new archi-

TRADE TIP

WHEN EMBARKING ON A RENOVATION, LOOK UP, DOWN, AROUND, AND INTO THE FUTURE. THE IDEA IS TO TAKE AS BROAD A SCOPE AS POSSIBLE AND ANTICIPATE ADDITIONS OR CHANGES YOU MIGHT MAKE DOWN THE ROAD IN ADJACENT SPACES. IF YOU ARE REDOING ONE BATHROOM, SAY, THE INCREMENTAL COST OF LAYING PIPEWORK FOR A NEIGHBORING BATH IS NEGLIGIBLE, ESPECIALLY WHEN COMPARED TO OPENING WALLS AND STARTING FROM SCRATCH, WHICH IS WHAT YOU'D HAVE TO DO IF YOU DIDN'T TAKE CARE OF IT AT THE TIME OF THE FIRST RENOVATION.

tect came up with a simple solution. By adding a peaked roof and an overhang on all sides, she was able to soften the squareness of the shape and visually connect the structure to the rest of the house.

Just two years later, the Loves decided they needed a spare bedroom for an au pair. The logical place to build was under the flying box, right below Hillary's office. Good idea, but bad planning. Had they thought of this earlier, the Loves could have plumbed, wired, and probably framed for the first-floor space while doing the office addition above, saving themselves the expense and inconvenience of bringing workmen and materials onto the site again.

Another few years came and went before the Loves had the energy and urge to renovate again. This time they zeroed in on the kitchen, which had always been cramped and confined, with nowhere to sit and eat. First they

[LEFT] THE INFAMOUS FLYING BOX, THE REVISED VERSION, WITH ADDED PEAK ROOFLINE AND MAID'S ROOM/PLAYROOM, VISIBLE BELOW AT THE FAR LEFT OF THE PHOTO. [BELOW LEFT] THE LOVES' EARLY DOUBLE-HEIGHT GREAT ROOM ADDITION. [BELOW RIGHT AND LEFT—INSIDE AND OUT] THE BUMP-OUT ADDITION ALLOWED SPACE FOR A BREAKFAST TABLE BAY IN THE RENOVATED KITCHEN.

punched out a deep bay, which gave them room for a breakfast table and a Welsh dresser for their china. In keeping with the farmhouse aesthetic, Hillary chose butcher block for the

[**ABOVE**] IN A HOUSE WITH THIS FEW ROOMS—NINE IN TOTAL IF YOU COUNT THE WALK-IN-CLOSET—EACH ROOM HAD TO SERVE MORE THAN ONE FUNCTION. THE LOVES DESIGNED THEIR DINING ROOM TO DOUBLE AS LIBRARY, GIFT-WRAP TABLE, AND ENTRY HALL. [**OPPOSITE**] A RAM-SHACKLE SHED WAS TURNED INTO A HOME EXERCISE STUDIO AS A BIRTH-DAY PRESENT. NO MORE COMPLAIN-ING ABOUT TRAFFIC ON THE WAY TO THE GYM.

countertops and two types of country-style cabinets: upper cupboards of pine, some with glass doors, and lower cabinets glazed with a deep green.

At the same time the Loves had the kitchen cabinetry built, they designed built-ins for the dining room, where they wanted floor-to-ceiling bookcases on two walls. This was a clever way to give the dining room, now seldom used, more than one use—adding purpose without square footage. The dining room now functions as a library and reading room, not to mention a place for gift-wrapping and game-playing.

The next renovation that came up, a decade later, was one the Loves *had* to do. In the backyard sat an old farm out-building, partially renovated by the previous owners, which Hillary and Jack had been using for catch-all storage. The foundation was collapsing, and in order to retain the structure on the property, they had to repair and renovate. As they began plans to shore up the foundation, the Loves thought about how they could most creatively use this separate space. They settled on the idea of a home gym the whole family could use (with the bonus of getting Hillary's bulky exercise equipment out of the small master bedroom). First the Loves had the structure weatherproofed; then they carpeted the floor, painted the walls a sea glass green, and installed plenty of mirrors. Outside they added French doors, a white picket fence, and an arbor to make a picture-perfect accompaniment to the main house.

When the children were grown, Hillary and Jack wrestled with the question of whether to stay or sell. The couple now owned a family ranch

TRADE TIP

CONSIDER GIVING AN INFRE-QUENTLY USED SPACE, LIKE A DIN-ING ROOM, MORE RELEVANCE. BY SIMPLY BUILDING BOOKSHELVES, YOU CAN MAKE THE ROOM DOUBLE AS A LIBRARY AND TURN THE TABLE INTO A COZY PLACE TO PAY BILLS, DO HOMEWORK, OR PLAY A GAME OF SCRABBLE (WITH THE DIC-TIONARY AT HAND).

TRADE TIP

YOU DON'T ALWAYS HAVE TO THINK LINEARLY. TRY
ANGLING FURNISHINGS TO ADD NEW DEFINITION AND
DIMENSION WITHIN A ROOM. SLANTING A BOOKCASE, OR
EVEN A CABINET ENCLOSING A REFRIGERATOR, AS THE
LOVES DID IN THEIR KITCHEN, INTO A ROOM CAN SUGGEST
DIVISIONS WITHOUT LITERALLY PARTITIONING THE SPACE.

the house, and so did their children. They decided to stay—
and renovate again.

The Loves thought it was time they had a bigger bedroom. But how? They glanced down the hall and eyed
Hillary's office, which she rarely used these days, having a
proper one at the office in Manhattan. Why not turn the
infamous flying box into a big closet and dressing room?
And that's what they did, adding wraparound storage cabinets and a vanity with a vessel sink. With windows on two
walls, the new dressing room/closet far exceeds what you
would expect to find in a little red farmhouse. And the

house out West. With their shared jewelry business (Jack
manages, Hillary designs) thriving in Manhattan, they considered buying an apartment in the city, giving up the farmhouse altogether. But ultimately, they couldn't. They loved

Loves gained in other ways, too. By creating a new place for clothes storage, they now could co-opt the closet space (that former balcony-turned-walk-in) and make the bedroom even bigger. Between the new square footage and the newly usable space created by removing all the old storage units, Hillary and Jack's bedroom could now accommodate built-in bookcases and a small TV next to the boxed-in chimney flue from the parlor below. In its third incarnation, the alcove houses a small desk for Hillary tucked under one eave and a cedar closet for out-of-season clothes under the other.

With the bedroom bigger and better, it was clear the Loves needed to update the master bath as well. The bathroom was outmoded and funky in the worst way, with an oversized angled platform tub that ate up a lot of floor space. The Loves realized they could add a little to the footprint of the bathroom by simply moving the door a few

[BELOW] GLASS IN A SHOWER IS EXPENSIVE, BUT NOTHING OPENS UP A BATH-ROOM LIKE AN ALL-GLASS SHOWER. RANDOM CHECKERBOARD TILES TIE TOGETHER THE SHOWER WALL AND THE FLOOR. THE WOOD FRONT ON THE TUB DECK WAS DESIGNED TO MATCH THE VANITY. [RIGHT] THE FORMER OFFICE BECAME A SHARED CLOSET/DRESSING ROOM. THE VESSEL SINK AND A "FALLING WATER" FAUCET ARE PERFECTLY SUITED TO A DRESSING SPACE—THE COMBINA-TION WOULD BE LESS PRACTICAL IN A PRIMARY BATH.

TRADE TIP

STONE IS ALWAYS 15 DEGREES COLDER THAN ANYTHING ELSE AROUND IT. CHOOSE SOMETHING WARMER FOR A SURFACE YOU WILL BE LEANING BARE FOREARMS AGAINST, LIKE A DESK OR DRESSING-TABLE TOP. WOOD, CORIAN, LEATHER, OR FORMICA ALL REMAIN AT ROOM TEMPERATURE.

feet down the small hall between the bedroom and the dressing room. That was all it took to make space for a generous shower, a separate tub, and a concealed toilet area. The Loves chose an arts-and-crafts leitmotif to finish their bathroom: art nouveau checkerboard tiles on the floor and inside the shower, copper wall sconces, and a handsome oak vanity with a marble counter.

Meanwhile, another upstairs bathroom called out for attention. The hall bath, with its old-fashioned claw-foot tub and handheld shower spray, had never had enough headroom for a full shower. With kids and grandkids coming to visit frequently, it was time to make a few adjustments. The Loves gutted the bathroom and added a dormer, which generated the necessary headroom for a legitimate shower.

It was also about this time that the Loves took a fresh look at the great room addition, which was now twenty-five years old. The attached atrium leaked and the Plexiglas was cloudy. They rebuilt it, using the renovation as an opportunity to reduce the number of panes and planes from ten to six and simplifying the design in the process. The peak was wired so a sweet little chandelier could be hung for a romantic touch.

The attached family room was also due for a little updating in the tech department. Jack decided it was time he could watch television without straining his eyes—even though, as he says, they're not television people. The problem was the placement of the TV, which was in the direct line of the sun, so that the light frequently washed out the screen. In the end, the Loves opted for a sleek plasma TV mounted out of range of the sun and directly across from the seating.

With the plasma screen in place, are the Loves finally content to sit back and relax? Are they finished with renovating? Jack believes so, but Hillary is less sure. They really need more first-floor storage, she says—after all, there's no attic and no basement. No doubt they'll be at it soon enough, making their little gem of a house slightly bigger and better.

HOUSE RULES

GET VIRTUAL. Hillary learned that it's hard to look at a two-dimensional blueprint and imagine a three-dimensional structure. She found it helpful to build a virtual room on her computer, tinkering with the design details, before the contractors built the real thing. (Architectural programs made for consumers include Chief Architects and the more layperson-friendly AutoCad 200 and AutoCad 2005.)

BE WILLING TO PITCH IN. When the Loves wanted to install central air-conditioning, they were hard pressed to find anyone to take the job. Contractors were put off by the age of the house and the attic limitations. Jack, who knew the house inside and out, finally agreed to lay the ductwork himself and found a firm willing to do the rest of the work. Sometimes, when you want something done, you have to do it, or begin it, yourself.

THINK OUTSIDE THE BOX—OR INSIDE THE WALLS. The Loves got creative when it came to rewiring the great room, making an inherent quirk work to their advantage. The upper portion of the walls was recessed from the lower portion and separated by a small ledge. The Loves decided to Sheetrock the upper walls, building them out flush with the ledge, and thus create a void behind the Sheetrock large enough to carry all new electrical wires.

REINVENT ROOMS. Just because a room starts out with one function—an office or a bedroom—doesn't mean it can't become another as a family grows and changes. In the Loves' case, a home office later became a dressing room and walk-in closet while an outbuilding was reconstituted as a home gym.

The glam great room was designed as the antithesis of the little red farmhouse. The room was set discreetly off to the side so it does not impinge on the historic look of the rest of the house.

THE ATRIUM IS A JEWEL BOX DRAWING YOU TO THE
END OF THE GREAT ROOM. PART OF THE LOVES'
FIRST ADDITION, IT WAS REBUILT WHEN THEY RENO-
VATED THE UPSTAIRS. THEY REDUCED THE NUMBER
OF FACETS FROM EIGHT TO SIX FOR A CLEANER
LOOK. A SWEDISH COUNTRY CHANDELIER HUNG IN
THE APEX SPARKLES MAGICALLY AGAINST ALL THE
BLACK GLASS AT NIGHT.

Reinventing the Ranch

[the program] Accomplished in sixteen months

- Add a second story to a one-level house, nearly doubling the space to 8,000 square feet
- Build a dramatic entry and staircase
- Give the living room and the dining room character
- Remodel three bathrooms and add five new ones
- Move the kitchen and style it with European flair
- Build a billiard/playroom for soon-to-be-teenage children

BART AND SUE BLATT ARE CONSUMMATE PROS. THEY'VE BEEN developing spec homes and renovating existing houses for more than fifteen years; it's an integral part of the family's construction business. More often than not, they've looked at renovating real estate as an opportunity—an opportunity they've taken advantage of by moving ten times in eleven years, frequently fixing up and selling their homes to generate new capital for the next project. The Blatts and their two children would up and move at the drop of a hat or a knock on the door.

When the Blatts bought their current home, a spacious 1960s ranch in a bucolic suburban neighborhood, they decided to finally stay put. This house would be "it"—their dream house, their pièce de résistance. It would also be a showcase for their firm's renovation work and a place to test-drive many of the newest home and building products on the market. The Blatts reasoned that if something worked for them, it would likely work for their customers— and if it didn't, better to know that, too.

While they knew their new house was right for them, it wasn't right as it was. The ranch was too tired and outdated to fit a modern lifestyle. The Blatts faced a dilemma familiar to many renovators: to renovate or to raze? Along with their longtime architect-collaborator, Justin Mineri, they

THE HUMBLE RANCH, TRANSFORMED. THE ENTRY COLUMNS, SUPPORTED BY STONE WALLS, TIE THE ENTRY VISUALLY TO THE STONE PIERS AS YOU ENTER THE DRIVEWAY AND TO THE RIVER-ROCK CHIMNEY, CREATING A THREE-PART HARMONY.

made the decision based on a single factor: ceiling height. A lot of older homes just don't have the ceiling height to allow taller doors, larger windows, and more prominent moldings. A 9-foot or, better yet, 10-foot ceiling has room not only for chandeliers but also for decorative features like beams or dramatic features like coffering. Luckily, both the step-down living room and the family room featured 9½-foot ceilings and didn't need to be touched.

Initially, the Blatts toyed with the idea of retaining the house's identity as a ranch, but no amount of headscratching or design-drafting could make the plan work. So, like many families facing a ranch expansion, they looked up and decided to add a second floor with four bedrooms. They also saw the chance to build a small wing behind the garage to house an au pair bed and bath, a mudroom and bath, and an expanded breakfast room, with a game room and home theater above. And, of course, they would revamp the first-

floor spaces as well, giving themselves a great room and a great kitchen.

Once they'd detailed the plans, the design process moved quickly. (It didn't hurt that the architect and the client have worked closely together for so long they can almost read each other's mind.) One of the first decisions they made was to leave most of the existing rooms in their original

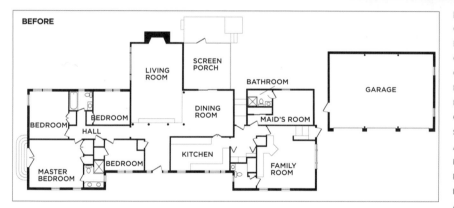

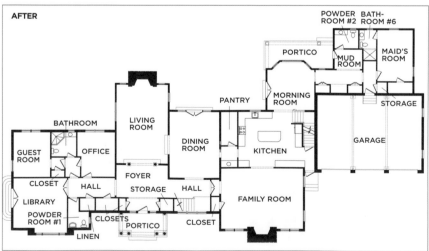

[ABOVE] THE RANCH HOUSE COULD BE THE BARGAIN OF THE REAL ESTATE MARKET, GIVEN ITS LARGE FOOTPRINT (AFTER ALL, THE LIVING SPACES WERE ON ONE FLOOR) AND THE EASY ADDITION OF A FULL OR PARTIAL SECOND STORY. TO RENOVATE THIS HOUSE, THE BLATTS LEFT THE FRONT DOOR IN PLACE BUT REROUTED THE DRIVEWAY INTO A GRACIOUS CIRCULAR DRIVE. [LEFT] IT IS SURPRISING THAT SUCH A COMPLETE OVERHAUL REQUIRED SO LITTLE ALTERATION TO THE EXISTING FOOTPRINT OF THE HOUSE. FROM THE FRONT HALL TO THE LEFT NOTHING AT ALL CHANGED. TO THE RIGHT, WALLS WERE MOVED AND SPACES RECONFIGURED BUT THE ONLY ADDITION WAS A SMALL SERVICE AREA BEHIND THE GARAGE.

THE POOLSIDE ARBOR WAS ENVISIONED TO SERVE AS BOTH A SHADE PROVIDER AND AS A VISUAL BUFFER BETWEEN THE POOL AND THE TENNIS/SPORTS COURT BEYOND. MORE THAN THAT, THE ARBOR CREATED AN OUTDOOR "ROOM." THE CHAISE LONGUES AND WICKER WOULD NOT NESTLE QUITE SO COMFORTABLY IF THEY WERE MERELY SITTING POOLSIDE.

locations and use them for their original purposes. The layout of these rooms was logical and livable. Dining room remained as dining room, family room as family room, and living room as living room. The three first-floor bedrooms were also left intact, though they were reassigned as guest room, paneled library, and ground-floor office for Bart. As the Blatts had learned from their many renovation projects, for themselves and for others, there's no point in tearing down a wall and reconfiguring a floor plan when something essentially works. If the size of the rooms and the flow between them works, as they did in this section of the ranch, why change them?

In the step-down living room, which was rather boxy and bland, the Blatts made a few key changes. They introduced a coffered ceiling, a series of decorative beams in a grid pattern, painted white, to create architectural interest. They replaced the windows on either side of the fireplace with taller, more elongated ones, which also emphasized the height of the ceiling. The fireplace itself they refashioned with exaggerated moldings for a simpler, stronger look, more in keeping with the classical lines of the new room.

TRADE TIP

ALFRESCO SPACES, LIKE A PORCH OR PERGOLA, ARE AN OPPORTUNITY TO REINFORCE THE WHOLE PRESENTATION OF THE HOUSE. WHETHER FORMAL OR COUNTRY IN DETAILING, THEY STRENGTHEN THE TONE OF THE HOME AND PROVIDE A SENSE OF CONTINUITY BETWEEN PUBLIC AND PRIVATE AREAS.

The only structural change the Blatts thought necessary was to open up the room to the foyer. They demolished the wall between the two spaces and added a pair of columns in its stead. They chose columns that both tied in with the ceiling woodwork to create a "framed gateway," as Justin said, and echoed the feel of the columns they had decided to use to support the portico they were building on the front of the house.

The dining room, formerly accessible only from the entry hall and the kitchen pantry, was opened up to the living room with a generous 6-foot entrance. This eliminated the dead-end aspect of the room, making it more central to the house. It also afforded a glimpse of the piano in the living room—a strong visual punctuation. A pair of French doors on another wall now lead to a stone terrace. These new doors bring in light and allow for easy indoor-outdoor entertaining, a particular priority of the Blatts, who also added a pergola and kitchen porch to the property.

The family room, which the former owners had con-

[ABOVE] ARCHITECT JUSTIN MINERI RAISED THE HEARTH, MAKING IT MORE VISIBLE AS YOU ENTER THE HALL TWO STEPS ABOVE THE LIVING ROOM. THE COFFERED CEILING BEAMS AMPLIFIES THE AXIAL RELATIONSHIP BETWEEN THE FRONT DOOR AND THE FIREPLACE. [BELOW] THE DINING ROOM SAT ABOVE AND LOOKED DOWN AT THE LIVING ROOM. THE ONLY OPENING BETWEEN THEM WAS A WINDOW. THE BLATTS HAD THE HALF-WALL DEMOLISHED, CONNECTING LIVING AND DINING SPACES BOTH VISUALLY AND LITERALLY.

verted from the garage, called for interior reconfiguration. Although a family room is typically not located at the front of the house, the Blatts saw no reason to move it and decided instead to rework the space from within the shell—all part of their pragmatic approach to renovation. They were able to get more usable space out of the room simply by gutting and co-opting a menagerie of small closets and odd nooks. Then, by borrowing several feet from the front hall, they were able to fashion a new double-door closet to house an array of audio and video components.

To give the family room its own character, the Blatts hung a striking iron chandelier at the room's double-height peak. Next, they built a massive rock fireplace with New England stones and extended the fireplace to the ceiling, which warms up the room literally and decoratively. By using the same stone for the fireplace as they did for the face of the exterior chimney, the Blatts created a dialogue between inside and outside.

The kitchen was the one room that had to be moved from its former location (where the staircase now sat). The Blatts took the old maid's room abutting the family room and turned it into the kitchen. They wanted to create the look and feel of old-world Europe, so first they put down a slate floor, which they sanded and sealed to prevent chipping or clefting, a practice Bart picked up from his vast on-the-job experience. The Blatts chose a simple recessed style for the cabinets and had them painted a pale khaki and then glazed in raw umber for an antiqued look. The finish is very forgiving, impervious to aging because it already has a patina. The cabinets extend all the way to the ceiling for a unified look, and the whole room is wrapped with mold-

THE FAMILY ROOM STARTED LIFE AS A GARAGE. FORMER OWNERS HAD TURNED IT INTO A DEN THAT FELT MORE LIKE A FLAT-CEILINGED BEDROOM. THE BLATTS STAYED WITH THE SIZE BUT RAISED THE ROOF, ADDED A TWO-STORY FIREPLACE AND NEW WINDOWS, AND RELOCATED A STAIRCASE TO ACCESS THE NEW BILLIARD ROOM AND HOME THEATER. THE EXTRAORDINARY LINTEL (STONE OVER THE FIREPLACE HEARTH) REPRESENTED MUCH WORK BY AN ARTISTICALLY MINDED MASON.

TRADE TIP

WHEN WALLS ARE OPEN DURING NEW CONSTRUCTION, THAT'S THE IDEAL TIME TO REWIRE THE HOUSE AND BRING TECHNOLOGY UP TO DATE. COMPUTERS, VCRS, TIVOS, AND FLAT SCREENS CAN ALL BE NETWORKED TOGETHER. EVERY ROOM SHOULD GET DATA LINES THAT NETWORK THROUGHOUT THE HOUSE. YOU'LL BE ABLE TO PLUG AND PLAY YOUR FLAT SCREEN WITH YOUR LCD.

ing for a polished finish. The counter-tops were cut from Montevideo lime-stone in a muted military olive. The Blatts had the stone color-enhanced, a treatment applied on-site by the installer both to bring out the depth of the color and to seal the surface. As a final touch of charm, vintage ice cream parlor oil lamps were rewired and hung directly over the island.

On the new second floor, the Blatts designed four new bedrooms, an office for Sue, and a billiard/media room for the whole family. The Blatts liked the idea of the children having a haven, with an all-important sound-absorbing cork floor, to hang out in when the grown-ups were entertaining downstairs.

As for bathrooms, the Blatts have, well, more than the usual—eight in total (two are half-baths). And there is

not an amenity the Blatts haven't installed and tried in the interest of showcasing and road-testing: deluge heads, body sprays, hydrotherapy baths, decorative subway tile, mosaics, tumbled marble, polished stone, toilet rooms, pedestal sinks, and furniture vanities. Bart's advice: Less is often more, and simple is usually better.

As the two floors neared comple-tion, the Blatts had to consider the staircase scenario. The key to connect-ing the two levels, to making the home read as a whole and not a second house grafted onto the first, lay in the two-story foyer. Justin designed a wide staircase and added a series of windows designed to step up in tandem with the stair treads. At the top of the stairs, he opted for a graceful, curved landing that directs traffic back to the new wing. In the ceiling of the double-

[ABOVE] FOR FLOORING, THE BLATTS USED CHINA SLATE, FROM STONE SOURCE, THROUGHOUT THE HOUSE—KITCHEN, FAMILY ROOM, BREAKFAST ROOM, BACK HALL, AND MUDROOM—VARYING BOTH THE SIZE AND DIRECTION FOR INTEREST AND DEFINITION. THEIR SUPERIOR-QUALITY SLATE HAS MUCH LESS CHIPPING AND "CLEFTING OR LIPPAGE" THAN A SLATE OF LESSER QUALITY; EVEN SO, IT WAS SEALED TO PROLONG ITS LIFE. [OPPOSITE, LEFT] A 13-INCH TILE WAS LAID ON THE DIAGONAL FOR THE FORMAL POWDER ROOM. [OPPOSITE, RIGHT] A 4-INCH TUM-BLED SLATE SUITED THE FAMILY'S KITCHEN BATH.

TRADE TIP

ALTHOUGH EXTREMELY WELL PRICED, SLATE CAN BE GLOOMY AND DIRTY LOOKING. IT'S AN OUTDOOR MATE-RIAL, MEANT TO BE SURROUNDED BY MOTHER NATURE'S COLORFUL BOUQUET, NOT YOUR SUB-ZERO. BE SURE TO GET SEVERAL LARGE PIECES BEFORE YOU DECIDE IF IT'S RIGHT FOR YOU.

height foyer, he designed a dramatic dome, which Sue had finished in an oxidized metallic paint. In an interesting (and economical) decorative counterpoint, she hung an oversized exterior lantern in the dome—a strong visual that catches the eye on the way up the stairs.

Once the renovation was complete, the exterior was virtually unrecognizable from its former ranchburger self. Now it was closer to the iconic New England country house. The architect, in fact, borrowed from the turn-of-the-century Shingle-style vernacular—deep porches, varying rooflines, and, of course, the shingles themselves, which wrap much of the house. In the end, the Blatts got just what they wanted—a classic-looking show home that's also a real home.

TRADE TIP

PURPOSEFULLY FINISHING A SURFACE TO MAKE IT LOOK OLDER OR DISTRESSED HAS MORE THAN A SUPERFICIAL DECORATIVE APPEAL. IT MAKES MAINTENANCE OF THE MATERIAL—KITCHEN CABINETS, WOOD FLOORS, EVEN WALLS—EASIER BECAUSE FINGERPRINTS, NICKS, AND SMUDGES BLEND INTO THE WOODWORK, SO TO SPEAK.

HOUSE RULES

HAVE PATIENCE WITH THE PUNCH LIST. Even when the owner is also the contractor, it's not unusual to have a few post-renovation items to do—the so-called punch list. Whether it's a little thing (a broken tile to be replaced, a cracked marble door saddle) or something larger (the library is not yet paneled—the case with the Blatts' house), try to keep perspective. Just talk to anyone else who's been through it; you'll be reassured that eventually all the glitches get taken care of.

DON'T BE SEDUCED BY GIZMOS. The Blatts learned through trial and error, using their own home as an idea lab for bathroom fixtures. They've found that the attachments and gadgets that cost the most don't always last the longest or work the best. For instance, they found rain showerheads unreliable and now always specify a classic showerhead (like the Speakman, at a modest $100), which provides a strong driving spray, day in and day out, for virtually a lifetime.

BUILD ON EXPERIENCE. Any house can be a foundation for your dream house. The Blatts knew from experience that they could take a standard-issue 1960s house and build up and out. If a house has enough intrinsic good qualities—like high ceilings or a gracious layout—there's no reason to tear it down.

BEWARE OF FEE TRAPS. Price is only one factor in selecting a contractor. The Blatts, who have been on both sides of the equation (client *and* contractor), advise that you also consider reputation, reliability, and availability—that is, how many other jobs the contractor is doing at the same time. Often the contractor with the lowest initial price gouges you later, adding extra after extra: Dumpster fees, carting fees, and surprised exclamations of "I didn't know you wanted that." You will live with this person for a year. You need to get along.

The Details . . .
Room by Room

Kitchens

The kitchen has always been the heart of the home. That's where Mom could most often be found and where kids checked in after school. Today the kitchen is family central, and everyone has a place there, not just Mom. It's where the family sorts the mail (and e-mail), where the kids do their homework, and where guests congregate before, during, or after a party. So it makes sense that we are devoting more of our renovation budget to kitchens than ever before, more per square foot than on any other home remodeling project. This year alone, five million kitchens will be renovated at a cost of more than 80 billion dollars. If it's any consolation, the dollar return on a kitchen remodel is higher than for any other renovation project, ranging from 74 to 100 percent or more.

Start your kitchen renovation by defining your objectives. Do you want an eating and seating kitchen? Island or table—or both? Walk-in pantry? Computer station? TV? More light? Better storage? Attached mudroom? Will your kitchen's existing size accommodate your grocery list of objectives, or will you need more square footage? If so, is additional space available within the house, such as an underused maid's room or porch, or do you need to add on? Once you've decided whether you are going to update and replace, expand within your home's existing footprint, or build on an addition, it's time to call the architect or the contractor. Based on your preliminary meeting, you can hope to walk away with a ballpark figure (and I mean *ballpark*—mentally add another 50 percent to be safe), provided your contractor has enough information. Keep in mind that, more than likely, your contractor's guesstimate will not include cabinets, countertops, and appliances, which you have yet to choose.

You'll have to ask yourself if the time, effort, and expense will be worth it—but the answer is almost always yes. After all, the kitchen is a 365-day-a-year room. It never gets a day off—and most days, it's working overtime.

TRADE TIP

LAYOUT LOGISTICS

In a from-scratch renovation, deciding where to locate the key elements—the major and minor appliances, the islands, and the breakfast nooks—is the top priority.

- CONSIDER THE NEW WORK TRIANGLE. The traditional doctrine was that the stove, sink, and refrigerator should be positioned as three points of an equilateral triangle, with no more than 22 feet connecting all three appliances. The new kitchen geometry is to think of an isosceles triangle—after all, we don't use the appliances equally. For example, the oven isn't used as

much these days, thanks to the microwave and the toaster oven. Although our kitchen layout is still determined by the three primary appliances, we now have a host of secondary appliances to incorporate, such as wine refrigerators, pot-filler faucets, and warming drawers, as well as secondary counter surfaces—islands and peninsulas.

- START WITH THE SINK. The first fixture to place is the hardest working, and that's the sink. With luck, you will be able to place it under a window. Light and view are infinitely preferable to upper cabinets, which can make you feel hemmed in. However, if you have no choice and your sink is windowless, try opting for an open shelf unit overhead to give you more breathing room. Make sure your sink has plenty of surrounding counter space—a minimum of 2 feet—for ample cleanup and to accommodate a dishwasher underneath on one side and a garbage door (twin bins for recycling) on the other.

- LOCATE THE FRIDGE. Most food preparation takes place between the sink and the refrigerator. Leave

enough uninterrupted counter space to comfortably prep, but not too much of a run so you're sloshing milk and eggs across the room. It may not be the workhorse that the sink is, but the refrigerator certainly hasn't lost its popularity—it's opened an average of 55 times a day!

- STAY WITHIN RANGE. Whether you choose a cooktop or an integrated range, you ideally want to position it on the opposite side of the sink from the fridge. You don't want to have to walk around a stove, especially one in use, to get from the refrigerator to the sink. Allow at least 3 feet of counter surface on the sink side of the range and 18 inches on the far side to make a landing spot for hot pots. Wall ovens need not be as central to the kitchen work area and can be placed far afield, either at one of the ends of a run of cabinets or on an independent wall of all tall pantry cabinets.

- CREATE AN IDEAL ISLAND. Islands are the progeny of the freestanding kitchen worktables of yore. Islands come in all shapes and sizes, the length and width of which are limited only by the square footage of your kitchen. A small one, at the very least, can serve as an extra prep surface. With stools, the island becomes an ad hoc table; if you're lucky enough to have room for stools on both the end and a side, you can actually carry on a conversation. A 15-inch overhang generously houses a comfortable counter stool (9 inches will do in a pinch). If the fit is snug, consider curving the overhang, keeping the deepest area to only a portion of the island. A curved shape also mitigates a blocked artery in a tight space. There is such a thing as too wide an island, however; one that spans more than 44 inches makes for a difficult reach across and may necessitate circumnavigation to clean and clear.

- WATCH THE AISLE. The distance between cabinets and island is a subject of much debate in kitchen design. Some experts say we need 4 feet. (My own experience is that 42 inches feels plenty generous.) Serious cooks sometimes prefer a 3-foot aisle where everything is within easy reach. Anything more than 4 feet compromises economy of motion.

- KEEP YOUR PENINSULA IN PROPORTION. As the name implies, peninsulas are exposed on three sides. Ideally, peninsulas should stay fairly short. The greater the length of the peninsula, the longer the walk around it to get from one side of the kitchen to the other. The most gracious peninsulas run between 5 and 7 feet long and about 3½ feet wide, with seating on one side only. Peninsulas make great breakfast and lunch counters for the kids (while keeping them out of the kitchen area). A peninsula also makes a wonderful serving station, bar, or buffet when entertaining.

TO PANEL OR NOT TO PANEL IS A PERSONAL CHOICE. WITH THE REFRIGERATOR A BIT FAR AFIELD, AS THIS ONE IS, PANELING CAN SERVE TO VISUALLY TIE TOGETHER THE KITCHEN. ADDITIONALLY, THE OVERSIZED HANDLE OF THE REFRIGERATOR WAS ORDERED FROM THE CABINET MANUFACTURER.

APPLIANCE PRIMER

The big three—refrigerator, stove, and sink—remain the cornerstones of kitchen appliances. Where once we selected our appliances from a single American manufacturer, like a prix fixe menu, today we have options . . . lots of options.

REFRIGERATORS

Most likely you grew up with a bulky box of a refrigerator with the freezer on the top. Simple, but not exactly stylish or even efficient (those standard units consumed a surprising 40 percent of the entire household's electricity). Refrigerators have been evolving ever since and now are better

Fridge Fringes

- BEVERAGE CENTERS. These versatile under-the-counter units are typically either 15 or 24 inches wide. With a combination of shelves and racks, they can store a few dozen drinks, from bottles of Coke to bottles of Cabernet. Beverage centers reduce your refrigerator's housing load, free up shelf space, and maintain your food at a more consistent temperature. As the refrigerator door is presumably opened less frequently, temperatures are more stable. The latest trend: black interiors.

- WINE CABINETS. Why hide your connoisseurship when a wine cabinet lets you show it off? The type of cooler below, with its ultraviolet glass door, holds between thirty and sixty bottles. Some wine cabinets, with a single interior temperature setting, only masquerade as the real deal. A true wine cooler, like Sub-Zero or Viking, has temperatures that range from 41 degrees (for the white wine shelves) to 63 degrees (for the reds).

built, quieter, and significantly more energy-conscious than even a decade ago. They're also better looking and designed to meld with their surroundings, look like handsome pieces of furniture, or project high-tech, pro-style chic. Built-in refrigerators sit flush with standard kitchen cabinetry. The sides of the Sub-Zero style are designed to be clad in panels that match your kitchen cabinets for a fully integrated look. The doors can be clad in matching panels or sheathed in gleaming stainless steel. Most modern models are shallower than earlier ones, extending only slightly beyond the line of the counters or cabinetry, because the compressor is more often located on the bottom or the top instead of the back. Inside, better lighting and glass shelves, along with the shallower depth, make it much easier to see what's in there for dinner. The freezer section, formerly found on top, is now all

Oven Extras

WARMING DRAWERS. Warming drawers range in width from 24 to 36 inches. They are usually stacked beneath wall ovens (one regular oven and maybe one microwave/convection oven); thus, your oven (usually 27 or 30 inches wide) determines the size of your warming oven. A warming drawer can also be used as a plate warmer.

INFRARED. Forget the electric coil broiler of yesteryear. Infrared grills throw a thousand tiny flames at your meat, generating enough heat for a steakhouse-style special.

over the place: on the bottom, on the side, or even off by itself, in which case the refrigerator is simply that—a refrigerator. Available in widths ranging from 27 inches to 36 inches, stand-alone refrigerators can be placed closer to your sink and cooktop, while your stand-alone freezer, used far less often, is farther away.

Another trend is multiple units. In addition to your refrigerator, you might have a wine cooler, an icemaker, and a couple of supplemental refrigerator drawers for produce or beverages. An undercounter beverage refrigerator might be located closer to the family room for easy refills or within reach of small children so they can help themselves to a juice box.

Integrated refrigerators come in three basic models: freezer on the bottom, side by side, and the outdated freezer on the top. The freezer-on-the-bottom design is popular for good reason. After all, most of us open the refrigerator far more than the freezer, so it makes sense

TRADE TIP

WITH THE RISING USE OF COMMERCIAL-GRADE STOVES, MANY HOMEOWNERS ARE TAKING THEIR CUE FROM RESTAURANTS AND INSTALLING POT-FILLER FAUCETS. THESE ARE TYPICALLY LOCATED ABOVE THE STOVE AND ALLOW YOU TO FILL A LARGE POT WITHOUT LUGGING IT ACROSS THE KITCHEN TO THE SINK. (BUT DON'T YOU STILL HAVE TO DUMP IT OUT?)

that those nice wide shelves are at eye level. No surprise that Sub-Zero's 36-inch-wide freezer-under style is its bestselling model. The side-by-side refrigerator freezer comes in three widths: 36, 42, and 48 inches. If you're going to go for this style—because you like its substantial look, or you *do* use your freezer all the time—try to make room for the widest model (4 feet). The size just below (3½ feet) costs almost as much, and you lose shelf space. Remember that side-by-sides have narrower refrigerator sections than under-over types, making it hard to fit a platter inside—impossible with the 36-inch model.

All flush refrigerators are not really flush. These so-called flush refrigera-tors come in two depths. One is the cabinet depth (27 inches). The refrigerator box is flush with the front face of the cabinets (24 inches), but the doors actually project beyond, a few inches into the room. Then there is the true built-in, which is a bit shallower (24 inches) and a lot pricier, though it looks more custom.

STOVES AND OVENS

When it comes to ranges (and ovens and cooktops), there are many options (in sizes, too, from 24 to 60 inches) these days, from professional, restaurant-grade stoves to infrared grills to convection ovens. In many

THE ISLAND IN THIS HARDWORKING KITCHEN HOUSES A SECOND SINK AND A DISHWASHER. WHEN YOU HAVE THE LUXURY OF DOUBLE DISHWASHERS IT'S BEST TO KEEP THE PRIMARY ONE NEAR THE LARGER SINK AND A SECONDARY ONE IN THE ISLAND TO AVOID CONFUSION ABOUT WHICH IS HALF-FILLED. BECAUSE THE ISLAND WAS OVERSIZE (10 FEET LONG) AND NO SINGLE STONE SLAB COULD BE FOUND, SOME CLEVER TRICKERY WAS NEEDED TO MAKE THE COUNTERTOP LOOK UNIFORM (INCLUDING USING THE FRONT AND THE BACK OF THE SLAB AND BOOKING THE TWO ENDS).

TRADE TIP

MICROWAVES ARE HANDY BUT NOT SO HANDSOME THAT YOU ALWAYS WANT THEM ON VIEW. MOST ARE TOO DEEP TO FIT INSIDE UPPER CABINETS. WHEN REMODELING, TRY RECESSING THE BACK OF THE MICROWAVE BETWEEN THE WALL STUDS FOR A FLUSH FIT, OR TUCK IT IN A PANTRY OR CABINET DOOR OUTFITTED WITH AN OUTLET.

kitchens you'll find two or more types of cookers. In the ideal kitchen, a serious cook would find room for a gas cooktop with four or more well-spaced burners, a gas oven with infrared broiling (far superior to electric for broiling), and an electric wall oven paired with a microwave/convection oven.

RANGES | A range (we used to call them stoves) was once a single oven on bottom and four burners on top. Now it often has an oven or two, a *minimum* of four burners, plus a griddle or a grill. As many stove styles as we have, there are almost as many cooking methods, but there's a reason: some suit certain cooks, and kitchens, better than others. Your range can cook with gas, electricity, via convection, or even induction.

Electric, or radiant heat, ranges contain two heating coils: one on the bottom, used for baking and roasting, the other on the oven ceiling, used for broiling. Electric ovens give off a uniform, consistent heat, which is great for baking. The coils are less effective for broiling, as they simply don't get hot enough.

A gas oven does not heat, or cook, as evenly as an electric oven, but it does bake moister; gas heat is not as drying. Cooks learn to use the uneven heat to their advantage (positioning potatoes, for example, which take longer to bake, on one rack, and meats on another). Unlike electric types, a gas broiler gets

grill-hot, which is great for searing and broiling. On the down side, most gas ovens are not self-cleaning.

In addition to these conventional cooking methods, we now have newer specialty options. The convection oven (a form of electric oven) uses a fan to circulate hot air equally around the food, pulling the air out of the oven, reheating it, and returning it to the oven. Superheating the air burns off odors, which means you can cook dissimilar foods (pizza pie next to apple pie) at the same time. Convec-

STOCK CABINETRY LOOKS ANYTHING BUT STANDARD WHEN PAIRED WITH A TRAULSEN REFRIGERATOR AND A HONED MARBLE COUNTERTOP. THE CASEMENT WINDOW ALMOST SITS ON THE COUNTERTOP. EVER TRIED TO LEAN OVER A SINK AND FLING OPEN A DOUBLE-HUNG WINDOW? SHAQUILLE COULD DO IT, BUT NOT ME.

tion ovens are so energy efficient that you can reduce the cooking time and the temperature (by 20 percent and 25 percent, respectively). Bakers love them. Some of the smartest new oven models can switch from conventional to convection. Some even include a built-in microwave overhead, but these are a bit more expensive than standard models.

COOKTOPS |

A cooktop can be integrated (on top of the ovens, as with a range) or stand-alone, and it can be powered by gas, electricity, or induction. Good-size burners and easily accessible controls are critical features; cooking style is second. A professional-style cooktop is determined by its heat output, measured in BTUs (which stands for British thermal units, a measure of heat). Standard cooktops have between 9,000 and 10,000 BTUs per burner. A pro-type cooktop has 15,000 to 17,000 BTUs. Multiplied by six or more burners, that's a lot of firepower, which means you can stir-fry at peak heat and boil a pot of pasta water in a flash. You can always tell when a gas cooktop's on because you see the flame. And you can easily adjust that flame, from low to high, simmer to sizzle. Surprisingly, a good-size electric burner can actually boil a pot of water faster than most gas burners, but it is harder to control and takes more time on both ends of the heat-cool cycle. What's more, while electric cooktops are less expensive than gas to buy, they end up being more costly to run. Induction, a smooth, ceramic-glass cooking surface, uses electromagnetic energy. It heats the pot but not the cooktop itself, so there's no worry about burns. The surface is easy to clean, and the temperature control is quite precise. The only drawback to induction cooktops is aesthetic: Some people simply prefer the look of a "real" stove.

VENTILATION |

Given all the attention fancy ranges and cooktops get, it's surprising how few renovators think about ventilation. Where are all those cooking smells going to go? A good ventilation system not only removes odors

TRADE TIP

AT 5 FOOT 7, I FIND THE DEEPER SINKS BACKBREAKING. DO A DEMO. STAND AT A DEEPER SINK AND SEE HOW IT FEELS FOR YOU.

but also protects counters, cabinets, floors, and walls from grease, smoke, and heat. Most top manufacturers—Viking, Thermador, and JennAir, along with old reliables like Vent-a-Hood—make a complete line of oven hoods, and with today's open kitchen plans, they are more important than ever, both in terms of how they look and how they work.

When selecting a hood, there are a lot of considerations to factor into your choice. Make sure the ventilator you choose can handle the heat output of the range. Oven hoods are rated by how much air they can move in a given amount of time, the standard measure being cubic feet of air per minute, or CFM. As a rule of thumb, the more heat your range puts out, the more CFMs you need. Pro-style hoods, for example, range from 600 to 1,500 CFMs. Typically, a 30-inch, four-burner range with 36,000 BTUs calls for a 600-CFM ventilator, while a restaurant-style 48-inch, six-burner range or cooktop with 90,000 BTUs requires one in the neighborhood of 1,500 CFMs. If you're doing construction, it's worth making sure you install the shortest chase (distance) possible between the vent and an outside wall. The shorter the chase, the better the draw.

If your cooktop is in an island, downdrafted ventilators are an unobtrusive option. These fans pop up at the push of a button when you're cooking, then retract to sit flush with the counter when not in use. Less efficient than a full-fledged hood, some people swear by them (others swear at them). There's also the option of a hanging over-the-cooktop hood (a hoodie), which works like an umbrella, trapping smoke, grease, and odor effectively. Effective, but perhaps contradictory to the premise of an island—all open and visible—as they tend to obstruct the view.

SINKS

The kitchen sink need not be banal. Sinks are available in countless shapes and forms, from the triple-bowl Euro style to deep-apron farmhouse styles, and in sizes ranging from diminutive (11 inches round) to daring (42 inches wide). Sinks can be self-rimming or integrated into the countertop, deep or shallow, stone or synthetic. As far as trends go, the bigger, deeper sink is gaining ground; instead of the standard 25-inch model, which is 8 inches deep, renovators are opting for a 30-inch or 36-inch sink that's 10 or even 12 inches deep.

A single deep sink makes it easier to accommodate large pots and helps control splatters, but it presents a quandary. While the big pots are soaking, the sink might as well be out of order; there's no room to rinse a glass or access the disposal. Two same-size side-by-side sinks, each with its own faucet set, make sense for many renovators. This setup allows them to rinse and scrape in one and soak and scrub in the other—and two people can be really working at the same time. The decision, however, is driven largely by available counter space. If you've got it, go for the duo.

Sink styles vary. Where once the single white porcelain drop-in sink was the prevalent style, currently it is the single oversized stainless sink. But I sense a directional shift as we move toward the so-called D sinks from Blanco and Franke (I endorse them). Two bowls, one large enough to soak a Pyrex baking pan *and* still have room to wash a dish and one smaller, both come with an integrated draining rack for the bottom.

Once you've determined the size and number of sinks you want, you must address how they are fabricated (if integral) and the method of installation. Here are some choices:

- UNDERMOUNTS. Today, as our countertops move increasingly to solid surfaces—Silestone, granite, marble, Corian—undermount sinks become an appealing option. They provide a cleaner look and a more sanitary surface. Undermount sinks are attached by means of clips to the underside of your countertop.
- INTEGRAL. For a seamless look, the sink and the countertop are fabricated of the same material. It can be a solid surface, like Corian, or a stone, like marble.
- RIMMED, SELF-RIMMING, OR FLUSH-MOUNTED. These sinks are attached to the top and not the bottom of your countertops, creating a small lip or rim. They don't sweep clean with as much ease as undermounted sinks but have a charming vintage look.
- FARMHOUSE. Also called self-apron front sinks, these sinks with an exposed front are usually deeper and larger than traditional sinks. Once they were deemed the provenance of the country, but no more. In materials as diverse as stainless steel, porcelain, and soapstone, they are newly chic.
- BAR SINK, PREP SINK, VEGGIE SINK. They're all the same thing. These second sinks are fine for rinsing vegetables or making a drink, but don't count on them to do any hard work. At a typical size of 13 or 15 inches (usually square or round), with no accompanying dishwasher or brigade of cleansers, a prep sink is more of a fashion item. So play it up. Don't try to match the small sink to your main sink. Instead, serve it up in a hammered or coppered finish.

No sink is a sink, of course, without a faucet, and again, there are myriad styles to chose from. A single lever with integrated hot/cold is an obvious and efficient (but rather prosaic) choice, especially when there are so many other options. Goosenecks are graceful to look at, but they splatter. Vintage styles with spokes and separate handles for hot and cold look charming, but it's hard to find a happy temperature medium, especially if your hands are full. If you have a double sink, be sure your faucet head pivots sufficiently to service both sides. An independent sprayer or a pullout faucet is indispensable.

As for the finish, satin nickel or stainless steel are both extremely popular, and classic chrome is always in style, but surprisingly, brass still outsells all others. For a more rustic look, oil-rubbed bronze is also an option; it looks weathered and natural, with an aged patina.

KOHLER'S SO-CALLED D SINK IS A MOST ACCOMMODATING MODEL. MAKE SURE
THE FAUCET YOU CHOOSE FOR A DOUBLE SINK SWINGS TOWARD THE PRIMARY
RATHER THAN THE SECONDARY SINK. (MINE DOESN'T, AND IT'S A PAIN.) THE OGEE
EDGE OF THE COUNTERTOP IS RICH AND REFINED LOOKING, BUT ADDED CONSID-
ERABLE COST TO THE STONE INSTALLATION. OFTEN I RESERVE IT FOR THE
ISLAND ONLY AND NOT THE PERIMETER COUNTERS.

TRADE TIP

ON A TRIP TO THE APPLIANCE STORE WITH A CUSTOMER, I
ASKED THE SALESPERSON WHY MY NEW, FAIRLY EXPEN-
SIVE EUROPEAN DISHWASHER SMELLED SOUR. I HAD BEEN
RUNNING THROUGH EMPTY CYCLES WITH LEMON JUICE
AND CLOROX TRYING TO REMOVE THE ODOR. HE ASKED ME
IF I'D MANUALLY CLEANED OUT THE FOOD FILTER. WHO
KNEW THERE WAS A FILTER THAT HAS TO BE EMPTIED
EVERY MONTH OR SO? THE FILTER IS MORE TYPICAL, IT
TURNS OUT, WITH EUROPEAN MODELS.

DISHWASHERS

What does one look for in a dishwasher? On the exterior,
you can let the appliance show or hide it completely, controls and all, behind a cabinet front panel (the buttons are
revealed on the top edge when the door's opened). As for
the inner workings, quiet is good, but loading capacity is
even better; don't sacrifice the latter for the former. Miele,
considered the Mercedes-Benz of dishwashers, has a rack
that adjusts to accommodate tall stemware on the top or 12-
inch dinner plates on the bottom by simply moving a few
levers; because the cutlery holder is on the top, there's
plenty of room for plates below. Like many other appli-

THE OH-SO-EXPENSIVE HAND-
PAINTED BACKSPLASH TILES
WERE CAREFULLY PLACED SO
AS NOT TO DISAPPEAR UNDER
THE LIGHTING VALANCE OR BE
OBSCURED BY THE POT FILLER
FAUCET. THE TILE MAN INSISTED
WE SUPERVISE THE PLACEMENT
OF EVERY SINGLE TILE. TEDIOUS
BUT WORTH IT.

ances, dishwashers are becoming more specialized. General Electric has designed one just for pots and pans, with a special racking system and hot-hot water.

The higher-priced dishwashers, with stainless-steel interiors, take the beating of high heat and chemical cleansers and can last twenty years or more. The less expensive types, roughly half the price, have vinyl-clad racks, which may chip or rust—and should give you about ten years of service.

CABINET FEVER

Cabinets—the color, style, patina—set the decorative tone of a kitchen. They certainly take up most of the kitchen's

floor space and an even bigger chunk of the budget—about 40 percent of your overall remodeling expenditure—particularly if they're detailed with architectural elements like corbels, pilasters, and decorative moldings.

Regardless of the look you're after, you have to start with the most basic cabinet construction decision: to go frameless or framed. Frameless, or European-style cabinets, have a clean contemporary look and slightly more interior cabinet space. Framed cabinets have a traditional look. The edges of the case or box are covered with a flat frame, much like a picture frame. Doors and drawers may be inset into that frame, exposing it, or may overlay it, concealing it slightly.

The next decision is the style of the

door itself. This can range from a molded mahogany English style to the simple painted scullery type and anything and everything in between. When looking at a cabinet door style in a showroom, try to visualize it in your kitchen in multiples. If you are planning to install many cupboards and drawers, layers of moldings can look busy (a box within a box within a box). Err on the side of simplicity.

In terms of workmanship, measure quality by the thickness of the doors and the construction of the drawer fronts. Don't be fooled by ornamentation and design details. A cheap cabinet door is ¾ inch or even ⅝ inch thick. High-quality cabinet doors are ⅞ inch to 1⅛ inches thick. You can see the difference, and you can feel it when you close the doors and drawers.

As for the material of the doors themselves, there are hundreds of options; certain favorites float to the top. Cherry, red birch, and maple are all popular woods for cabinet doors (interiors are almost universally MDF or plywood). If the cabinets are to be painted, consider even doors made of MDF, also known as particleboard, or other aggregate species. They're less expensive, but more important, they are dimensionally stable, meaning they don't expand or contract with moisture and humidity. And they can take stronger cleansers.

In terms of design, the whole approach to kitchen cabinetry has changed and broadened. For years, cabinets were fitted, meaning all of them matched in style and finish. Now, cabinets are often unfitted and can include a range of finishes and heights, all in the same space. The height of the base, or lower, cabinets have long been built to a

TRADE TIP

AN ADVANTAGE OF FRAMED CABINETS IS THAT THEY GIVE YOU A CONCEALED RECESSED CAVITY IN WHICH TO HOUSE UNDERCOUNTER LIGHTING. FRAMELESS CABINETS DON'T, UNLESS YOU ASK FOR IT. TO CONCEAL YOUR UNDER-COUNTER LIGHTS ON A FRAMELESS CABINET, ASK THE MANUFACTURER TO INSTALL A LIGHT VALANCE TO THE BASE OF THE UPPER CABINET OR, PREFERABLY, TO RECESS THE BOTTOM OF THE CABINET, AS THE LIGHT VALANCE CAN LOOK GRAFTED ON.

Cabinet Makers

Depending on your taste—and your budget—there are three basic types of cabinetry.

- CUSTOM. Made expressly for you by a millwork shop in any size or format. The sky is the limit in terms of customization, and you're not hemmed in by standard sizes if you want an unusually large or small cabinet made.

- SEMICUSTOM. Ordered expressly for you from a cabinet manufacturer working with standard components, sizes, and increments. Boxes or cases come in 3-inch increments. For example, a drawer can be 21, 27, or 36 but never 28 inches wide. Offered in myriad styles and finishes, the built result of a carefully considered semicustom plan can look like a custom kitchen.

- STANDARD. In standard designs and standard sizes, cabinets from the IKEAS and Home Depots of the world offer the least flexibility. Still, if you have a simple space, they can work, and you can always change the hardware to give the cabinetry a little more personality.

Details

- DRAWER GLIDES. Ask if your drawers come with the Blum Motion drawer glide. The Blum Motion pulls your drawer closed softly and slowly.

- PROPORTION POINTERS. Proportion counts. I find cabinet drawers look best at about 18 inches wide. A pair of drawers creates a 36-inch-wide cabinet above or below. It's just a good proportion—important in a room where you are basically stacking a bunch of boxes.

- TOUCHUP KITS. If you buy painted or stained cabinets, ask your vendor to give you a small jar of the paint or stain for touchups down the road.

[ABOVE, LEFT TO RIGHT]
AMONG THE MYRIAD AMENITIES
OF A "FULLY LOADED" KITCHEN
ARE STORAGE OPTIONS FOR
BASE CABINETS, FROM THE
OBVIOUS TO THE SURPRISING. A
TWIN-BIN GARBAGE DRAWER
FOR TWO 30-GALLON TRASH
CONTAINERS, PEGGED DISH
STORAGE FOR BASE CABINETS—
ESPECIALLY USEFUL WHEN
THERE IS A PAUCITY OF UPPER
CABINETS—CUTLERY DRAWERS,
DIVIDED TO MATCH THE SIZES
OF A CLIENT'S FLATWARE,
AND A HEAVY-DUTY ROLL-OUT/
SWIVEL-UP DRAWER FOR
WEIGHTY APPLIANCES.

standard 34½ inches; add the countertop for a height of 3 feet, the same
as standard inset ranges and dishwashers. The height of upper cabinets is
another story altogether. With homeowners increasingly favoring 9- and 10-
-foot ceilings, it makes sense to max
out the upper cabinet size. Once a
mere 30 inches tall, the new standard
is 36 to 42 inches tall, and custom cabinets extend to a towering 50 inches.
Upper cabinets are also being mounted
closer to the countertop, sometimes
resting right on it like a china cabinet.
If your cabinets stop short of the ceiling (after all, who can reach the top
shelf?), you have to decide whether to
finish them off with molding or to

extend them to the ceiling with a false
front, called a soffit starter, which can
also be embellished with moldings.

STORAGE TRICKS AND TIPS

Interior storage options—from rollout
trays to swing-out shelves—are so
plentiful you don't have to waste an
inch. Start with the basics: Locate
trash pullouts near the sink, cutlery
drawers near the dishwasher, utensils
and pots and pans storage near the
stove. That's called point-of-use storage. A lazy Susan is ideal for corner
cupboards or any place that's hard to

TRADE TIP

TO MAKE THE MOST OF STORAGE—
ESPECIALLY IF YOUR KITCHEN IS
SHY ON UPPER CUPBOARDS—
EXPLOIT THE BASE CABINETS.
MANY STYLES NOW COME WITH A
SYSTEM OF PEGS THAT LET YOU
DESIGN YOUR DISH STORAGE
DRAWERS TO SUIT YOUR NEEDS—
AND YOUR CHINA.

reach; store canned goods, spices, or anything that won't wobble around when you swivel. A cousin of the lazy Susan is the so-called magic corner—a wire half-moon shelf that rotates out so you can get to things in a dead corner. Spice drawers are another advan-

tageous storage amenity, and it's nice to have all your spices laid out where you can see them. The ideal is a stepped spice drawer. If you can't give up the drawer space, you can hang a spice rack on the inside of a cabinet door. This solution is not as efficient or accessible, as the door-mounted rack shrinks your interior cabinet shelves and puts some of the spices out of easy reach range. Two-tiered cutlery drawers come in handy if you have two sets of silverware. The overall drawer is only 6 inches deep, so whatever you store on the bottom tier needs to be flat.

Useful base cabinet storage amenities include the twin-bin garbage recycling

unit that accommodates a drawer above and a pair of 30-gallon trash cans stacked back to back below. Use the drawer above for garbage bags and dish towels if you're squeamish about housing food and utensils over waste. Interior rollouts let you open a cupboard to reveal a pullout shelf—great for accessing pots at the back of the cabinets. Just make sure to open doors a full 90 degrees or you will have dings on the inside of your cabinet doors. Trays, cutting boards, Pyrex casseroles, and cooking tins can all be slid into a base cabinet with built-in dividers. Divide the space both vertically *and* horizontally, and slide in the trays front to back rather than top to

bottom; you'll be able to store twice as much. A vertical storage unit that pulls open like a drawer makes good use of a narrow space and provides great storage for canned goods.

ON THE SURFACE

Surface considerations—countertops and flooring—are the final factors in defining your kitchen's style and personality. Looks do count, but these surfaces will really take a beating. With so many new material options, from solid surfaces to stones to aggregates, untested by previous generations of cooks, the choices can be perplexing.

FROM THE GROUND UP

Wood has covered American floors for centuries. Today, some 75 percent (!) of kitchen renovations have wood floors. Although old heartwood pine, with its scars and blemishes, engenders a charming rustic look, oak holds up better. But put a spin on your oak. A wider strip size—3, 4, 5 inches—in a quarter-sawn cut (the tree is cut across the

grain) eliminates all knots and gives a wonderful historic look. (The cost of the wood increases, but the labor to install and stain the boards remains unchanged.) Maple does not hold stain as well as oak and therefore has less of a color range. Maple just wants to be maple-colored—a contemporary urban look. Mahogany is a durable hardwood but expensive and perhaps too dressy for a kitchen space.

As for color, check the Minwax stain chart at a home improvement store and identify the stains you are drawn to (Jacobean, Red Oak, and Ipswich Pine are three of the most popular). Ask your floor refinisher to do some in-house samples; that's the only way to be sure of the outcome on your floors in your light. Stand there with him, cheek to jowl. You may have to mix and match, adding 50 percent of one stain to another to get the color you want. When the floor is finished, ask for two coats of oil-based polyurethane in the kitchen area for added protection. Water-based polyurethane dries quicker and is odorless but does not hold up as well in a kitchen.

Stone floors are also durable—after all, centuries-old châteaux stand with their original stone floors intact. Sanitary and easy to clean, stone choices include limestones, granites, marbles, and beautiful ceramic and porcelain tiles. Some of these slabs must be sealed by the installer (be sure to ask) to increase their stain resistance. (You might also consider adding radiant heat beneath the stone, as laying the heating cables is relatively easy when your home is opened up.) On the downside, just as dishes shatter if they hit the stone, so, too, does noise clatter off a stone floor.

COUNTER CULTURE

The countertop is the real workhorse of the kitchen, so ask yourself if your selection will stand up to years of wear and tear. Will it scratch or scorch? Will spaghetti sauce seep into the grout, grain, or pores? Your choices are more abundant than ever before—and many renovators go with an unmatched look, choosing more than one. Each, of course, has its trade-offs.

• PLASTIC LAMINATES. Formica, Pionite, Nevamar, and Wilson Art, the four major manufacturers, are the least expensive option by a significant margin, and they come in hundreds and hundreds of colors. They are easy to clean, too, with readily available Soft Scrub. Plastics can burn and scratch, however, and once damaged, you need a total replacement.

• SOLID SURFACES. Corian, Avonite, and Surrell are 100 percent synthetic—and what's wrong with that? As the name implies, the color goes all the way through the surface, so any damage can be sanded or buffed out. More expensive than laminates, solid surfaces can take direct heat and absolutely will not stain. But unless you want your kitchen to look like a hospital laboratory, it's best to introduce another material, perhaps stone or tile, on another counter somewhere in the space.

• STAINLESS STEEL. The ultimate in water and heat resistance, stainless can be shaped to include its own sink and nosings. The look is modern but also historical,

WHAT COULD HAVE BEEN A COLD WHITE INTERIOR WAS COZIED UP WITH SWEDISH ACCENTS: A WAINSCOT-CLAD CENTER ISLAND, MARBLE COUNTERS, PETTICOAT-DRESSED IKEA CHAIRS, AND A BLUE TILT-TOP TABLE. THE SPACE'S WARMTH COMES FROM LIGHTING: RECESSED FIXTURES, A RISE-AND-FALL DOUBLE HANGING PENDANT, AND A GILT-EDGED CHANDELIER.

recalling the 1930s "modern cooking" kitchens. On
the plus side, stainless is reasonably priced, especially
if you order from a restaurant supply house. On the
downside, it can scratch and be cold to the touch.

- AGGREGATES OR STONE-SYNTHETIC COM-
POSITES. Made of 90 percent quartz (stone) parti-
cles and 10 percent acrylic or epoxy binder, these look
like real stone—just not one you can put a name to. A
cinch to care for and impervious to heat, the compos-
ites never need to be sealed (unlike natural stone).
Costs are slightly less than for granite. The color is
completely consistent, so seams and matching are not
a problem.

- STONES. Granite is the hardest of the stones, followed by marble, limestone, and soapstone. Other
stones are too soft for countertops. The benefit of
stone is undeniable: Each piece is unique and individual—and natural beauty is never not a good choice.
The drawback, to some at least, is maintenance. Red
wine and tomatoes eat through the polish. The way
around this is to have the stone honed (a process that
makes it matte) at the marble yard. Honed finishes are
not affected by acidic food spills. Remember, stone
comes in sizes determined by nature and not man.
When you go to select a slab, be sure to know the
largest size you need. You may not find a 7-foot slab of
your stone to cover your island in one piece.

PROOF THAT A SUCCESSFUL DESIGN CAN BE BORNE OF SIMPLE ELEMENTS OF QUALITY: HONED CREMA DELICATA MARBLE AND AN 8-INCH BACKSPLASH PAIR WITH A FOG-COLORED PAINTED WOOD CABINET.

TRADE TIP

THERE'S HONED, AND THEN THERE'S HIGH-HONED. USING A HIGHER-GRADE SANDING PAPER, SAY 220 AS OPPOSED TO 110, CREATES A FINISH THAT'S NOT POLISHED AND YET NOT AS MATTE AND PASTY AS HONED SURFACES CAN BE. SORT OF LIKE BUFFED FINGERNAILS—LUSTROUS AND SILKY TO THE TOUCH. BUT REGARDLESS OF THE DEGREE OF HONING, IF YOU FIND A STAIN, DON'T BE AFRAID TO SAND AWAY AT IT WITH EITHER A POT SCRUBBY OR STEEL WOOL. THEN JUST APPLY A FINISHING SEALER AND IT'S LIKE NEW.

Bathrooms

Bathrooms have come a long way—from small utility rooms with Formica vanities and plastic shower curtains to spa-worthy spaces. Our remodeled bathrooms are room-size affairs loaded with appurtenances. Steam showers with multiple heads and secondary spray sources are now the second most asked-for home feature (after granite kitchen countertops). Today's toilet (commode, in bath-speak) is likely to be located in a separate water closet the size of the typical 1950s bathroom. Amenities might include heated towel bars *and* heated floors, a telephone, and a TV (flat-screen, of course).

The fact is, the average American bath is middle-aged and everything needs to be replaced: the lead pan in the shower leaks, the toilet runs, the faucet threads are stripped bare, the tiles are cracked, and the grout is missing. Wading through all the renovation decisions can be intimidating (so many choices!). Your bath is the first thing you see in the morning and the last at night—it should be wonderful. Ultimately, a pristine and perfectly functioning bath is well worth the time and trouble.

WHERE TO BEGIN

Bathroom renovations are one of the best home investments you can make; the return on your expenditure is over 70 percent. No wonder bath renovation has grown into a $21-billion-a-year business.

So where to start? Before you even call the contractor, make a trip to the local plumbing or bath supply store. Renovating or adding a new bath still centers around the trinity of tub, toilet, and sink. Start by selecting these. If space allows, layer in the add-ons: whirlpool bath, separate shower stall, second sink or vanity. The dazzling array of options is overwhelming, and it's hard not to be confused by the shapes, sizes, and finishes: Spokes or levers? Brushed or polished? Satin nickel? Legacy brass? Chrome? Pewter? That's just the faucet.

Armed with research and spec sheets, call in the contractor. Your advance efforts will not only reassure him that you are serious about the project but will also help him come up with a preliminary cost estimate. If you want to enlarge your existing bath—through either an addition or the inclusion of adjacent space from, say, a spare bedroom or an extra closet (does such a thing really exist?)—you will most likely need an architect. You can usually avoid the expense of hiring an architect if your bath renovation is straightforward and doesn't involve adding space or moving walls. Your contractor can give you an idea of both what is possible and what is improbable. When you've explored your options and recovered from the sticker shock, you can move forward.

Now it's time to revisit the plumbing and bath supply stores to verify your original selections. The time since your preliminary research visits may now be several months. This time delay aids in your education. During the interim, you have likely become hyperaware of bathrooms and look at them in a new way—as a consumer and as a potential user, not just as a visitor. Your bath antennae are up. Often, I find renovators get over their initial fascination with the limited-edition diamond-faceted sink and make more classic choices.

TRADE TIP

WHEN IN THE MIDST OF FANTASIZING ABOUT A BATHROOM RENOVATION, ASSEMBLE ALL YOUR MAGAZINE AND BOOK TEARSHEETS TO REFLECT YOUR INNER SYBARITE. TAKE THESE REFERENCES TO THE BATH STORE. ONE PICTURE REALLY IS WORTH A THOUSAND WORDS, ESPECIALLY IF YOU'RE USING THE WRONG WORDS. A LAVATORY IS . . . A SINK?

LAYING IT ALL OUT

Did you ever wonder why the men's and ladies' rooms in hotels and airports are either adjacent to or backing on to each other? Sharing water and waste lines is efficient. If you are creating an entirely new bath, rule one is to try to keep the room either directly above or adjacent to an existing bathroom. Next, put the least-used fitting farthest from the door. The usual progression is sink closest to the door, toilet, and then tub/shower. If at all possible, don't put the toilet directly across from the door. The prospect of a door swinging open, exposing you enthroned to family or guests, is terrifying. (And when it's not in use, who wants to look at a toilet?) The sink is much more attractive and visually creates the illusion of a more expansive bath.

Another rule of thumb: Avoid relocating the toilet if at all possible.

GENEROUS HIS-AND-HER VANITIES REPLACED THE RECESSED MEDICINE CABINETS. ELECTRICAL OUTLETS WERE POSITIONED INSIDE THE DRAWERS SO HAIRDRYERS, ELECTRIC TOOTHBRUSHES, AND RAZORS NEED NEVER SIT COUNTERTOP. FOR A CLEAN, FINISHED LOOK THE MARBLE BASE WRAPS AROUND THE ENTIRE PERIMETER OF THE BATH, INCLUDING THE VANITY BASES. THE RESULT: A DOUBLE BORDER OF STONE, ONE ON THE HORIZONTAL PLANE, ONE ON THE VERTICAL PLANE.

TRADE TIP

WHEN REDESIGNING AND RENOVATING YOUR BATH, NO TWO TRADESPEOPLE ARE MORE VITAL THAN THE PLUMBER AND THE TILER. WITHOUT A GOOD PLUMBER, NOTHING WILL WORK RIGHT, AND WITHOUT A TILER WITH AN ARTISTIC BENT, NOTHING WILL LOOK RIGHT. BE SURE TO HAVE YOUR CONTRACTOR MEET WITH KEY TRADESPEOPLE BEFORE YOU START YOUR PROJECT.

Toilets plug into the primary waste line. At 4 inches in diameter, plus framing, the line creates quite a significant bump to relocate and bury, and it is costly to move. You can, however, rotate your toilet. And you can move it a very few inches without compromising flow, but that's all. Sinks, showers, and tubs are easy to reposition. Their secondary water and waste lines are smaller and easier to move.

A powder room can be squeezed into a minimum of 3 by 6 feet, and a full bath (albeit a modest one) can be shoehorned into a 4½ by 6-foot space. But if your bathroom is that small, forget about the latest shower designs with multiple spray sources, or the new taller toilet, and the dual-sink vanity.

THE FIXTURES

TOILETS

Like Ford's Model T car, toilets once came in a single color and style. Now the choices are almost endless. They can be one piece or two piece, elongated bowl or regular bowl, standard height or the new comfort height. Toilet styles range from the sleek and streamlined to "prettier" models. Whatever style you choose, remember this: A toilet is only as good as its flushing mechanism. This seems rather obvious, but since the government mandated restricted water flow in the 1980s, not all toilets flush equally. Toilet tanks use

[**OPPOSITE**] DUST BUNNIES BE DAMNED. THE VANITY WAS COMMISSIONED WITH A REAL FURNITURE FOOT (RATHER THAN ONE WITH TOEKICK CLEARLY VISIBLE). AN OFF-CENTER SINK ALLOWED FOR A SIGNIFICANT EXPANSE OF COUNTER SURFACE RATHER THAN TWO ITTY-BITTY PORTIONS. [**ABOVE**] TO CREATE THE SENSE OF A TOILETTE WITHOUT ACTUAL WALLS, THE VANITY WAS SITUATED JUST SO, BALANCED ON THE LEFT BY A SHALLOW STORAGE CABINET WHILE A DEEPER SHOWER STALL FACES THE TOILET AREA.

• IF YOUR TOILET IS A FAST FLUSHER (less than 1.5 seconds), you will need to keep a toilet brush at hand. A toilet with a high water mark and a sustained swirling flush generates enough water contact with the bowl to clean the surface.

• THE MAKERS OF THE PEACEKEEPER, a toilet seat with a slow regulated closing mechanism, claim it keeps the peace in a shared bath. And I thought the problem was when the toilet seat was left in the *up* position.

• NOW THERE'S EVEN A HEATED TOILET SEAT for those of us who don't have the luxury of heated floors or towel bars. Those who have it love it.

• WHEN YOU SELECT YOUR TOILET ON THE SHOWROOM FLOOR, more than likely it is shown with an upgraded seat (pressed wood, factory-sprayed white) and a chrome or nickel press lever. Then your toilet arrives with a flimsy plastic lid and press lever. *Quelle surprise!* Ask about these extras at the time of purchase and have your model delivered with them. It will save the plumber time.

• A TOILET WITH A LARGE WATER SURFACE in the bowl keeps down odors because the waste is below the water line. Hence the odor is buried.

IN THE ABSENCE OF A MEDICINE CABINET, TRAYS AND BOXES SERVE TO ORGANIZE COUNTERTOP TOILETRIES. IF THE COUNTERTOP TILE DOES NOT HAVE A FINISHING TILE, AS THIS ONE DOES, A BIT OF MOLDING STAINED TO MATCH THE BASE CABINET MAKES FOR A GRACEFUL EDGE.

TRADE TIP

IF YOU ARE THINKING OF RUNNING A VANITY COUNTERTOP OVER YOUR TOILET, CONSIDER A ONE-PIECE MODEL, WHERE THE TANK AND THE BOWL ARE MOLDED TOGETHER. ONE-PIECE TOILETS ARE ALWAYS ELONGATED AND ALWAYS HAVE A LOWER OVERALL HEIGHT. TWO-PIECE TOILETS ARE TALLER.

gravity to force-feed the water, and other improvements, such as glazed (hence more slippery) trapways, larger traps for easier passage, and rim jets at the top and siphon jets at the bottom of the bowl, all help do the job better. Still, all flushes are not created equal. Kohler's Welworth, the best buy in the industry, is reputed to be the best flusher. Toto, from Japan, also has a reputation for excellent flushing.

After asking the salesperson about flush performance, next address comfort. You'll need to sit a spell. Until 1999, every toilet introduced since 1900 was a child-size 15 inches high. Then Kohler finally introduced its new "comfort-height" model. At a normal chair height of 17 inches, it is a bestseller. True to their name, chair-height toilets are comfortable. Pro-

vided your bath can accommodate the added depth (comfort-height toilets are always elongated), I would not consider anything else. Toilets can range in depth (front to back) from 25 inches to 30 inches. An elongated toilet is 2 inches deeper than standard. Be sure you have enough knee room. In a tight space, 2 inches matters.

SINKS

Mankind probably first got the idea for a sink by observing rainwater trapped in naturally formed rock depressions. Today, your sink can be made of enamel, china, cast iron, hammered stainless steel, synthetic materials, glass, and even stone. It can be round, oval, square, or faceted, deck mounted or undermounted or wash-stand style.

An overmounted or drop-in sink rests on its rim on the countertop and is sealed with silicon. An undermounted sink sits beneath the countertop and is attached with clips and, again, sealed with silicon. The newer washstand, or vessel sink, sits entirely on top of the counter with the bowl exposed. These decorative models are more suited to powder rooms than master baths, since cleanup is difficult. The undermounted models provide a neat look and make cleaning your countertop a breeze. An integral sink molded into a synthetic countertop, such as Corian, is the most sanitary of all.

A pedestal sink, perhaps better suited to a powder room, precludes a vanity and provides very little counter surface. Even so, the simple charm of a vintage (or newer lookalike) pedestal is hard to resist, especially if you have a convenient storage closet located within your bathroom.

TUBS

Baths can be a true indulgence. If you've got the square footage, there is no substitute. Sandra Bullock and Barbara Walters are legendary bathers. Ms. Bullock says a really good day is a two-bath day; I agree.

The new standard tub is 66 inches long, 32 inches wide, and 16 to 17 inches deep—a vastly improved proportion over the shorter, shallower old tubs. As for shape, a tub can be freestanding, claw-footed, deck-mounted, or drop-in. Cast iron is the classic tub material. Such tubs typically last the life of the house. Their porcelain coating, however, is prone to chipping and eventually may need to be refin- ished. Cast iron has high heat retention when warmed (colder than an acrylic tub when empty, cast iron stays warmer longer once filled with hot water), but it is rarely used for oversized tubs (Jacuzzi, whirlpool, or two-person) because of its weight. Hence most oversized models are either acrylic or fiberglass. Both materials are lightweight and can be easily molded and shaped for back support, but they do have drawbacks. Fiberglass tubs, the least expen-

sive, are so lightweight they can sound like a beating drum when water from a shower hits them. They can also warp and scratch easily. Acrylic tubs are the most popular because they are easy to clean and repair (the color is solid all the way through, so scratches can be sanded out).

When shopping for a tub, you need to take the plunge and actually lie down in the ones that appeal to you. Simply get in and try them on for size. If you are 5 feet, 6 inches tall, a 6-foot tub is too long, assuming you would like to keep your head above water. In a too-large tub, you will either be treading water or supporting yourself with your hands. The ideal length is 60 to 66 inches. Torso height is the next consideration. To keep a consistent body temper- ature—that is, stay warm—you want your knees and shoul- ders to be under water. A tub that is 18 inches deep does that beautifully. Any deeper and you can't rest your arms on the sides of the tub to read. Also, the wider the exposed surface of the tub water, the faster it will cool off. So an oversized tub takes longer to fill and cools faster.

SHOWERS

We are no longer satisfied with a single showerhead. The shower has turned into a true sybarite's delight, with rain heads, multiple body bars, and handhelds. Multiple spray sources mean more water flowing. You will need to upgrade your plumbing lines from ½ to ¾ inch to sustain simultane- ous operation of more than one shower spray at a time.

The good news about all the shower accoutrements is that they can be used independently or together. Each spray source typically has its own thermostatic control and pressure volume control. A typical upgrade might include a

Spas

Whirlpool baths were once the province of health clubs, but they are being added to homes with a vengeance. A typical whirlpool tub runs up to 72 inches long, 54 inches wide, and 24 inches deep and comes with six or seven standard jets. Base models start at around $1,200, with prices quickly tripling with added features or dimensions.

A few other points:

- Water jets are more powerful than air jets and produce a stronger blast through fewer but larger openings. Sensations can range from a soft stroking feel to the chop, chop, chop of a jujitsu massage, depending on motor speed.

- Air tubs deliver the massaging action through more numerous and smaller jets, up to 40 on some models. The feel is much lighter, like wind on a beach or the feel of rushing water. Air-jet tubs are also quieter, and you can add bath oils, bubble bath, sea salt, or therapeutic herbs—not so with a water-jet tub.

- Consider an in-line heater to maintain water temperature. If a tub has a capacity of 60 gallons, then you need at least 40 gallons of hot (140-degree) water. A factory-installed heater will prevent the cycle of draining and then adding more hot water as the tub cools.

- Be honest about how often you'll go under the jets. According to one study, whirlpool baths are used an average of four times a year. Unless you are a devoted bather, you might be better off investing in a killer shower.

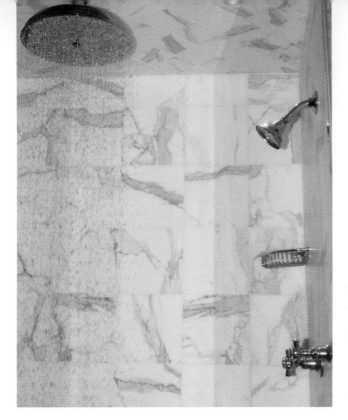

rain head, a handheld spray, a standard fixed showerhead, and two or more body bars. That means at least ten thermostatic controls and ten volume controls.

Your standard showerhead should be positioned as first control. That is not only the one you turn on first but also the one you use day in and day out. The Speakman (large), reminiscent of old country club showerheads, has a classic look and a driving spray, and it will last a lifetime. Place your adjustable handheld on an opposite or a perpendicular wall from your standard head. That way you can surround yourself with water. Your handheld should be on an adjustable bar so it can be raised or lowered for a child.

A shower stall should be a minimum of 32 inches square —if you like showering in a phone booth, that is. A more comfortable minimum is 36 by 39 inches, and that's without additional spray sources. Multiple spray sources require a shower that is a more comfortable 39 by 42 inches.

Shower design is also rapidly evolving. The emphasis is on glass walls—clear, textured, or etched with designs that create an open spa feel. Taking the trend toward greater open-

- RAIN HEADS or deluge heads are gravity downpours consisting of oversized droplets (like rain). With 200 holes or more and 8, 10, or 12 inches in diameter, they drop a ring of water the diameter of the rain head itself—no wider.

- BODY BARS or body sprays are wall-positioned showerheads used in multiples of two or three. They allow you to position the spray at specific heights: the nape of the neck, the small of the back, the buttocks. Body sprays can be piercing, needle-like, or pulsating.

- STEAM SHOWERS are not as complicated as they sound. A shower door with transom above, a vapor-tight stall, and a steam generator are all you need. The generator uses very little power. Because a steam shower takes between fifteen and twenty minutes to heat up, it is smart to get one with a programmable timer. (If your shower is lined with marble or stone, you will need to double your generator capacity, because these materials are poor insulators.) Generators can be located in remote locations, from an adjacent room to an insulated attic. When you're steamed up, it's good to vent. The same goes for a bath. Today's fully loaded designs use a lot more water, which increases humidity and condensation. Proper ventilation cuts down on mildew and mold. If neither a window nor an operable skylight is an option, use a ventilating fan, which can be placed anywhere in a bath.

TRADE TIP

TO ACCOMMODATE THE INCREASED WATER FLOW FROM MULTIPLE SOURCES, YOUR WASTE DRAIN MAY ALSO NEED TO BE ENLARGED FROM 2 TO 3 INCHES. SOME PEOPLE EVEN PUT IN TWO DRAINS. IF YOU CHOOSE THAT ROUTE, WATCH OUT FOR MORE RED TAPE: SOME MUNICIPALITIES HAVE RESTRICTIONS ON DRAIN SIZE! WHEN SELECTING ALL OF YOUR SHOWER SPRAY SOURCES, CONSIDER NOT JUST THE COST OF THE UNIT ITSELF BUT THE ADDITIONAL EXPENSE FOR VOLUME AND THERMOSTATIC CONTROLS FOR EACH SOURCE AS WELL.

ness to the extreme, some designers are eliminating the shower stall door altogether. But take note: A doorless stall should be at least 60 by 96 inches to allow for enough slope in the floor to keep water moving toward the drain. Also, the water action tends to create an internal draft, which could chill your shower if you don't have added heaters. Be sure to check the hot-water heater as well. A higher rate of water flow might demand a larger water heater to avoid suddenly cold showers.

VANITIES

As you shop around, you are likely to discover that sink vanities, also called sink cabinets, are growing in size. Up from the century-old standard of 31 inches tall, today's vanities are usually 34½ inches plus countertop, which brings them to an ergonomically correct height (even shorter people love them). You may also notice that vanities are starting to look a lot like fine furniture. Manufacturers are using the same construction, style, and finishing treatments as your living room tables to give baths a more elegant, refined look. To that same end, moldings, trims, and pilasters are cropping up all over the bathroom to finish the look.

Complementing furniture-quality vanities, some homeowners are taking the next logical leap and adding armoire-style units for storage, music and television systems, and chairs for reading and relaxing. Vintage vanity chairs are also finding a home in the bathroom, as are full-size makeup tables. If you are really serious about spa-quality amenities, think about including an aromatic steam system, a hydrotherapy tub, a shiatsu massage table, or a portable hyperbaric oxygen chamber. Talk about stress release!

If you plan to install a second vanity, consider separating it from its mate, either on another wall or via a tower—a vertical storage unit–cum–medicine cabinet that sits on the vanity top to segregate his-and-hers real estate. Also think about fog-free mirrors and perhaps magnifying mirrors, which can be recessed into the wall. For the truly pampered, go for towel warmers.

Today's bathrooms often give short shrift to serious storage space. While countless shelves are allocated for rolled towels and scented candles, medicine cabinets are regularly eschewed in favor of in-cabinet storage—which, though useful, is no substitute for eye-level, at-hand, above-sink storage. Medicine cabinets are available in depths of 4 to 8 inches (complete with interior electrical outlets for hairdryers and razors) and can be built in or semi-built in to the wall. The style and size options offered for in-wall medicine cabinets are a bit limited. However, your contractor can build one to any size and specification and with any kind of frame.

FAUCETS AND FINISHES

Renovators choose the sink faucet first and then match the tub and shower fittings to it. Spokes, or wagon-wheel lookalikes, have been in the fashion forefront for a decade. Coupled with wainscoting, they evoke a cottage charm. Levers, however, are fast replacing spokes as the bath handle du jour. When selecting a spout, inquire as to splatter and spray volume. A super-high spout, say 7 to 9 inches in height, falls with a more forceful splash, often spraying trouser fronts in

A SIMPLE STAINED WOOD "FURNITURE" VANITY WAS TOPPED WITH A VESSEL SINK AND A "FALLING WATER" FAUCET. HOW WONDERFULLY ELEGIAC. GRANDMOTHER'S OLD MIRROR BECOMES PART OF THE MIX.

the process. Be sure your spout is deep enough to project into the body of your sink basin. You need enough room to be able to cup your hands under the faucet.

The brushed nickel finish reigns supreme, with back-orders of up to eight months on bath amenities like towel bars and toilet paper holders. But polished nickel and chrome are fast-rising contenders. Nickel has a slightly warmer—that is, yellower—base note than chrome. It is also significantly more expensive. Polished brass, unpolished brass, rubbed bronze—in the end, it's all just fashion. What's in this year will be on the wane a few short years from now. The best advice is to be true to your instincts and trust your own taste.

TRADE TIP

IF YOU WANT YOUR MEDICINE CABINET TO BE FULLY BUILT IN (WITH NO PROJECTION FROM THE WALL), BE SURE TO GIVE YOUR CONTRACTOR A HEADS-UP. OTHERWISE YOU MAY FIND THAT WATER PIPES OR VAPOR LOCKS HAVE ALREADY BEEN LOCATED—OVER THE SINK. AS FOR *CLEANING* THE MIRROR ON A MEDICINE CHEST, BE CAREFUL NOT TO SPRAY DIRECTLY WITH CLEANSER (IT CAN CAUSE BLACK SEEPAGE AROUND THE EDGES). INSTEAD, SPRAY A CLOTH AND *THEN* WIPE THE SURFACE OF THE MIRROR; YOU'LL PROLONG ITS LIFE AND LOOKS FOR DECADES.

APPURTENANCES

Those we love:
- Heated floors
- Wall-mounted telephones for that inevitable early-morning call about the car pool, snow day, or sick housekeeper
- Privacy walls, partial or full
- Shower benches
- Wall-mounted shower baskets, easily accessible and mold free
- Robe hooks
- Built-in or wall-mounted soapdishes and cup holders
- Scrub brush and washcloth hooks inside the shower
- A functioning window—the best ventilator
- A pristine chrome-framed glass shower door

Those we can live without but wouldn't mind having:
- Separate toilet rooms
- Furniture-footed vanities
- Shower niches
- Bracketed flat-screen TVs
- Music, music, music
- Exhaust fans
- More glass

Those we abhor:
- Over-the-top tile trims and finishing pieces
- Exposed lightbulbs
- Unflattering light fixtures wall-mounted over the mirror
- Climb-up-into tubs
- Showerheads that trickle
- No medicine cabinets
- Plastic toilet seats

Safety makes sense

Falls in bathrooms, a significant cause of accidents and even death, are on the rise. With today's bigger bathrooms, you can really pick up speed when crossing from tub to toilet. Oversized tiles mean less grout (grout grips, giving good traction) and even more cause for slippage.

Other safety points to keep in mind:

- Watch out! Most accidents occur while stepping into or out of the shower or the tub.

- Check beneath your soap dish or shower niche for potentially slippery soap spills.

- Anchor your towel bars and shower curtain rod securely to the wall studs for safety and support.

- Install grab bars near a bath that's difficult to get out of.

- Use heavy-duty bath rugs (not flimsy, easily tripped-on bath mats) in an oversized bath to absorb water.

- Consider a 14-inch-deep tub, which is easier for elderly people to step into and out of. It is also best for bathing small children.

[ABOVE] FOR MANY, AND I COUNT MYSELF AMONG THEM, THE NEED TO HAVE TOOTHPASTE, FLOSS, Q-TIPS, AND CREAMS AT EYE LEVEL MEANS THERE'S NO SUBSTITUTE FOR A FULLY RECESSED MEDICINE CABINET. IN TERMS OF OVER-SINK LIGHTING, THE MORE DIFFUSE THE LIGHT, THE MORE FLATTERING. THREE IS PREFERABLE TO TWO. [BELOW] IF YOU WANT YOUR VANITY DRAWER FRONTS TO APPEAR UNIFORM BUT NEED A DEEP DRAWER ON ONE SIDE ONLY, LAMINATE TWO DRAWER FRONTS ONTO A SINGLE INTERIOR DRAWER.

Family Rooms

Our homes, and our home lives, have evolved in the last century. Nineteenth-century sitting rooms have transformed into today's family rooms; they've simply followed the technology. The shift from sitting room to family room began with the advent of radio in the 1920s, when the hearth lost its place as the focal point of family life. The radio gave way to boxy black-and-white rabbit-eared television sets atop TV stands. Today, new technology is still driving the market. Televisions are giving way to integrated media centers, which are becoming the raison d'être of the modern family room.

Most of us live in older homes that reflect the tastes and needs of earlier, more formal, generations. The converted family room is often a long, narrow former sunroom at the far end of the house from the kitchen, necessitating the long trek through dining room, entry hall, and living room. The solution, of course, is to renovate. And today, the most requested renovation is an expanded kitchen with an adjacent family room added to the back of the house.

Planning and designing a successful family room is a complex endeavor. These rooms house a plethora of electronic components and encompass countless hours of diverse family activity. They need to look good, work hard, and accommodate the entire family—often all at once. No matter what we call it or how we decorate it, it is where we all congregate. Americans spend one-third of all leisure time in front of the TV; that's four times more than any other leisure activity. I may not advocate quite that much viewing time, but your family room warrants a great deal of design time and commensurate decorating dollars.

DETAILING YOUR NEEDS

Before meeting with the architect or the contractor, develop a use plan for your new space. Ask yourself what you intend to do in the family room—that politically correct euphemism for TV room. Is it all about the audio/video, or are you game players, too? Perhaps you have some nascent gamblers at home, as I now do, or maybe your family does jigsaw puzzles or plays Monopoly or chess. Do you want a reading corner? A window seat? How many people do you hope to accommodate? Is your family room strictly a family affair, or are neighbors and friends invited in? Are you going to incorporate a computer, thus creating the new great room of the twenty-first century?

Do an area assessment, too. Your seating and activity goals will help you estimate the necessary size of your new room. Try to assign an appropriate square footage to each activity: game table, 42 square feet; reading area, 39 square feet; seating, 48 square feet. Circulation, or traffic patterns, also needs special attention. A simple and direct route feels best. You don't want to have to circumnavigate a game table to reach your seating area. This may sound like an enormous amount of real estate, but the room I've just described works out to be just 15 by 17 feet, a well-proportioned room but by no means grand.

Once you've sized up your proposed addition, it's time to define the amenities you want to include. A fireplace is always a real draw (along with a built-in firebox or a log bin for wood storage). Perhaps a window seat with an almost mattress-size cushion for visiting

A TABLE IN THE FAMILY ROOM BECOMES THE SPOT FOR MORE THAN JUST MEALS: FAMILY MEMBERS PLAY GAMES, DO PUZ-ZLES, WRITE THANK-YOU NOTES, AND ASSEMBLE MODELS ON IT. THE NEARBY ARMOIRE CONTAINS A COMPLETE KITCH-ENETTE. AN ORIENTAL RUG MIGHT SEEM TOO PRECIOUS A CHOICE HERE, BUT IT HAS PROVED INDESTRUCTIBLE. THERE'S A REASON THOSE BEDOUINS TOOK THE RUGS CAMEL-BACK FOR DESERT-AIR DINING.

TRADE TIP

THE RACK, AS THE VERTICAL STACK OF ELECTRONIC BOXES (CABLE BOX, DVD/VCR, ETC.) IS FONDLY CALLED, SHOULD OPTIMALLY BE PLACED ON A WALL OTHER THAN THE TV WALL. IDEALLY, THE TV SHOULD BE ON AN UNCLUTTERED WALL. YOUR EYES NEED TO FOCUS ON ONE OBJECT AND ONE OBJECT ONLY TO AVOID OVERWORKING.

cousins (a bay window would do it). A ceiling fan, ceiling height allowing, to stir the family air. And what about your storage needs? Built-ins specifically designed for DVDs and electronic detritus and deep drawers for toys, books, and games are neat and efficient. Where will you place them, and on what walls? Think of the built-ins in relation to your doors and windows. You need to develop a rhythmic, repeating pattern: door/window/cabinet/window/door, tall/short/tall. If the elements are balanced, they support one another. Architecturally, will plain Sheetrock and a flat-ceilinged six-sided box suffice, or do you want to incorporate paneling or wainscoting and beamed ceilings?

Research your material options. If your family room is an addition, your design can depart from the mainstream of your home. The fireplace can be clad in fieldstone, antique brick, or limestone. The floors can diverge from the standard 2¼-inch oak strips to wide heart pine or chestnut flooring. Or go in another direction altogether and use

a handcrafted fired tile or a rustic stone.

Think about furniture placement in relation to windows and doors and, of course, the almighty TV. Create furniture clusters and then address how to light them. Will you need floor outlets (these are a snap to install in the building stage), wall sconces, or recessed or hanging lights? How will you keep *out* the light? Unfiltered sunlight washes out the TV screen, making the picture almost invisible. (Blackouts aren't needed; wood blinds or shutters will do.) Window treatments are important in a family room for more than light control and privacy. Noise is always an issue in a multipurpose room. Fabric window treatments, rugs, and upholstered furniture are all sound-absorbing. And what of transmitting noise between rooms—will doors be needed? If so, do you have ample space

A COMPLETE TRANSFORMATION WAS ACCOMPLISHED VIA A FEW SIMPLE CHANGES, NAMELY PAINT AND SQUARING-OFF THE ROUNDED BOOKCASES. THE CABINETRY, PULLED FORWARD TO THE FRONT FACE OF CHIMNEY, CAPTURES ENOUGH DEPTH TO RECESS A STANDARD TV AND ATTENDANT ELECTRONICS. THERE ARE PLANS AFOOT TO PLACE A PLASMA OVER THE MANTEL.

TRADE TIP

YOUR FIREPLACE MANTEL WILL NEED TO BE DEEPER—SAY 15 INCHES DEEP—THAN A STANDARD-ISSUE MANTEL TO PROTECT YOUR FLAT-SCREEN TV FROM SMOKE DAMAGE.

[ABOVE] BLINDING LIGHT AND LATE AFTERNOON SUN? LINED AND INTERLINED DRAPES, PREFERABLY ON A TRAVERSE ROD FOR EASY OPENING AND CLOSING, PROVIDED THE MOST OPAQUE SOLUTION. A PATTERNED CARPET AND NUBUK OTTOMAN ENSURED THAT DOG'S HAIR AND SOIL WERE LESS VISIBLE; ALMOST INVISIBLE, IN FACT. [RIGHT] THE ATTRACTIVE CABINETRY CAME FROM A SURPRISING SOURCE: CALIFORNIA CLOSETS. QUICK DELIVERY AND EASY INSTALLATION MADE FOR A PAINLESS, AND WELL-PRICED, SOLUTION.

TRADE TIP

CALCULATE THE CORRECT VIEWING DISTANCE FROM TV TO SEATING VIA THIS FORMULA: THE SIZE OF THE SCREEN TIMES SEVEN. (SO FOR A 36-INCH TV, THAT WOULD BE 21 FEET.)

for door swing, or are hidden pocket doors an option?

Finally, what mood do you want to evoke: cottage casual, metropolitan cool, traditional tenor, or bohemian clutter? There is no right or wrong answer (other than durability, because who needs the stress of fragile, hard-to-maintain surfaces?) as long as your family's comfort and storage and activity needs are met.

ELECTRONICS: THE GOOD AND THE BETTER (AND THE UGLY)

Because technology is driving family room renovations these days, why not start with the easy and the obvious and first define the electronic components of your family room? A trip to any electronics store will yield spec sheets detailing the size and shape of your desired components. A purchase would be premature, but planning is helpful for drawing up an accurate budget and construction plan.

Today, audio/visual questions are more perplexing than ever before. We are being swept away on a wave of plasma envy, but the technology is changing so rapidly it's worth the effort to keep checking for the latest developments. Flat-plasma television screens, for example, were once considered unreliable. Who really knew how long they would last? But today's plasma

screens have gone through six or seven generations of development. The newest models are vastly improved, and prices are plummeting. Today, media centers are increasingly made up of separate components. Traditional analog television sets (that's the plain old TV we know and love), which have been perfected to the point of lasting virtually forever, include a bulky picture

tube, a television tuner, and one or more speakers. Flat-screens are the future, and virtually every renovation I am involved in incorporates one.

Unlike the cabinet-model television sets of old that hugged the floor or portables that were plopped on counters or cabinets, flat-screens are being hung on walls as much as 6 feet off the floor—and to the surprise of many, the height works well. As in an old-fashioned movie theater, looking up is actually easier on the eyes. Just make sure you have enough space between the screen and the chairs so the viewing angle isn't too steep. That could be a pain in the neck. Before you decide to hang the screen above the fireplace mantel, decide how you intend to deal with all of the cables connecting your VCR/DVD player, cable box, sound system, and computer. They'll need a surface to sit on as well, and the mantel isn't deep or long enough. If you don't want cords dangling everywhere, you'll need to wire before the walls are closed up.

Audio systems are also turning up the volume of technology. Today's state of the art is surround sound. Traditional stereo systems reproduce sound recorded through two channels, mimicking the way we hear with our two ears. Surround sound is recorded using three or more channels. When sound is reproduced on such a system, it sounds as if it's coming from all around you, hence the name.

FURNISHING AND FINISHING

Just as electronics are the centerpiece of the modern family room, they also define how to think about seating and other activities. Where will we place a napping couch or a sitting/reading couch or perhaps one of each? What about swivel chairs that rotate from fireplace to big screen to outside view, leaving shared ottomans on casters to be fought over? If you want to seat the maximum number, think about a sectional sofa. A sectional with only two arms (one at each end) outseats a pair of sofas (with two arms per sofa). For me it is important for a family room to have a private napping/cluttered corner, well lit (from behind my shoulders), with comfort a huge factor and lots of table surface for all my too often ignored piles of books and periodicals. Mine is the corner seat in my 8 by 11-foot sectional.

Lighting plays an integral role in any family room. Technically, no light source brighter than the TV screen should be placed between you and it. Think of theater lighting as a model here. Reading lamps should be behind you. Any hardwired overhead lighting should be on dimmer switches. It's a good idea to put the dimmer on a remote in a nearby room so no white-noise whine competes with the audio.

Sconces or recessed lights on the perimeters of the room, with perhaps one center fixture (on a dimmer), provide ambiance. Lamps provide task lighting; to get one to your seating area, especially in a large room, you may need to plan on floor outlets.

TRADE TIP

LIGHTING CAN BE USED TO EMPHASIZE OR MODIFY SPATIAL PERCEPTIONS. IT SETS A MOOD. DIM LIGHT IS INTIMATE AND COZY. DIFFUSE, EVEN LIGHT FLATTENS EVERYTHING OUT. USE A MIX OF OVERHEAD LIGHT AND LAMPLIGHT TO CREATE DIFFERENT ROOMS WITHIN A ROOM.

MORE IS BETTER: IN A ROOM CHOC-A-BLOC WITH AUDIO/VIDEO EQUIPMENT, MUSIC, ELECTRONICS, BOOKS, AND FAMILY, MORE PATTERN, MORE WOODGRAIN, AND MORE PRINTS WERE NECESSARY TO BALANCE AND SUPPORT ALL THE ROOM'S "STUFF." COUNTERINTUITIVE MAYBE, BUT THINK ABOUT IT: A CLEAN-LINED SPACE NEEDS TO BE EMPTY, PRISTINE. DOESN'T SOUND LIKE THE FAMILY ROOM TO ME!

Home Offices

If the kitchen is the heart of the house, the home office is its pulse, radiating energy and connecting us to the ether world. After all, we live in an era when we check our e-mail before our snail mail, when computers double as photo labs and printers as graphics centers, and when new technology enables us to sit in on a virtual business meeting without getting out of our pajamas. We spend more and more time in these multipurpose spaces not only to *work* work but also to deal with the stuff of daily life. This is the place we pay bills, order books, backpacks, and movie tickets, even communicate with our children. I often instant-message my teenage son from my office to his room, even though we are separated by a mere flight of stairs. And you know what? I usually get a fast response —and a polite one at that.

Working at home is hardly a new phenomenon. Home was, in fact, the original work environment. It was technology (in the form of manufacturing jobs) that drove us out of the house and into factories in the eighteenth century. Ironically, it is technology (in the form of Internet connections) that is returning us home in the twenty-first century. Even in

IN AN OLD-WORLD STUDY, ANTIQUE FURNISHINGS AND LIGHTING WERE AUGMENTED WITH STATE-OF-THE-ART ELECTRONICS, WIRING, AND TECHNOLOGY, ALL CONCEALED BEHIND MAHOGANY CABINETRY. WHAT'S BEHIND CLOSED DOORS IS ANYTHING BUT ANTIQUE.

my lifetime, change has been dramatic. I logged on at age thirty-eight; my kids logged on at age three. We are raising a generation of screenagers. And they, like the rest of us, need to be accommodated.

Depending on a family's needs and the layout of a house, a home office can take on different roles and guises. The space itself can be a simple little nook tucked under the stairs or a turned-out

office-away-from-the-office. The room can be a grown-up zone or a free-for-all family information center. Some families need more than a single home office. Increasingly I'm asked to help situate two or even three under the same roof.

No matter the number of rooms you allocate, my feeling is that if you're going to have a home office, you want to feel like you're at home. Or what's the point? Do you want to walk into the room, close the door, and think you're in some cookie-cutter high-rise somewhere? When it comes to renovating and outfitting a work area, remember: You're the boss of your home, so you can design your office to suit yourself.

SIZE UP THE SPACE

While there are no hard and fast rules about where and how to set up shop in the house, a few guidelines do hold true. Ideally, you want to pick a room or a spot with natural light and air. Forget cramming a desk into a closet unless you have absolutely no other choice. Poor air circulation and lack of natural light mean you'll hate going in there. And if you are going to spend lots of time in the office, you'll want a door for privacy and quiet. A room with a door also means you can close it at the end of the day—psychologically, this helps separate work and family life—and hide the messiness of any projects in pro-

A HANDSOME PARTNER'S DESK HAS BECOME THE SPOT TO THINK, REFLECT, DAY-DREAM. THE ARCHED, RECESSED COMPUTER TABLE HAS AN ERGONOMICALLY CORRECT PULL-OUT KEYBOARD TRAY AND ENOUGH SURFACE AREA FOR DOUBLE DATA COMPUTERS. TALL STORAGE UNITS HOUSE THE PRINTER, FAX, AND HARD DRIVE.

gress. Some people like the idea of housing (and concealing) a mini-office inside an armoire in a bedroom, say.

This certainly makes space-saving sense, but it may not make aesthetic sense. Chances are you won't bother closing the armoire up when you're done, leaving your work life (and clutter) on display. But if you're neat and organized and have good-looking equipment (computers are getting so chic!), who cares? After all, a computer is a sign of intelligent life.

The family-style home office calls for a few additional considerations. Everyone will be logging onto computer central at all hours of the day and night. Think of the home office as an interactive information center, a modern take on the telephone table—a place to check the weather, plan a trip, Map Quest directions to a party. You'll want the office (which may

TRADE TIP

IF YOU'RE GOING TO PUT TWO COMPUTERS IN THE SAME OFFICE AND ON THE SAME SURFACE, IT'S BEST TO SEPARATE AND SEGREGATE. BISECT THE COUNTER SURFACE WITH A FULL-HEIGHT CABINET—FROM FLOOR TO CEILING. THIS PREVENTS NOT ONLY CHAIRS AND PEOPLE BUT ALSO PAPER AND MINUTIAE FROM INVADING ANOTHER'S SPACE.

TRADE TIP

A HOME OFFICE DOESN'T NECESSARILY MEAN MILES OF
DESKTOP. SOMETIMES IT SIMPLY MEANS A QUIET PLACE
AWAY FROM THE REST OF THE HOUSEHOLD WITH A DOOR
THAT CAN BE CLOSED AT WILL. WITH LAPTOP AND LAP, A
HOME OFFICE WILL TRAVEL.

A BACKLIT SOFA HAS BEEN TRANSFORMED INTO THE PERFECT AD-HOC OFFICE
FOR A LAWYER PARTIAL TO USING A LAPTOP. THE BOOKCASES HAVE BECOME
THE RESEARCH LIBRARY; THE COFFEE TABLE THE FOOTREST.

simply be a desk space) in the eye of the storm, near the kitchen—even *in* the kitchen, if it's big enough. This way you can keep an eye on the kids and their online activities.

Of course, if the size and layout of the house allow for more than one office space, then why not set up both types —the public and the private? In my home we started with one office, conveniently located between the front hall and the kitchen and outfitted with an antique trestle writing table and a carpenter-built cabinet (to house printers and hard drives). Recently, however, it became clear that if the grown-ups were to ever log on, we'd need a second home office. With two teenagers, a college student, and one all-grown-up kid, we adults reclaimed the old playroom at the top of the stairs.

ORGANIZE AND STREAMLINE

No matter the size or shape of your office, or how many bells and whistles you need or want (scanners, copiers, plasma TVs), an office is ultimately only as smart as its setup. The average American spends five days a year looking for misplaced things: receipts, bills, phone numbers, play tickets—where did they go?

The basic word for keeping an office organized is *storage*— both open and closed. Open, in the form of shelves, bins, or baskets, should house the stuff you reach for every day: school directories, class lists, dictionaries, correspondence, current projects. Into closed storage—cabinets with doors, closets—goes anything you don't need to see all the time: computer manuals, reams of paper, stationery, film, family photos, office supplies. Classic, standard filing cabinets— which can save space by doubling as supports for a desk— are still one of the best and sturdiest options around. I find that, in general, the less visible clutter in the office, the easier it is to get work done. Try to keep the bare minimum on the desk: your computer screen, modem, and phone. That way you have elbow room for writing as well as enough space for projects in progress. A pencil drawer—I call this a clutter catcher—is indispensable. No matter how much technology we have, we still need scissors, paper clips, colored markers, and all the other tools of desktop work. The computer "brain" can go below the desk, and bulky printers and faxes can be placed on adjacent bookshelves or tables. Surface space is hot real estate. The most coveted size: 8 linear feet (6 is the minimum). You can always add more by simply adding a second unit, creating an *L*-shaped extension with a simple, streamlined parson's table or storage unit.

FIND THE RIGHT LIGHT

Any type of work that requires reading and writing calls for good lighting. There are two main types to consider: overhead, or general, lighting and desk, or task, lighting. In overhead lights, look for fixtures with a lens, shade, or alabaster globe to diffuse the heat and the glare. Halogens, provided they are low voltage, generate less heat than standard incandescent lightbulbs—a good option in a tight space. Don't overlook fluorescents—the new ones, that is. They give off no standing heat whatsoever and can be color-corrected to appear less harsh. Dimmers are always a good idea. They allow you to adjust the amount of light, they're inexpensive, and they're easy to install—but they can create a hum, so consider mounting the switch just outside the door.

While an overhead may cast enough ambient light in the room, a desk lamp is good for close-up work like paying bills and reading, especially when daylight has faded. The best desk lamp design is one that swivels—like the classic Tizio—so you can pull the head in close and then push it aside when you go back to working on the computer screen. If you choose a standard table lamp, make sure the shade is tall and deep enough to avoid catching sight of a bare bulb. Your eyes are attracted to the brightest light in the room, and that should be your computer screen, not your lamp. Imagine an old theater. All the lighting is on the perimeter.

EVEN CHILDREN WANT AN "OFFICE." THIS GARDEN TABLE WAS PRESSED INTO SERVICE IN A TEENAGE DAUGHTER'S ROOM AND HAS BECOME THE PREFERRED PLACE FOR NOT ONLY ALGEBRA AND WORLD HISTORY, BUT JEWELRY MAKING, SHELL PAINTING, AND THE ALL-IMPORTANT DOODLING.

- If parents and kids are sharing, put the adults in the inner circle and the children on the perimeter. That's because children will run in and out, shedding juice bottles and stray clothing. If you're on the inside, they'll use their own (outer) desk as the surface of first resort.

- Don't put your light source directly above your head unless you want to bake all day.

- Make sure the kids' monitor is facing out so it can be easily seen by parents walking by. Also, make sure to keep the monitor dust-free

- Like the refrigerator motor, it needs regular dusting, both inside and out.

- Don't spray Windex or other cleansers on your computer screen. Use the alcohol pads sold at computer stores.

When the lights dim and the film starts, your eyes go right to the screen. That's the way your home office should be.

UP THE AMPS

If you were to count the number of gadgets you need to plug into that duplex outlet under your desk, you'd be shocked. Five? Ten? Try as many as twelve. And you never know when you'll decide you *must* add the latest tech toy—a plasma TV, speakers for iPods. The office is one place people tend to

underestimate their electrical needs. That's why you want to plan for your outlets. The motto here: More is better.

Wire management sounds tedious, but it is necessary. Think about what you need where before you arrange your furniture and equipment. You'll need a couple of outlets above the desk; place them on the outer corners so they're not in your line of sight. The majority of outlets should go below. If possible, bring what's called a dedicated circuit to the office. This puts all the outlets on the same circuit breaker, helping prevent power overloads down the line. (A quick aside: Many old houses have become a tangle of overextended circuits and jury-rigged cables. Renovation is an ideal time to replace old cloth wiring, pre-1980, which can become brittle and crack and is the leading cause of house fires.)

Next order of business: organizing all those wires snaking across your desktop. The best solution is to drill a couple of holes, or grommets, in the desk. Forget the cute little brass ones; go for big openings, 3 inches in diameter. These allow you to thread clusters of wires through the desk

MODERN AND HISTORICAL MAKE A
GOOD MATCH IN THIS AT-HOME
"REAL" OFFICE. AN ANTIQUE TABLE
AND FAMILY ORIENTAL RUG PART-
NER WITH MODERN CABINETRY
AND ELECTRONICS. THE OFFICE
REQUIRED EXACTING LIGHT. FORTU-
NATELY, DAYLIGHT FLOODED THE
ROOM, BUT AFTER DARK A DOUBLE
RISE-AND-FALL PULLEY PENDANT
PULLS DOWN TO DRAFTING TABLE
HEIGHT.

and out of sight. A bonus: You can push your desk flush against the wall without bumping up against bulging cords and coils. Skip bundling or wrapping wires inside a coiled hose, sometimes called a wire caddy. If you need to access a particular wire, as you undoubtedly will, figuring out which one in the caddy you need will be a nightmare.

GET WIRED— OR WIRELESS

The connected future is close at hand. In fact, you could say that doing an office renovation that doesn't plan for a computer network is like renovating a century ago and ignoring indoor plumbing. It's that important. The Home Automation Association has a great Web site devoted to teaching consumers and builders about the latest in network technology (check out www.homeautomation.org). At first blush, the idea of a grand plan that connects hardware, software, and office equipment may sound vaguely Orwellian, but new devices promise to make connecting to a network as simple as plugging in a toaster.

When wireless technology—also

called Wi-Fi (rhymes with hi-fi)—works, there's nothing better. A laptop really earns its name; you can take it with you out to the lawn or into the laundry room. But Wi-Fi has its limitations. Walls, lead pipes, and floors can get in the way of the wireless signal. In my house, the attempt to create a wireless second-floor study was a miserable failure. We had to get hardwired the regular way. In fact, for families with multiple computers, some combination of systems—wireless where it works, hardwired where it doesn't—is a common scenario.

One emergent technology you're likely to hear more and more about is BPL (Broadband over Power Lines), which transmits digital information more quickly than cable or DSL lines. Better yet, it uses plain old electric wires to carry data— the very wires that already exist in every room of the house.

If your head is spinning, at least it's in good company; it's hard for all of us to keep current with all the tech advances. This much is clear: Check with your resident computer geek or digital diva (if you're lucky enough to have one) before you commit to an Internet server. Cable was the savior five years ago; now techies eschew the extra wires and the so-called last mile problem (meaning it's hard to connect to the bedroom, kitchen, den, or basement from the main entry port without running unsightly wires all over the place).

MAKE IT COMFORTABLE

Sitting in front of a computer for hours on end may benefit the business (or the brain) but not always the body. From muscle spasms to carpal tunnel syndrome, the information age can take its toll—if you let it.

- SCREENS. Eyestrain isn't only caused by the obvious: staring too long at the screen. Another contributing factor is light bouncing *off* the screen. To avoid light overload, position your desk perpendicular to the window, not facing it *or* with your back to it. If that's not logistically possible, think about moving your computer closer to the center of the room and using curtains or blinds to block out direct sunlight. Some of us, of course, crave the view outside for daydreaming or inspiration. If you're one of those, be sure to take your computer breaks when the sun comes glaring in.

- SURFACE. Counters count, too. Blue, green, and cool neutrals are less likely to cause glare than hot colors like yellow or orange. Also consider the surface itself. Granites and stones are luxurious, but they bounce light around. Plus, they're cold to the touch, which restricts blood flow to your wrists and fingers, which can lead to circulatory problems down the road. Laminates and micas are more modest (and modestly priced), but they're also durable and practical. As for good old wood, it provides a soft, forgiving surface and brings welcome warmth to the chill of high-tech equipment. No matter the material, if you tend to rest your forearms directly on the desk surface, make sure the edge is eased or completely rounded in a bullnose.

- ERGONOMICS. The term may sound New Age, but the subject is hard-core science. For healthy alignment of the body, the computer monitor should be positioned 2 feet straight ahead of you. To keep your arms and shoulders relaxed, place the keyboard at a height of 27 inches from the floor (unless you are a professional basketball player, in which case it can be a few inches higher). Most desks are the standard 29-inch height, however, so you may want to install an undercounter keyboard; you can pick up a pull-out at any home office store. If you like, as I do, to angle your keyboard this way and that as you write, consider a custom-made, adjustable pull-out.

- CHAIRS. You will be seated in your desk chair 98 percent of the time you spend in your new home office. A chair conscripted from the kitchen table may not have the required waterfall edge and thus may restrict blood flow to your lower legs, which can be a serious health problem. The right chair has a soft rounded front and should tip or tilt forward. Your feet need to be firmly planted on the ground.

CONSIDER THE KIDS

If your children will be using your home office, you'll need enough linear desktop for two or more kids (at least 4 feet) so they can sit side by side, as mine seem to love to do. Face it, wherever you put the computer is where your school-age children will be. In our house, the home office now out-ranks even the family room as the top spot—that is, the messiest room in the house.

In our home, the kids' computer table went from a single surface with a single computer to an *L*-shaped unit housing two computers, color printers, speakers, CD burners, three lamps (two would do but, hey, I'm a decorator), and every form of youthful detritus. The computer table once sat soli-tary; now it floats perpendicular to a new base cabinet (loaded with storage) in a commanding position.

A GROWN-UP TAKE ON THE BASEMENT PLAYROOM. THIS ART CURATOR AND SERIOUS MODERNIST BELIEVED IN TAKING HER WORK SERIOUSLY AND HER HOME OFFICE LIGHTLY. SHE CONCEALED A LIGHT BOX AND SLIDE STORAGE BELOW THE STAIRCASE. THE EBONY STAIR RAIL AND A STAINLESS-STEEL RAIL MAKE THIS COLORFUL AND PLAYFUL SPACE FEEL LIKE ANYTHING BUT A BASEMENT.

Talk the Talk

When it comes to tech terms, I often find myself at a loss for words (a rarity!). Every step of the office renovation process, it seems, involves buzzwords that baffle. Here, a quick translation of the most common terms being bandied about.

broadband	Broadband refers to high-speed data transmission in which a single cable can carry a large amount of data. The most common types of Internet broadband connections are cable modems (which use the same connection as cable TV) and DSL modems (which use your existing phone line).
browser	A Web browser is the program people use to access the World Wide Web. It interprets HTML code, including text, images, and hypertext links. After interpreting the HTML code, the browser displays a legible formatted page. Some common browsers are Microsoft Internet Explorer, Netscape Communicator, and Apple Safari.
byte (B)	A byte (B) is a set of 8 bits that represent a single character in the computer's memory. Bytes are typically used to measure hard disk storage and computer memory.
ethernet	Ethernet is the most common type of connection computers use in a local area network (LAN). An Ethernet port looks much like a regular phone jack, but it is slightly wider. This port can be used to connect your computer to another computer, a local network, or an external DSL or cable modem.
firewall	A computer firewall is used to protect a networked server or a client machine from damage by unauthorized users, commonly known as hackers. The firewall can be either hardware- or software-based. A network firewall allows only certain messages from the Internet to flow in and out of the network
gateway	A gateway is either hardware or software that acts as a bridge between two networks so that data can be transferred between a number of computers. An Internet gateway allows your computer or computers on a network to access the Internet and browse Web pages.
gigabyte (GB)	A gigabyte is approximately 1 billion bytes. There are 1,024 megabytes or 1,073,741,824 bytes in a gigabyte. In today's computer systems, storage capacity (the size of the hard drive) is usually measured in gigabytes.
Internet	The Internet was created in 1969 by the United States military. It was meant to be a communications network that would operate even if under nuclear attack. Many computers communicating together instead of relying on one main computer is much less vulnerable to a widespread attack.
network	Two or more computers connected to each other forms a network. The purpose of a network is to enable the sharing of computer files and peripherals (printers, scanners, disk drives) by multiple systems. Computer networks can be connected through cables, such as Ethernet cables or phone lines, or wirelessly, using wireless networking cards that send and receive data through the air and communicate through a central access point.
ping	A ping is a test to see if a system on your network or your Internet communication is working properly. Pinging a server tests and records its response time. Pinging multiple computers can be helpful in finding Internet bottlenecks, so data transfer paths can be rerouted more efficiently.
router	A router is a hardware device that routes data from a local area network (LAN) to another network connection. A router allows only authorized machines to connect to other computer systems.
TCP/IP	TCP/IP is an acronym for Transmission Control Protocol/Internet Protocol. These two protocols were developed in the early days of the Internet. The purpose was to allow computers to communicate over long-distance networks. The TCP part has to do with verifying delivery of the packets. The IP part refers to the moving of data packets between nodes. TCP/IP has become the foundation of the Internet. It is also the most common way computers talk to one another on an internal computer network.
Wi-Fi	Wireless fidelity, or Wi-Fi (sounds like hi-fi), refers to wireless network components that are based on one of the Wi-Fi Alliance's 802.11 standards. The Wi-Fi Alliance created the standard so that manufacturers can make wireless products that work with other manufacturers' wireless network cards, network access points, Internet routers, and so on.

Dream Retreats

Wine cellars, billiard rooms, media centers . . . more than ever, homes are catering to our pasttimes, our wants and desires. We are creating or carving out havens and getaways in a private context. Houses today go beyond the roll of shelter to provide dream destinations within their walls.

Baby boomers are no longer down scaling when they become empty-nesters. Instead, they are turning vacant rooms into true dream retreats. Homeowners with active families are doing the same. According to the American Society of Home Decorators, specialty rooms such as wine cellars, billiard rooms, home theaters, gyms, and music rooms are increasingly being added through remodeling or as new home options. Consumers spend almost $5 billion a year on home exercise equipment, and almost one out of every four households has some kind of home theater, even though prices start at $20,000 and go up (and up) from there.

The other aspect of this trend is the role of technology. From flat-screen televisions to sophisticated home theater systems to health club–quality exercise equipment, technology is not only driving down costs but also raising quality. We don't seem to mind paying for it. But there is more to this than hanging a flat-screen TV on the wall or throwing a pool table in the basement. Because true specialty rooms involve a high degree of form *and* function, they are almost as complicated to design as bathrooms and kitchens. A poorly planned home theater or gym not only fails to provide a meaningful experience, in the end it becomes an underused room and misspent money. To avoid the pitfalls, here are key issues to consider before you create your dream retreat.

WINE CELLARS

Before you even consider *whether* to add a wine cellar, first decide if you really *need* a wine cellar. Like swimming pools and that extra fireplace, wine cellars do not pay back their investment in increased home value. Unless you

THE DECISION WAS MADE TO "GO WITH" THE KNOTTY PINE PANELING IN THIS BASEMENT RENOVATION—BUT WITH A HOME THEATER, WEIGHT ROOM, AND WINE BAR ITS FUNCTION IS ANYTHING BUT REC-ROOM RETRO. THE DESIGN OF THE NEW CABINETRY MIMICS THE EXISTING PANELING.

Wine: Climate Control

If you decide to go the wine cellar route, remember, a good wine must be stored properly. Overheating accelerates the chemical reactions within the bottle and causes wine to age prematurely, so climate control should always be the prime consideration. That means no excessive heat or cold (57 degrees is ideal), and no excessive moisture or dryness (65 to 70 percent humidity keeps the corks fresh). In addition to a room unit that controls temperature and humidty, all walls and ceilings must have vapor barriers (typically, 6 mil polyethylene plastic) and insulation (minimum R-19). The floor, if concrete, also needs a vapor barrier.

Key Wine Cabinet Considerations

- Preferred units have quiet-running, fully digital programmable electronic cooling systems.
- Glass doors should be Thermopane UV-safe.
- High-temperature alarm: Sensor calibration controls should be included.
- An air- or liquid-sensing probe (digitally operated) should be installed.
- At least a one-year warranty with extended warranty available from the factory should be acquired.

Sizing the Cooler

Size the cooling system to your room based on its volume. Most large cellars use a split refrigeration system. The fan coil is located in the wine cellar and the condenser is placed outside, much like any central air system. Cooling unit size is based on cooling needs. A cooler big enough for a 300-cubic-foot cellar typically runs about $900, while a unit for a 2,000-cubic-foot room could cost $2,000 or more.

plan to do some serious collecting (five hundred bottles or more), you may not need a full-blown wine cellar. Think about buying a good wine cabinet instead. Wine cabinets hold anywhere from a few dozen to five hundred bottles and can be built into your kitchen or an adjacent room (perhaps a butler's pantry).

Many brands are on the market in a variety of finishes and materials, but not all wine cabinets are created equal. Most use the same cooling system, but the real test is in the quality of construction. Does the wine cabinet, for example, use true refrigerator hinges or common door hinges? The latter might be an invitation to trouble down the road. Is the cabinet's construction furniture quality, with dovetail joints or better? Remember, the typical bottle of wine weighs 3 pounds. Cheaply made cabinets can warp under the weight over time and cause your door seal to fail.

What's the best location for a wine cellar? Under the stairs? In the garage? How about the attic? Almost any out-of-the-way place would seem to work to store a few bottles —or so one would think. But ask any oenophile worth his or her 2000 vintage Lafite Rothschild Bordeaux ($400 to $700 per bottle), and the short answer would be *"Absolutment non!"*

Wine can also spoil if it's agitated, even slightly. Little (or big) feet running up and down the stairs can create enough vibration to damage a fine wine stored undernearth or even nearby. Excessive light can also send a good wine south. This is why, historically, wines were stored in caves or cellars. So when you think wine cellar, think cool; think dark; think refrigeration. While your basement is the logical

TRADE TIP

WHEN IT COMES TIME TO CLOSE THE DOOR ON YOUR WINE COLLECTION, THINK CREATIVELY. SINCE YOU NEED ONLY ONE DOOR AND IT DOESN'T NEED TO MATCH ANYTHING ELSE IN THE HOUSE, LOOK FOR AN OLD EXTERIOR DOOR AT A SALVAGE YARD. ETCHED GLASS AND ELABORATELY CARVED PANELS WILL ADD ROMANCE TO YOUR CELLAR. IF YOU CAN'T FIND AN OLD ONE, THEN GET A SINGLE GLASS-PANED FRENCH DOOR.

[**ABOVE**] A 1,500-BOTTLE WINE CELLAR PAIRED NEW CABINETRY WITH AN ANTIQUE WINE STORAGE RACK ON THE REAR WALL AND A PETITE WINE TASTING TABLE IN THE FOREGROUND. AS LIGHT WAS NOT AN ISSUE IN THE DARK INTERIOR SPACE, A GLASS DOOR WITH SIDELIGHTS WAS SELECTED AS A WAY TO SHOWCASE THE COLLECTION AND THE CELLAR.

[**OPPOSITE**] BILLIARDS HAVE BECOME THE NEW PING-PONG, THE REC ROOM MUST-HAVE OF THE TWENTY-FIRST CENTURY. KIDS LOVE TO CONGREGATE HERE, AND THE TABLE (WHEN COVERED) MAKES A GREAT SURFACE FOR ENTERTAINING, SORTING, ASSEMBLING.

choice for a wine cellar, it can also be built in any room in your house, provided the room has no ambient light and can be insulated and temperature controlled.

While a wine room or cellar can be as big or as small as you like, experts say that a wall 10 feet wide by 8 feet high provides enough space for about 1,250 bottles of wine stored in a 22½-inch double rack. So, roughly, you need 1 linear foot of wall for every 125 bottles of wine. To store 750 to 800 bottles, a wine room can be as small as 4 feet by 7 feet. A 7 by 10-foot room can handle about 2,100 bottles of wine.

Unlike most house walls, which are built with 2 by 4-inch wood studs, the walls of your wine cellar should be framed using 2 by 6-inch studs to leave enough space between them for adequate insulation. If your rooms are being insulated with spray-on polyurethane, make sure your studs

TRADE TIP

SLATE, TILE, MARBLE, AND VINYL ARE THE MOST COMMON MATERIALS USED FOR FLOORING IN A WINE CELLAR. NEVER USE CARPET, AS THE COOL, DAMP ENVIRONMENT WILL CAUSE IT TO MOLD AND MILDEW. THE SAME GOES FOR WALL COVERINGS.

don't rest against the exterior walls so that foam can fill the space behind the studs. If your basement is cold, you may even have to insulate under the wine cellar floor. Moisture-resistant drywall (called greenboard) should be used for all walls and ceilings. Be sure to use an exterior door for this interior room to provide a proper weather seal.

A number of factors come into play in designing the racking system for the wine cellar. How many bottles? What does the current collection consist of? Once these questions are answered, the design can begin to take shape. Racks typically come in two sizes, 9 inches and 13 inches wide, with spacing for half-bottles, wine, champagne, magnums, and larger sizes. Before having your contractor build custom racks, check out specialty manufacturers that make modular systems. They probably cost much less and include design features you might not think of. If you have the room, include a tasting bench or table in your cellar (if you can't show off your collection to your friends, what's the point?). Mix things up and integrate an antique wine-tasting table or wine rack among the newer system components.

Lighting should always be dimmable. You might as well add audio, too. Glass panels in your door ensure that your wine cellar can be admired and appreciated when not in use. If you used recessed lighting, set it at least 16 inches from the wall if you are using single racks and 28 inches for double-rack systems. This prevents the lights from heating the wine next to them.

BILLIARD ROOMS

The popularity of billiards has risen and fallen and risen again for most of the nation's history. During the nineteenth century's Gilded Age, it was considered a gentlemen's game, and the homes of the nation's wealthiest families often included ornate billiard rooms. Prince Albert and Queen Victoria had a billiard table. Antique tables from that era easily fetch six figures today. Pool is one of today's fastest-growing leisure activities and the centerpiece of most home game rooms. While 62 percent of all pool players are men, women and teenagers are the fastest-growing segments of new players.

In fact, pool has become so popular that some—okay, a few—homeowners are turning their formal living rooms (which are never used) into billiard rooms (which are used often). Billiard rooms are an effective way of keeping the kids and their friends at home under watchful eyes. My

Billiards by the Numbers

- A regulation-size billiard table is 4½ by 9 feet.
- A home-size table is 4 by 8 feet.
- A bar table is 3½ by 7 feet.
- A rack consists of fifteen balls; seven solid, seven striped, and the eight ball.
- A regulation cue is 57 inches long. (You can cut down a regulation cue if you are short the necessary setbacks in certain areas.)

friend Rachel put a pool table in her basement so she can always know where her daughter is. The teenage boys love to come over and play.

Like all activity-intensive form/function rooms, however, a billiard room has special requirements. For one, the room must be big enough to accommodate your table. Most home tables are 8 feet long, as are most barroom tables, although manufacturers also make 6- and 7-foot tables. To accommodate a 7-foot table, the room must be at least 13 by 16 feet in size; an 8-foot

table requires at least 13½ by 17 feet, and a regulation-size 9-foot table needs at least 14 by 18 feet of space. And those are just *minimum* room sizes. Another approach is to plan for at least 5 feet of free space all around the table. That just barely accomodates a rail shot with a regulation 57-inch pool cue. Don't try to cram too much table into a small space.

Like furniture, pool tables come in a variety of styles. Midpriced models start at around $2,000, and the range goes as high as $15,000 for a full-size regulation table. For antique tables, the sky is the limit. The playing surface on a high-quality table is made of a single piece of slate. Surprisingly, homeowners often fail to consider its weight. A typical table can tip the scales at 600 to 1,100 pounds, depending on size and quality, so don't overlook structural issues in your floor. Also be sure doorways and stairways can accomodate moving a table into an attic room or the basement. Pool tables also have specific lighting requirements—classic pool table hanging globed double and triple lights—which may call for some rewiring.

You should also think about who will use the room: adults, teens, kids, or a mixed crowd. What about a television and video games? Typically, a billiard room may contain a mini-refrigerator or kitchenette and perhaps a children's area with board games and seating for people waiting to play. Some manufacturers make special elevated spectator chairs like the ones used in turn-of-the-century billiard rooms.

Depending on space, some homeowners are going beyond billiards and adding dartboards, poker tables, and foosball. And don't forget all those game room accessories like sports posters and beanbag chairs. Shop for them online, at flea markets, or at local billiard supply stores. If your billiard room is an adults-only affair, add a card table and line the walls with bookshelves and trophy cabinets for that clubby English look.

HOME GYMS

The hardest part of exercising is getting motivated to start the workout in the first place. We all know the health benefits, but getting to the gym is often a pain for busy parents and professionals. Whether the problem is the commute or someone hogging the machines, it's all too easy to avoid going. You won't have to—if you build a gym at home.

Today, gyms are second only to home theaters on the list of most desirable dream retreats. And they should be, as our days are spent increasingly in front of our computers and our evenings in front of the TV. Yoga rooms, basketball and tennis courts, and swimming pools are all part of the growing home fitness trend. The more elaborate gyms can include everything a commerical gym has excluding the membership fees and single socializing patrons. Televisions and sound systems are also becoming must-have items. If you're going to hop a treadmill, climb on a stepper, or board a stationary bike, you should certainly be able to channel surf. Correct lighting, between you and the mirror rather than behind you, ensures a true view of your exercise form.

While basements are the traditional site for home gyms, this is slowly changing. An inviting, well-ventilated location with sufficient lighting is what we all want and need. Therefore, homeowers are increasingly converting spare bedrooms or adding an enclave off the master bedroom to make exercise an integral—and inescapable—part of modern

Getting Going on a Gym

- ASSESS FAMILY FITNESS NEEDS. Your home gym should work a full range of muscle groups and have a wide array of settings so you can increase—or decrease—resistance, incline, or duration for both weight training and cardiovascular exercise. Make sure your gym equipment is suitable for men, women, and children if you have them in the house.

- SIZE UP THE SPACE. You need as much open space around each machine as the machine takes up itself. Some high-quality home gyms are extremely heavy and can't be moved easily. Others use light-weight resistance materials and fold up for convenient storage.

- CONSIDER YOUR BUDGET. You get what you pay for. Look for club-quality machines with free-moving parts, plenty of padding, and a solid, stable frame. Specialized machines are always better than multipurpose machines.

- SHOP SECONDHAND. Inquire at your local gym equipment store about secondhand machines. I did and was able to buy a top-of-the-line wide-bodied treadmill for less than half-price. My salesperson assured me that most dilettante owners tire of equipment shortly after they purchase it and want the latest, newest incumbent, reclining, elliptical, Nordic whatever.

- ENCOURAGE, DON'T DISCOURAGE. A home gym is more important than new living room sofas or dining room drapes. Spend your money where your family will really benefit. Encourage your children to be fit and your spouse to work out, too.

- LOCATION, LOCATION, LOCATION. The basement, with its thick stone walls, is naturally considerably cooler than the rest of the house—always a plus when working out. Stone walls and cement floors provide privacy and buffer sound from the rest of the household. With nothing below, you needn't fear shaking loose a chandelier from its fittings.

living. In designing a home gym, consider safety, traffic flow, desired equipment, and future expansion possibilities.

Once your space is mapped out, and provided you have plenty of it, you need to decide which exercise machines you want. Treadmills continue to be the most popular home exercise machine, largely because they burn calories and help shed weight more efficiently than any other machine. Look for models with a continuous-duty motor that's rated at 2 horsepower or better. The deck should be at least 18 inches wide, but believe me, you want 20 inches unless you plan to take a few side trips off the deck. Fifty-three inches in deck length is ample unless you are tall (over 6 foot 2). You tall guys should check out extended-length models to accommodate your longer stride. Cushioned decks are available to ease the stress on your feet, ankles, and knees. If your room is carpeted, it pays to put special mats under the mechanized equipment because greasy grime accumulates underneath and around the base, staining the rug.

Elliptical trainers are gaining in popularity because they offer a no-impact workout that exercises the legs, arms, and upper torso. Like treadmills, they are designed for weight-bearing exercise, which helps preserve bone density. Look for motorized models and road test the stride to make sure it feels right for you. Exercise bikes, whether upright or recumbent, are also a staple of home gyms. Your calorie-burning aerobic excercise machine should be complemented by an apparatus that provides strength training. Generally, those are machines where you work against resistance.

The big quandary in strength-training equipment involves choosing between multistation gyms and specialized machines. Experts say the best systems employ weights and pulleys; second best are machines that rely on stretchable bands or bows. In addition, equipment should have ergonomic features that ease the stress on your joints. Most of all, it should operate smoothly. Consult an expert, and don't forget: it pays to keep it simple. Step benches, mats, exercise balls, and inclined benches are all inexpensive and effective.

Very heavy free weights often aren't recommended for home gyms because they require spotters, and who has one of those? The alternative, working out alone with very heavy free weights, can be dangerous.

Besides the home gym's must-haves—an aerobic component (bike, treadmill, etc.) and weights (free and/or machines)—don't forget a phone intercom system. It is imperative that you can reach your darling while he's sweating off the holiday pounds or working on his abs.

HOME THEATERS

Building a home theater means more than setting up a big-screen TV and plopping down in your favorite chair. To create a dedicated home theater, you are going to need far more than the local contractor to outfit the room. Designing a home theater requires the skills of an acoustical engi-

neer, a sound system specialist, a video specialist, and a heating and ventilating specialist. That sounds daunting, but, thankfully, audio/video companies that provide all the necessary expertise—and furniture, too—are sprouting up all over. The project is complex because you are doing more than building a room; you are creating an experience. At least that's what the experts tell us.

With today's technology, it's possible to exceed even movie-theater quality in your own home. Projects can easily run from $75,000 to $250,000. Because home theaters are

THE FIREPLACE HEARTH AND OPENING WERE REMNANTS FROM EARLIER RATHSKELLAR INCARNATIONS [OPPOSITE]. A NEW AN-TIQUE MANTEL AND THE ELECTRIFICATION OF THE GAS HEARTH LEND A WARM GLOW TO THE GOINGS-ON IN THIS HOME THEATER AND PERFORMANCE SPACE FOR A FAMILY WHO LOVES THE ARTS. THE CONTRACTOR FABRI-CATED THE NEW STAGE PROSCENIUM.

Screen and Projection Systems

TYPE	MAX SIZE	ADVANTAGE	DISADVANTAGES	COST: 15" OR LARGER
LCD-TV	40"	Reasonable price below 35"; low operating cost; slim size; good brightness; HDTV capable	Subject to pixel failure; no true black in picture; fast-moving images blur	$325 to $10,000
plasma	63"	Higher resolution; HDTV capable; no scan lines; slim size; broadest field of vision	Potential for image burn; size limited to 37" or bigger	$579 to $10,000+
rear projection	65"	Larger screen sizes; lower initial cost; HDTV capable	High operating cost; replacement bulbs expensive; bulky size; narrow field of vision	$1,000 to $20,000
front projection	120"+	Sharp images; jumbo screen sizes; HDTV capable	Susceptible to room reflections; needs large, dark room	$2,700 to $30,000+

Equipment Basics

MACHINE	EXERCISE	DESIRED FEATURES	ADVANTAGES	DISADVANTAGES	SPACE REQUIREMENTS
treadmill	Aerobic	18" by 53" deck; continuous-duty motor, 2 hp or better; cushioned deck	Most popular; efficient weight reducer	High impact on joints; belts prone to breaking; stride may not match deck if tall	30 sq ft
elliptical trainer	Aerobic	Motorized; digital controls; varying resistance	Low impact; works legs and upper torso; reduced machine time	Can be difficult, unwieldy to operate	20 sq ft
exercise bike	Aerobic	Upright and recumbent models available; digital controls	Low impact; good aerobic exercise	Uncomfortable seats; limited upper body workout	10 sq ft
multistation gym	Strength	Weights and pulleys; allows multiple users; smooth operation	Provides full range of exercises	Can be bulky; wide-ranging quality; some machines gimmicky; can be difficult to operate	50 to 200 sq ft
single-station machine	Strength	Weights and pulleys; heavy-duty construction	Specialized machines tend to provide better strength conditioning for specific muscles	Takes up a lot of floor space; mutiple machines required; wide-ranging quality	35 sq ft
rowing machine	Aerobic	Multiple workout feature; magnetic resistance; digital controls	Full-body workout; silent operation	Puts a lot of load on your lower back	20 sq ft
free weights	Strength	Stackable weights	Provides best strength workout; simple, durable equipment	Spotters needed; mutiple benches needed; bulky	20 to 50 sq ft
stair climber	Aerobic	Magnetic resistance; digital controls	High-level workout; low impact; mainly works posterior, thighs, calves	Awkward to use; bulky size, weight; stresses lower back; knee injuries	10 to 20 sq ft

so tech heavy, it's not easy to streamline your expenditures. Spring for a sound system but skimp on the room's acoustics, and you compromise the quality.

Ideally, your home theater should be located in an underused, lightly trafficked, out-of-the-way spot with little or no ambient light. You're trying to create a tomb, and it sounds like the basement to me. Because they are mostly belowground, basements are naturally soundproofed against outside noise. Usually, only the ceiling must be insulated to create full soundproofing.

Unlike many other renovation projects, the room's size *and* shape are important considerations. It's no accident that most commercial theaters are rectangles, and, as is often the case with home theater ingredients, there is a prescribed ratio: The length of your home theater should be 30 percent greater than the width. Room size is also dictated by the desired screen size. The larger the screen, the greater the viewing distance needed. There is, naturally, a prescribed ratio, and viewing distance calculators are available online or at your local electronic store.

For the best sound, you must deal with the room's acoustics. Poor acoustics can diminish your home theater experience. Avoid rooms with multiplaned walls and angled walls or ceilings, all of which distort sound. Avoid square rooms; same-size walls tend to bounce sound waves back and forth, intensifying sound in certain areas and creating dead zones in others. Sounds echo off hard surfaces and become fuzzy or distorted. Deaden (remember, it's a tomb) the room with fabrics, carpets, and wall upholstery. Even the ceiling should be upholstered.

Save the plasmas and the LCDs for the family room. In a true dedicated home theater, the options are front- and rear-projection televisions. The big advantage of projection technology is the large screen at a reasonable price.

Rear-projection TVs are self-contained in a cabinet. They look like big, bulky conventional TVs and can be as large as 4 feet square and weigh up to 300 pounds. Rear-projection screens are best viewed from directly in front. Images tend to

Tomb Tips

A dedicated home theater is not the place for slick sound-bouncing surfaces like stone, mirror, and glass. Colors should be deep and dark—no lights and brights to reflect light back into the room. Fabrics should be textural and dense, like chenilles and velvets. Slick cottons and linens do not absorb enough sound.

Windows not only let in ambient light, they also leak sound in from the outside.

Home Theater Wiring

- Avoid using extension cords and outlet splitters to supply components. Make sure outlets are grounded, unless you want the buzz of the electronic components to accompany the sound track.

- Safeguard your electronics with surge protectors. Some manufacturers include them in home theater cabinetry.

- Call in an electrician early in your planning to determine your system's needs. Can the household wiring handle the load? You may well need to upgrade your electrical system or add another circuit.

- Most home theater cabinets are designed with wire management in mind. They have channels and holes to accommodate wires safely and out of sight.

Theater Threat: Heat

- Cabinets can trap heat generated by electronic equipment. In fact, overheated equipment is a major cause of home fires. Pay close attention to projectors, line doublers, DSS receivers, and amplifiers.

- To avoid heat buildup, install fans in your theater cabinets. So-called media fans are made specifically for this purpose. They also are designed to run quietly.

- Cabinets designed for home theater systems should have extra room in the rear for fans and vents. Build custom cabinets with adequate extra space (2 inches on all sides) around the equipment.

the room. A key comparison to keep in mind is the throw distance—that is, the distance the projector can be placed from the screen and still produce a sharp 100-inch image. Most high-end units have throw distances of 5 to 22 feet, an important factor when you're planning room size.

Front projectors have shortcomings as well. They require a big room, and they perform best when the room can be completely darkened. Professional installation is a must. Even so, most experts say the image looks so real, it almost seems as though you can walk into the screen.

If you intend to invest in a full-blown home theater with a high-end front-projection television system, opting for less than theater-quality sound would only undermine your investment. We live in a three-dimensional world, and to get three-dimensional sound we need five speakers, a sub-woofer, and a Dolby Pro Logic or Dolby Digital receiver as a starting point. That's what's known as surround sound. It's always best to consult a specialist, but as a rule of thumb, your six-speaker system should be set up so two speakers are positioned to the left and the right of the screen with your center speaker above it. The horizontal speaker, the center speaker, reproduces most of the dialogue. As sound travels more slowly than light, the center speaker must be near the screen so the actors don't appear to be lip-synching. The two rear speakers should be on

fade as your viewing angle moves off center, and the screens are prone to excessive reflection. They also have a limited aspect ratio (screen size ratio of height to width). That means you can't see movies as they were originally filmed. Still, rear projection is a popular and inexpensive way to get a top-quality picture (albeit for a limited number of viewers).

Technology experts say front projectors provide a more cinema-like experience for slightly more money. For the price of a high-quality 64-inch rear-projection television (about $7,500), you can buy an HDTV-compatible front-projection system with a higher-quality 100-inch screen image.

In front-projection units, the projector is located in the room and beams the image to a wall-mounted screen, much like an old-fashioned movie projector. Front projectors can generate a picture four times the size of rear-projection and flat-screen TVs. Typical sizes range from 70 inches to 120 inches, but even bigger screens are available if you've got

TRADE TIP

DVDS AND CDS MUST BE STORED IN A COOL PLACE OUT OF DIRECT SUNLIGHT. IF YOU DON'T STORE THEM VERTICALLY, THEY CAN LOSE THEIR RIGIDITY.

either side of the seating area. The side speakers should be angled at 45 degrees and not too close to the corners of the room. The subwoofer—that's the one that makes the walls shake—should be to the left or the right of the TV.

After you have determined the what (equipment) and the where (basement or spare room), start thinking about the how—how you're going to lay out and light your home theater and how you are going to furnish it. Be aware of traffic patterns when locating furniture. Ideally, position the entrance door at the rear of the seating so that you don't create a thoroughfare between the viewer and the screen. Try to incorporate risers into your floor, elevating the rear seating sections above the front. This, of course, depends on ceiling height, and it may mean you have to place your screen higher on the wall. And where will you put the gear rack (DVD player, receiver, CD storage)? Does the room have a closet? You can even place the rack in a neighboring room and use an infrared repeater system for control. Appliances like mini-refrigerators should also be located in a closet or in an adjacent area. Refrigerator compressors are noisy.

You will need two kinds of lighting in your home theater: task lighting and ambient lighting. Task lighting allows you to read the DVD cover. Make sure your selection gives a focused light that doesn't spill over into the rest of the room. Pharmacy lamps or lamps with dark shades work well. Ambient lighting gets you in and out of the room without stumbling. Ideally, your ambient lighting should fade in and fade out, giving your eyes time to adjust. Sconces, so often used in theaters of old, are a great choice

for your home theater. Theater seating, available through your audio/video consultant and at furniture stores, consists of attached reclining seats—sort of a combination movie theater seat and recliner. Tactile transducers or buttshaker seats vibrate with the sound system for a true Space Mountain experience. Use theater seating in pairs so you can punctuate it with side tables, unless you want to hold your popcorn and sodas on your lap. Be sure your seat backs aren't too high, or the peanut gallery in the back will complain. A gas fireplace adds a nice ambient glow, and chenille throws at each seat warm up a basement space. Allow floorspace in the foreground for squirming little ones, wrestling adolescents, and schoolgirl slumber parties.

[OPPOSITE] WITH TODAY'S INFRARED REMOTES, NO ELECTRONICS NEED BE LEFT OUT IN THE OPEN. THE TRANSMITTER CAN PENETRATE SOLID WOOD! [ABOVE] WE'RE NOT SURE WHAT THEY OPERATE BUT WE'RE STILL SAVING THEM...JUST IN CASE.

Utilitarian Rooms

All too often we design our renovation around the rooms in which we entertain. Fine, but how about where we *live?* As much thought and effort should be put into the utilitarian spaces as our living and dining rooms. This point is not lost on savvy remodelers. Architects and contractors are finding that the desire for behind-the-scenes spots—laundry rooms, mudrooms, walk-in closets, and play spaces—is rising on remodeling wish lists. In fact, in a survey of the most in-demand *extra* rooms for convenience or luxury, laundry rooms topped the list at a whopping 92 percent. Far beyond the typical kitchen/family room renovation, today's remodelers are adding room-size closets—with a window, please. Mudrooms with individualized storage for Mom, Dad, the kids—and the dogs—are also high on lists, as are project, craft, and hobby rooms and designated playrooms.

Utilitarian rooms not only support our homes and our lives, but they also keep clutter at bay. They are the rooms where we warehouse and maintain our belongings, from soccer cleats to ballet bags, from golf clubs to shopping bags and the newspaper recycling bin. The chief source of friction (and disorder and wasted effort) in a household is a lack of storage space. You can't train people to put things away if there's no "away" in your home. The average American spends 150 hours a year looking for things. Translate that into waking hours, and that's ten full days. If I had those ten free days, plus the amount of time I spend transferring seasonal clothes from one tiny closet to another, I'd have enough time for a month's vacation.

Underused rooms and unfinished spaces within our existing footprint are the first places to look to for utility rooms. Your laundry room or playroom or project room can be carved out of an unused bedroom or unfinished basement. Basements typically have 9-foot ceilings, often with tons of natural light from welled windows.

LAUNDRY ROOMS

The first washing machine was invented in the 1850s, but it took the advent of the modern spin washer in the 1950s to make the washer a common household appliance. And therein lies the problem. A great number of homes were built prior to 1950, and washers and dryers were an afterthought. They were typically tossed in the basement simply because the space was available and access to water and electricity was easiest. Later, we stuck stackable washers and dryers behind pantry doors off the kitchen, as if that were the best place to pile lights and darks, soggy towels, and sweaty workout clothes. We learned the hard way that an inadequate or a poorly placed laundry room is more than a minor headache; it's a major inconvenience. Laundry is not a weekly chore. It's ongoing!

Today's laundry rooms are becoming true room-size rooms. Many are taking on multiple roles and becoming activity centers; along with two washers and dryers, some families have cable TV and Internet access. The room can be a place to enjoy crafts, check your e-mail, or eavesdrop on Oprah while taking care of small home repair projects, like regluing a vase.

The location of the laundry room is usually determined by space and availability. A second-floor laundry room is the best location, with the basement next, and an off-the-kitchen room third. Upstairs simply makes the most sense because that's where most of the laundry is generated. In those frantic moments before school or work, having a laundry close to your bedroom means you can sprint down the hall in the morning to retrieve a garment from a drying

AT FIRST BLUSH, THIS LITTLE MESSAGE CENTER TUCKED INSIDE A KITCHEN PANTRY SEEMED SILLY. NOW I WISH I HAD ONE!

[LEFT] EXTRA CABINETS FROM THE KITCHEN RENOVATION WERE PUT TO GOOD USE IN THIS SMALL LAUNDRY ROOM. DOORS WERE REMOVED ON THE UPPER CABINETS; THE LOWER CABINETS WERE DRESSED UP WITH GREEN GLASS KNOBS. FRENCH COUNTRY WALLPAPER UNIFIED WHAT PREVIOUSLY SEEMED LIKE TOO MANY DISASSOCIATED COLORS AND SURFACES: COBALT BLUE WALL TILE AND TERRA-COTTA FLOORING. [BELOW] THIS EFFICIENT LAUNDRY ROOM ACCOMMODATES UNDER-COUNTER APPLIANCES, A LAUNDRY CHUTE, AND A SMALL TV. AN EVER-ROTATING EXHIBIT OF CHILDREN'S ARTWORK GETS DISPLAYED OVER THE PERFECTLY WONDERFUL LAUNDRY SINK WITH DRYING RACK BELOW.

TRADE TIP

THE FRONT-LOADING WASHER IS THE NEWEST TREND IN LAUNDRY ROOMS. THEY DON'T HAVE AN AGITATOR LIKE TOP LOADERS, WHICH MIX, TWIST, AND SOMETIMES RIP OUR CLOTHING, AND THUS THEY LEAVE FEWER WRINKLES. FRONT LOADERS USE 50 PERCENT LESS WATER THAN TOP LOADERS. THAT TRANSLATES INTO LESS ENERGY USE, LESS SOAP, AND LONG-TERM SAVINGS. FRONT LOADERS CAN HANDLE LARGER LOADS AS WELL, ABOUT 3.8 CUBIC FEET IN THE LATEST MODELS, COMPARED TO 3 TO 3.2 CUBIC FEET IN TOP LOADERS. THAT MEANS FEWER LOADS OF LAUNDRY PER WEEK. DURING THE SPIN CYCLE THEY ALSO EXTRACT MORE WATER FROM THE CLOTHING, WHICH MEANS LESS DRYING TIME.

[**FAR LEFT**] FOR THOSE OF US WHO LOVE TO LINE DRY, A SOLUTION: A CENTRAL DRAIN INSTALLED IN THE FLOOR OF THIS CERAMIC-TILED LAUNDRY ROOM ALLOWS THE OWNER TO DRIP DRY TO HER HEART'S DELIGHT. [**LEFT**] LESS ACCESSIBLE UPPER SHELVING WAS PUT TO GOOD USE TO HOUSE THE OWNER'S BACK ISSUES OF GARDEN-ING, COOKING, AND ART MAGA-ZINES.

rack. If your second-floor laundry room is large enough, you can add a closet or keep your sewing machine permanently set up. (A basement laundry room is a great place for a backup refrigerator or freezer and an added pantry.)

The basement wins points as a location for a laundry room because it typically has underused space. Just as important, you won't flood the living room below if your washer overflows. If you're pulling apart your home and opening up the walls and you have a basement laundry room, think about trying to configure a laundry chute. At least that way you only have to carry the laundry up the stairs and not down. While they may seem practical, off-kitchen laundry rooms add too much noise, heat, and activity to an area of the house that's already plenty busy. Laundry rooms produce high amounts of humidity, dust, lint, and vapors from cleaning solutions, to say nothing of damp, smelly sports clothes—not exactly appetizing.

Appliance manufacturers are taking a cue from renovators and coming out with washers and dryers that are smarter and more sophisticated. Many are now digitally operated. Some washers and dryers communicate with each other to preset

drying cycles. Others have the capacity to wash up to 22 towels per load (Wow!). Some European models are 24 inches wide and 28 inches deep. The larger-capacity machines are 31 inches deep. Leaving room for waste and water traps, you need to allow another 6 inches from the wall to the back of your machine. (If you want machines that fit under the counter, of course, go with front loaders.) If you are tight for space, put a small stackable washer and dryer in a closet that is at the very least 36 inches deep. These are great for second-floor laundry rooms where space is limited.

Appliances aside, you want to think about how to lay out your laundry room, including workspace and a large table or counter for folding. Because this room is utilitarian, let form

TRADE TIP

WHEN IRONING, I FIND THAT I PREFER TO MOVE MY BOARD AROUND A BIT. THE STATIONARY MODEL DOESN'T SUIT MY STYLE, AND I THINK MOST IRONERS WOULD AGREE. IF YOU'RE THE SAME, AVOID PULL-DOWN OR HIDEAWAY IRON-ING BOARDS AND STICK WITH FREESTANDING.

follow function. Some new laundry room sinks, for example, have built-in wash ledges for delicates and detachable drying racks. You'll need space for a freestanding ironing board, but pull-down, or hideaway, ironing boards are an unobtrusive option in tight spaces. High shelves or a closet are a must to store soaps, detergents, bleach, and other cleaning products. (If the shelf is over your washer, allow 6 inches of space above the open washer lid for clearance.)

Utility does not have to mean ugly. Tile, vinyl, or ceramic makes the best sense for flooring. A commercial-grade vinyl tile in a two-tone checkerboard pattern is vintage appropriate. Make sure your laundry room has good overall lighting. This is not the place for recessed lighting. I frequently suggest a pair of milky-white schoolhouse globes for good, even lighting.

WALK-IN CLOSETS

When we read advertisements for new homes and apartments, the phrase pops out at those of us who are deprived: "walk-in closets." These spaces even have their own little acronym, WIC. When we see it, we feel envy, and we secretly, desperately want one—or two. More than a home theater, more than a billiard room, more than a wine cellar (way more), most people would kill for a good-size walk-in closet.

HOOKS MOUNTED ON THE FRONT FACE OF THE SHELVING UNIT PROVIDE EXTRA
HANGING SPACE. AS THE HOOKS AREN'T AS DEEP AS HANGING (17 INCHES DEEP)
OR SHELVED STORAGE (10 TO 16 INCHES DEEP), THEY WORK ESPECIALLY WELL
FOR SHALLOW SPOTS WHERE PASSAGE MIGHT BE A CONCERN.

But what actually constitutes a walk-in closet? Well, for one, you can walk into it. That means it should be at least 6 feet wide. That creates enough space for a 32-inch door and aisle and a 40-inch space for hanging clothes (20 inches on each side of the door). There is no maximum size—the bigger, the better. Many upper-end homes have his-and-hers walk-ins off the master bedroom. Window seats, dressing tables, ironing boards, shoe racks, and a bench to sit on when we put on our hose are among the amenities you can add (in which case the closet should be a minimum of 10 feet by 10 feet, according to builders).

Two walk-in closets, one off the kitchen and the other off

the master, constitute the best possible adjuncts to our busy lives. In the morning, one spouse can get dressed without disturbing the other. Just as desirable is a walk-in closet that also connects with the master-suite bath. This makes effortless the flow of activities associated with dressing and undressing. Beyond that, space should dictate where to put a walk-in closet. Many renovators simply take over an adjacent bedroom. What you lose in total bedroom numbers is more than made up for in the convenience of having all of your clothes in one place.

There is no shortage of firms like California Closets and Alternative Closets to help you outfit your new closet spaces. And companies like The Container Store have made a science of closet design. Many closet fixtures, whether made of

TRADE TIP

SKIP RECESSED LIGHTS WHEN ILLUMINATING A CLOSET. THEY CREATE FLASHLIGHT BEAMS, LEAVING LOTS OF AREAS UNDERLIT. IF YOU WANT TO BE CERTAIN THAT BOTH YOUR SWEATER AND PANTS ARE BLACK, INSTALL TWO (OR FOUR) CEILING-MOUNTED FIXTURES, EVENLY SPACED, FOR GOOD OVERALL LIGHT.

More Mortal Closets

Most closets come with a single hanging rod about 5 feet, 8 inches from the floor with a shelf above. If you need more space but can't expand, consider double hanging, where you divide the vertical space and put up two clothes rods. You'll have to fold pants to hang them and put full-length items in another closet, but you'll double your linear feet of hanging space. If you opt for only a lower rod (positioned approximately 36 inches from the floor), you generate space for three to five deep shelves above it for folded sweaters and athletic clothes. You don't need 20 inches of depth for shoes, so store them in a shallower spot.

wire grids or solid cherry, are modular, and you can mix or match units to get the storage you need for your wardrobe.

If your new closet really is room-size, think about what else you might want to do with the space. A center back-to-back chest-height bank of double drawers would give you plenty of space for socks and smalls and serve as a sort of island for folding and unpacking. A lawyer's or investment banker's closet might have a small morning desk with a fax. A mirror should be standard (full length). Consider a makeup sink to cut down on the crowding at the bathroom sink when you're both dressing for the day or an evening out. A safe or a locked drawer for valuables is another appropriate consideration.

PLAYROOMS

Homeowners are rediscovering the charm of a place for play and designating a playroom separate from the so-called great room. Playrooms keep the kids (and most of the mess) out of the kitchen and TV room without banishing them to their bedrooms. Playrooms also mean the kids can leave their toys out. If you keep the TV out of the picture, they encourage creative fun beyond cartoons and DVDs. Playrooms can be located just about anywhere, depending on the

[OPPOSITE] A SMALL TV ON A PULL-OUT SWIVEL SITS OVER PULLOUT DRAWERS AND BEHIND CURTAINED GLASS DOORS. THE DRESSING ROOM ALSO DOUBLES AS A NIGHTTIME SITTING ROOM. [ABOVE] THE GIGANTIC WALK-OUT BASEMENT YIELDED A VOLUMINOUS PLAY SPACE. TO TAKE FULL ADVANTAGE OF THE VOLUME, A PLAY BALCONY AND SECRET SPACE WERE BUILT ON-SITE. THE COLOR SCHEME WAS INSPIRED BY FISHER-PRICE. WALLS PAINTED WITH BLOCKS OF COLOR ADD DEPTH AND DIMENSION TO THE BIG ROOM.

age of your children. The ideal spot is a room adjacent to the family room and the kitchen—say, a converted sunporch. The room at the bottom of the basement steps works, too, as does an unused upstairs bedroom or finished attic.

For flooring, think about using commercial-grade vinyl tiles, like those from Mannington. Washable and cushiony, they make a great play surface to skate on, run a Matchbox car race on, or march an action hero over. Sealed cork floors are a chic alternative.

To furnish the room and to spark play, hang a mirror so your little action heroes and playacting princesses can try on and discard personas. Add a

reading chair, a bookshelf, and lots of storage. For capacious toy storage, consider a separate closet lined with shelves and bins and baskets. An 18-inch-deep painted plywood ledge running along one or more walls at 16 inches high (eye level to a standing toddler or kneeling child) makes a wonderful surface for children to set up their play worlds.

In terms of style, think utility and

TRADE TIP

IF YOU CHOOSE TO CARPET, GO WITH A LOW-PILE FLAT WEAVE OR REPLACEABLE CARPET SQUARES, WHICH MAKES A GOOD PLAY SURFACE AND WON'T TRAP TOO MANY BITS OF CRAYON.

gracing our back doors. They are often the new main entrance for families, and sometimes they are the guest door as well. A mudroom is not about hanging things on a hanger in a closet but rather about putting them away. It's a place to stop, drop, and enter, without bringing myriad appendages of a day's activities into the main house.

A modern mudroom is anywhere from 50 square feet to 500 square feet. Renovators who are bumping out a kitchen typically include a mudroom as part of the expansion. A mudroom can also be added between the main house and a detached garage or carved out of the garage itself. It can have as much charm and style as your kitchen. Wainscoting is an option for a look reminiscent of the room's agricultural origins; try cladding both the walls and the ceiling with it. Flooring should be waterproof and cleat-proof. A rugged tile, sealed slate, an outdoor stone like a quartzite, or brick is ideal. Add a window if possible. Higher-end mudrooms have heated floors, built-in benches, pet-washing sinks, and even a second refrigerator or large freezer. Think about adding outlets, too, for rechargeable cell phones and Palm Pilots. Choose lighting that is direct and bright.

A mudroom should include individual cubbies for family members and closed closets for hanging ski jackets and out-of-season coats. Consider shelves for hats, mittens, scarves, and suntan lotion. This is also the place for plenty of hooks to hold hats, dog leashes, umbrellas, and beach bags. A ball box is handy for the kids' gear, and many remodelers reserve space for paper/can/bottle recycling bins as well. Gardening supplies can have a section, and if you have pets, the mudroom is a good place to keep their food and water, not to mention a doggy bed.

durability. Walls should be painted with washable eggshell or semigloss paint—or, better yet, covered with even easier-to-clean vinyl wall covering (if you haven't looked at wallpaper lately, you'll be surprised by how good it looks). Surfaces must be smooth, sturdy, and durable to last from the toddler years through high school. As for color, just let go of all your preconceptions and coordinate with their toys. Nothing wrong with Barbie bright.

MUDROOMS

Mudrooms were born down on the farm; today, they're invading suburbia. We're not going back to plowing and planting, but thank goodness mudrooms are once again

TRADE TIP

TO KEEP TRACK OF EVERYONE'S COMINGS AND GOINGS, MANY FAMILIES HANG A CHALKBOARD IN THE MUDROOM. THEY ARE DECORATIVE—AND INEFFICIENT. HOW DO YOU POST A RECYCLABLES SCHEDULE OR A SOCCER SCHEDULE ON A CHALKBOARD? FOR A BETTER MESSAGE CENTER, HANG A BULLETIN BOARD IN YOUR MUDROOM.

THESE CUBBIES WERE BUILT TO BE OPEN AT THE BOTTOM—THE EASIER TO STUFF WITH STUFF. ANY GOOD MUDROOM SHOULD CONTAIN A COMBINATION OF OPEN (SHORT-TERM) AND CLOSED (LONG-TERM) STORAGE OPTIONS. A PRACTICAL— I.E., IF I CAN'T SEE THE DIRT THEN IT CAN'T BE THERE— FLOORING SURFACE WAS A CRITICAL CONSIDERATION.

Comings
and Goings

A house makes an impression in many ways, but the first, and often most indelible, is right through the entrance. From there the story of the house unfolds to the right, to the left, through doors, via hallways, and up and down staircases. Often we don't make enough of a home's passageways, the viaducts from one room or one floor to the next. As we renovate, we are apt to focus on the size of the dining room, the length of the kitchen island, the number of linear feet of closet space. We weigh in on coffered ceilings and dentil moldings. But rarely do we inquire about the vital and integral components that make up an entrance or a hallway.

As necessary as entries, halls, and staircases are, they tend to be undervalued and, unfortunately, underdesigned. Traditionally, the front door opened onto a center hall, with stairs up to the second floor—end of story. Today, halls go to the other extreme, meandering to connect playroom wings over three-car garages or build-outs over the kitchen/ family room. As a result, homes seem to stretch on forever, linked by uninspiring windowless halls and straight stairs without the space or grace of a landing.

Before you get too deep into dreaming of new wings and added-on rooms, start at the beginning—with how you enter and connect with the landscape on the exterior and the spaces within your home. After all, we can't visit our family or enjoy our new rooms without passing through halls, stairs, and entries.

ENTRYWAYS

It's at the front door that we greet our guests and open our homes—and this is also a logical place to consider renovation. The pleasure of a gracious entrance is enjoyed by more than just our family and friends; it is shared by passersby as well. The New England charm of a white picket fence, a stone wall, or a privet hedge signals that our home is loved. Think of this vis-à–vis your own experience. Imagine pulling up to someone's home and getting that frisson of pleasure when you see an engaging entrance with real street presence. Then imagine pulling up to an underwhelming entrance; the burden falls to the rest of the house (and its owners!) to make up for the poor first impression.

The focal point of any entrance is, of course, the front door itself, a key feature of the exterior architecture. If your house is older, chances are previous owners tried to update

THE OPENING SIZE STAYED THE SAME BUT CHANGING THE BACKDOOR FROM SOLID TO GLASS-PANED ALLOWED BETTER LIGHT AND A VIEW. A WHIMSICAL PAGODALIKE OVERHANG COMPLETE WITH FAUX BAMBOO COLUMNS ENHANCED THE ENTRY.

ENTRIES THROUGH THE AGES

Entrance halls have always played a distinctive role in architectural design, going back to the days of ancient Greece. Then, as now, they offered visitors the first glimpse inside the home and made a statement about the person who lived there. The higher the rank or greater the wealth, the more elaborate the home's entrance. Isn't that still true today, as we install columns and add pediments and oversized moldings with processionals of topiary trees ascending to our doors?

The desire for a dressed-up door is reflected in the architecture of federal and neoclassical homes from the late eighteenth and early nineteenth centuries, which feature large, front-to-back center halls. Although designed to make a statement, large entrance halls also had a functional use. In the highly proper Victorian America, only family and announced guests were granted access to formal rooms such as the parlor. Strangers and unannounced guests were seated in the entrance hall. And in colonial houses, the front-to-back center hall helped ventilate the house in summer. Remember when we had doorstops to keep doors from slamming shut before we retreated to an air-conditioned world?

In the great post–World War II housing boom, the emphasis in design shifted to functionality rather than formality, typified by the ranch house. But entrance halls never *really* went out of style. Today, the soaring, two-story entrance hall has become a signature feature of homes sometimes referred to as McMansions. They are clearly designed for a touch of grandeur, complete with dual staircases, large chandeliers, and overscale Palladian windows.

a dramatic difference. Unlacquered brass, beautiful and bronzer as it ages, can replace shiny-bright. Mullions can be added back where they once were. And if you have to replace the whole door, manufacturers make a wide variety of raised-panel wooden doors, just as they always have.

Any good entrance is more than a door. Ideally, the entry also has an overhang—if yours does not, think about adding one. Solutions can range from the classic portico with white columns and a wainscot ceiling to a cantilevered wrought-iron balcony creating a sheltering hood over your door. Ask your contractor or architect about how to bring your front door, and your family and guests, in out of the rain.

Once you pass through the front door, you enter the front hall or the foyer—a chance to create the initial impression of a home's interior style. Often, in a renovation, more can be made of the foyer by widening doorways to give the room stature. Sometimes, though, less needs to be made of an entry. The foyer may be the only room in the house with a double-height ceiling, and you may feel the need to humanize the scale of the space with wainscoting,

the door at some point to reflect the tastes of their time. With today's emphasis on authenticity, that remodeling may be considered a remuddling—and may require reevaluation. Take, for example, the insulating plastic doors popular during the energy-starved 1970s and 1980s. Another 1970s-style artifice: glaringly bright lacquered brass door hardware, artificial-looking in its perfection. Faux-leaded glass doors and doors with mini-fanlights are a more recent affectation. Fortunately, even the smallest change can make

moldings, light fixtures, and furniture. The hall requires little in the way of furnishings, merely a chest or a table for keys, packages, and presents, a chair or a bench for coats of unexpected guests, and—always—a beautiful lamp for a soft, sequestered evening light. Area rugs add texture and warmth and help trap moisture and dirt from shoes.

THIS HALL WAS FIRST RENOVATED WITH LOTS OF SISAL RUGS AS BEFITTED ITS BEACH-HOUSE PERSONA. AFTER A FEW YEARS, THE OWNERS REPLACED THE SISAL IN THE HALL WITH THESE COLORFUL, DIRT-CONCEALING KILIMS, THOUGH THEY KEPT THE SISAL ON THE STAIRS.

TRADE TIP

USE A DEEPER TREAD, AND YOUR CARPET WILL LAST LONGER. YOU WON'T BE HITTING THE NOSE OF THE TREAD ON YOUR WAY DOWN, WEARING IT AWAY.

STAIR LINGO

Stairs command their own set of rules and their own unique vocabulary.

THE COMPONENTS

THE STRINGERS are the sides of the stairs. They are cut to accept the treads.

THE TREADS are the parts you step on.

THE RISERS are the vertical parts that connect one step to another.

THE NEWELS are the larger posts at the bottom and top of a run of stairs.

THE BALUSTERS, or spindles, are the smaller, more numerous posts that support the handrail between the newels.

THE BALUSTRADE is made up of newels, balusters (spindles), and a handrail.

THE STYLES

STRAIGHT: As the name implies, these stairs rise straight up from one floor to the next. They are the most common type.

FLARE: The first few steps are longer than the subsequent steps, creating a gracious ascent. This style is mainly used to add drama and give the effect of a curved stair.

CURVED: The shape follows a constant radius or the arc of a circle. This style can be combined with a flare.

SPIRAL: Originally designed to spin inspirationally heavenward, spiral stairs are available in easily assembled kits to provide access to a townhouse garden or an attic. Spirals are used mainly where space is limited.

GOING UP: STAIRWAYS

The rise and run of the stair determines its gracefulness, as do the turn of the newel post and the height of the handrail. If you have a disappointing entrance hall, you can reinvent it by redesigning the staircase. Palladian architects developed the concept of a magnificent staircase as the hall centerpiece in the 1700s. Now stairs are significant features and often the most interesting architectural element in a home. Stairs *are* architecture.

Together, the riser and the tread determine the slope of the stair and, therefore, the ease of its use. A 9-inch tread with an 8-inch riser is the minimum required by most housing codes. If the tread is wider, the riser must be lower. Higher risers mean shorter treads. (A 12-inch tread warrants a 5½-inch riser.)

OFTEN A HALL IS THE MOST INTERESTING ARCHITECTURAL FEATURE OF A HOME, A PLACE FOR PEOPLE TO CONGREGATE. IN THIS HOME THE OWNERS CHOSE TO OVERSCALE THE HALL (ALL THE BETTER TO ADMIRE ITS GRANDEUR) AND, DURING PARTIES, TO SET UP THE BAR FRONT AND CENTER.

TRADE TIP

IF YOUR HOME HAS A VESTIBULE (A SMALL ANTEROOM THAT PRECEDES THE ENTRANCE HALL), TRY PAINTING IT IN A CONTRASTING COLOR, A SPLASH OF EXAGGERATED AND INTENSE SATURATION ON THE WALLS AND THE CEILING. ADD A WHIMSICAL LIGHT FIXTURE. IT MAY SEEM COUNTERINTUITIVE, BUT IT'S GOOD TO OVERDO SMALL SPACES. COLOR AND LIGHT MUST TRANSITION. FROM THE CLOISTERED, LOW-CEILINGED VESTIBULE, YOUR HOUSE OPENS UP ONTO THE TWO-STORIED ENTRY HALL. THE ENTRY HALL IS LIGHTER AND AIRIER BY CONTRAST.

It's hard to believe that Victorian halls could be quite so beautiful.

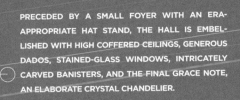

PRECEDED BY A SMALL FOYER WITH AN ERA-APPROPRIATE HAT STAND, THE HALL IS EMBELLISHED WITH HIGH COFFERED CEILINGS, GENEROUS DADOS, STAINED-GLASS WINDOWS, INTRICATELY CARVED BANISTERS, AND THE FINAL GRACE NOTE, AN ELABORATE CRYSTAL CHANDELIER.

When we are designing stairs, we are designing within extreme limitations. Narrower treads and higher risers take up less linear space but are harder to climb and dangerous on descent. (With my pointy shoes, I can't even tell if my whole foot is on the tread.) A deeper tread is safer because your entire foot is on the tread; this reduces the chances of slipping on your way down or tripping on your way up.

The stair's various ornamental components lend a sculp-tural design presence to the entry. The handrail, typically in a handsome wood (or, if marred, painted black), should be easy to grasp—ideally, not more than 2⅝ inches wide. Handrails can be set at any height from 30 inches to 38 inches from the floor of the tread, though I find 34 inches a convenient modern height. The newel post may be richly carved or turned and topped with a finial or banister ball. Balusters can be straight, round, graduated, or faceted. Railing systems may be oak, mahogany, walnut, or any good-quality hardwood.

Many homes built before 1950 had not only front but

back staircases. Narrower and more utilitarian, the back stairs were meant to be used by servants, usually linking one or more small bedrooms with the kitchen. Without balustrades, these back stairs were in fully walled stairwells with no redeeming feature other than transportation. My house has one. When two visiting architects recommended separately that I open up my back stairs, knocking out the roomside wall, I complied. First, I opened up the ground floor by removing a full wall that concealed an eight-step run of stairs, the small lower landing, and two additional bottom stairs. Then I opened the second floor, and finally the stair to the basement. Now as we descend our back stairs to the kitchen, we do so on a staircase with detail and charm that is open to the hall windows above and below. Today, back staircases from the upstairs bedrooms to the kitchen are once again popular in new construction, and smart remodel-

[**OPPOSITE**] WHENEVER AND WHEREVER POSSIBLE, OPEN UP A STAIRCASE. THEY CONVERT A SPACE FROM TUNNEL TO TERRIFIC. AND THE STAIR, WHICH IS ALL ABOUT COMMUNICATION—ALBEIT FROM ROOM TO ROOM AND FLOOR TO FLOOR—IS SUDDENLY MUCH MORE GREGARIOUS. [**ABOVE**] A CHINESE CHIPPENDALE-STYLE DOGGY DOOR WAS INSTALLED TO SEGREGATE ENTRY FROM HALLWAY AND TO CORRAL TWO SPIRITED DOGS. A SCROLL-LIKE FLOURISH AT THE BOTTOM OF THE BACK STAIRCASE SOFTENS A RATHER SEVERE SPINDLE AND NEWEL POST.

ers are adding them as part of a major kitchen upgrade or addition. We need them to connect our expanding homes. With more "towns" (rooms), we need more "roads" (halls). From the massive sculptural structure to simple utilitarianism, our stairs do more than a pedestrian (pun intended) job.

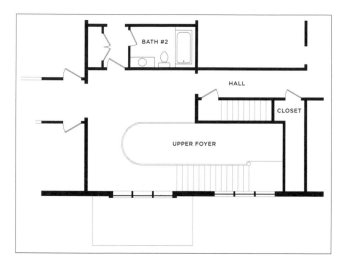

THE LONG AND WINDING HALL

In new home construction, homeowners are asking for designs that deemphasize or eliminate hotel-like hallways in favor of less claustrophobic layouts. Instead of long, nar-

row corridors, they are opening up double doors to compartmentalized side rooms, creating fluid, integrated spaces. The bedroom lets the light shine through, sharing its windows with the hall. Pocket doors and glass doors with sidelights are increasingly being incorporated to allow the rooms to flow visually while retaining the option to separate them.

Upstairs halls in most homes don't lend themselves to decoration; wallpaper is a traditional choice for stairwells and halls because it is washable and wipable. A simple run of chair rail molding installed at 30 to 36 inches high can add detail and dimension. Halls are usually windowless, which makes a good lighting plan critical. With the exception of sidelights and transoms over doors and perhaps a landing window, your hall is an interior room, and it travels to a lot of locations. Lighting sources should be dispersed over the entire hall area. Lighting can be like a trail of bread crumbs leading you to and through the home. An oversized hanging lantern, pendant, or chandelier in the heart of the stairwell is classic. Oversizing makes the look more contemporary. A chandelier with too many candles (bulbs) means you'll always be on a ladder swapping them out. Sconces on the landings generate additional intimate lighting and a sense of place; the hall landing becomes a room. Recessed lights help illuminate the corners and far reaches of long upstairs halls.

TRADE TIP

CEILINGS ARE GREAT PLACES TO FEATURE ARCHITECTURAL OR ORNAMENTAL DETAIL. THEY ARE A BLANK SLATE, AND THERE ARE LOTS OF WAYS TO DRESS THEM UP—FROM PUNCHING THEM UP INTO THE ATTIC AND CREATING A HALF-DOME, AS THE BLATTS DID, TO HANGING EXOTIC LANTERNS OR ADDING COFFERED BEAMS. IT GIVES THE HOUSE ANOTHER DIMENSION; YOU'RE NOT ALWAYS LOOKING DOWN OR STRAIGHT AHEAD—BUT UP.

Outdoor Living

The line between inside and outside the house has never been less clearly delineated. Homeowners are adding outdoor rooms, making the grounds outside the house an extension of the rooms inside. In the last decade, spending on outdoor improvements has more than doubled. What is it about this magic space between inside and outside? Our love of outdoor spaces—patios and porches—reflects a renewed interest in gardening, now our fastest-growing leisure activity. But the appeal goes beyond a desire to be out in the fresh air. It's also about taking the time for friends, family, and reflection. With utmost satisfaction, I slide into a wrought-iron chair on my terrace every morning from spring through early fall. The demands of to-do lists are replaced by the ancient rhythms of life. Outside, it seems, everything is better. Parties are more entertaining and lunches more convivial, reading is more enjoyable—even grooming the dog is fun.

THE OWNERS OF THIS BEACH RETREAT QUESTIONED THE WISDOM OF HAVING A MARBLE-TOPPED TABLE ON THEIR PORCH. MUCH TOO HEAVY TO MOVE INSIDE COME WINTER, HOW WOULD THE TABLE WITHSTAND THE CLIMATE 365 DAYS A YEAR, YEAR IN AND YEAR OUT? BEAUTIFULLY, IT TURNED OUT. AFTER ALL, STATUES AND MONUMENTS ARE MADE OF MARBLE, TOO.

If you are embarking on an interior renovation project, explore how you can take your lifestyle and your decorating outside as well.

PORCHES AND DECKS

Porches are a classic American architectural fixture, yet for years, builders made them so narrow that they were little more than rain covers. Lately, proper deep front and back porches have become the most asked-for extras in new home construction.

Since porches date back to ancient Greek and Roman times, designs can range from the simple farmhouse style to the ornate revival style, complete with fluted columns, carved balustrades, and curlicued support brackets. Like inside rooms, porches can take on any form or shape—even gingerbread—as long as they complement (that doesn't mean conform to) the architectural style of the house. They are typically roofed, elevated, and wood-framed, with tongue-and-groove wood flooring. The ceilings are often made of beadboard, a narrow tongue-and-groove material, and filled with fretwork.

The overwhelming majority of

porches—and decks, for that matter—are made from pressure-treated lumber, usually southern yellow pine. Some decks, out West or in the mountains, carry a rustic motif throughout the design with tree limbs as supporting posts and deck railings. If you don't want pressure-treated wood, consider mahogany, cedar, or fir, all of which are weather-worthy. Redwood is also an option, although it is scarce and expensive. Some new composite woods, like Trex, are also gaining in popularity.

Although procedures vary widely depending on where you live, homeowners generally must submit plans for a porch or a deck to their local regulating body. You may also be required to have a series of inspections; first, when the footing is dug (in climates where the ground freezes, footings must extend below the frost line, typically 30 inches deep); next, when the rough framing is finished; and finally, when the project is completed.

As you consider adding a porch, also think about where and how the sun moves through the day and the seasons. Which side of the house gets too much sun? You can add a porch to shade the interior of the house. Which side gets the cool early sun? That might be a perfect spot for an uncovered morning terrace.

Decks differ from porches in that they are less formal and usually are not roofed or enclosed. Consider a deck for an informal backyard or a vacation home, or where cost is an issue. Decks are less expensive to build than porches and often come prefabricated from the manufacturer, but they are no less enjoyable, although their uses are more limited. There will be no faded porch florals or seagrass rugs on the

TRADE TIP

OVER TIME, WATER, HEAVY USE, AND NATURAL AGING CAN DISCOLOR THE WOOD OF PORCHES AND DECKS. A GOOD SCRUB-DOWN WITH A HIGH-PRESSURE POWER WASHER WILL RESTORE THE LOOK.

deck—nor should there be. Somehow, redwood and cedar furnishing seems more appropriate.

Those of us who fondly remember growing up with expansive porches know that they evoke not only memories of sights and sounds but also of scents. No plan for a porch is complete without some thought to plantings. In spring, the scent could be lilac blooms; in summer, it could be gardenias,

THE OWNER ADDED A SIMPLE PORCH TO THE DECREPIT "BARN." CHARMINGLY IN KEEPING WITH ITS PREDECESSOR, THIS ADIRONDACK-STYLE ROCKIN' AND SITTIN' PORCH WAS WELL SITED TO OVERLOOK THE VALLEY BEYOND.

honeysuckle, or Linden oak. In the fall, chrysanthemums could complement the turning leaves. If you love the smell of summer rain on fresh-cut grass, plant trees near your porch. They absorb the water and make the smell more redolent.

A screened porch shelters your furnishings better than an

TRADE TIP

PORCHES SEEM TO HAVE A LIMITED COLOR RANGE. WHITE ALWAYS WORKS. IF YOUR BEADBOARD IS NATURAL, A SIMPLE VARNISH LENDS A SHIPSHAPE SEASIDE CORRECTNESS. SKY BLUE FOR PAINTED BEADBOARD CEILINGS IS AN ALTERNATIVE TO WHITE, AND SO-CALLED PORCH GRAY AND PORCH GREEN ARE TIME-TESTED COLORS FOR PAINTED FLOORBOARDS.

open porch, and it means you can be outside without the bugs, even with the lights on. Copper and bronze screens provide a richer, more authentic look, and they are extremely durable. While aluminum screens don't rust, they do oxidize. Aluminum, however, is far less expensive, and if cost is an issue, fiberglass screening is an alternative that doesn't rust or corrode. Reinforce bottom screens with stiff mesh hardware cloth. That way, a cat, dog, or toddler will not push through.

PATIOS

Patios, or terraces, also trace their origins to antiquity, giving you license to be as grand or as simple as you desire. In the tradition of ancient Greece and Rome, some homeowners are adding patio entries (called porticos) to their houses, much like the gated and walled porticos of Mediterranean homes.

Patios and terraces are almost always made of masonry or stone and usually are built on the ground, or close to it. To start the planning process, make a trip to a local supply store and check out the paving materials. Don't rely on pictures or catalogues. The colors of the stones can vary, sometimes significantly. Generally, choose a material that complements or contrasts with your house. It will be

almost impossible to match materials, so don't even try. (The same stone, years later, is not the same stone.) But you can pick up on a historical reference from your house and continue it on the patio. If your house is a federal style, for example, then brick is a natural choice. As for color, darker

TRADE TIP

IF YOU ARE ADDING A PATIO FROM SCRATCH, YOU CAN EXPERIMENT WITH VARIOUS SHAPES AND SIZES WITH ROPE. BUY A 200-FOOT LENGTH OF CLOTHESLINE ROPE AND USE IT TO OUTLINE THE PERIMETER OF YOUR PLANNED POOL OR PORCH. TOO BIG? ROLL IT UP AND TRY AGAIN.

[ABOVE] A PICNIC-INSPIRED TABLE, RENDERED IN A CHIC SQUARE, PROVIDES A SPOT FOR ALFRESCO DINING IN THIS PRISTINE PORCH. SIMPLE SUPERSIZED X LAT-TICED BOARDS KEEP DOGS FROM RUNNING RIGHT THROUGH THE LOWER POR-TION OF THE SCREENS. [OPPOSITE] A FLORAL "WALL" CREATES A BACKDROP AND SENSE OF PLACE FOR AN ANTIQUE WROUGHT-IRON LOVESEAT. A FLAG-STONE BORDER ON THE GRASSY BED FURTHER DEFINES THIS OUTDOOR "ROOM."

PATIO PAVERS. These flat square or rectangular blocks of pressed concrete can be colored. Typically, they come in 2-foot and 2 by 3-foot squares. They are usually used for informal patios or where price is an issue. Because they are not cemented in place, they can be easily replaced if they crack. They can even be made to look like brick.

STONE/SLATE. Also known as flagstone, this is a natural material that can be cut in standard sizes, but it's also laid in a random pattern. Pieces almost always vary somewhat in thickness.

BRICK. Bricks are the most popular surfacing material for patios and terraces. Today, they come in a wide variety of colors and are rated for weather resistance based on the density and type of material used. The more weather resistant, the higher the price.

AGGREGATE. Made of crushed granite, aggregate has been used for years on paths and in outdoor areas. One popular trend is to combine aggregate with brick edging.

CONCRETE. Thanks to new technology and modern techniques, this is not yesterday's patio material, and cold, gray concrete patios are largely a thing of the past. Concrete comes in all sorts of colors and textures these days and can make an extremely attractive and durable patio surface.

tones usually offer advantages. They cut down on glare and absorb the sun's rays, radiating heat even after sunset. But if your patio gets a lot of direct sunlight, dark materials may get too hot to walk on comfortably.

Of course, patios are customarily used for eating outdoors, but the charcoal kettle cooker is being supplanted by more sophisticated equipment. Dining alfresco has become a virtual art form, and old-fashioned barbecue pits are giving way to sophisticated outdoor kitchens. New heavy-duty gas

TRADE TIP

THE USE OF PRESSURE-TREATED LUMBER, USUALLY IMPREGNATED WITH A PRESERVATIVE AND AN INSECTICIDE TO WARD OFF TERMITES, HAS COME UNDER FIRE IN SOME QUARTERS BECAUSE THE CHEMICALS CAN CAUSE A REACTION IN SOME INDIVIDUALS. KNOW YOUR OWN TOLERANCE AND CHECK WITH THE MANUFACTURER OR YOUR CONTRACTOR BEFORE USING IT.

Patio Pointers

When selecting a mason for your patio or terrace, you are looking for an artist and not a mere tradesperson. The true stonemason has a feel for and a love of stone and recognizes the uniqueness of each piece. Putting together an assemblage of irregular sizes and shapes is an elaborate puzzle.

The stone you select for your new outdoor project should suit with nature and the surrounding homes. A stone can be a pretty color and yet quarrel with nature. Fortunately, many colors look good with leaf green. Indigenous stones always seem to be an appropriate choice. If you are building a stone wall, ask your mason to rake back the joints for a more natural and organic look.

If you are matching two different stones or species of stone, contrast the sizes. Two small stones can start to swarm (move or vibrate) when positioned side by side. Two large stones side by side will look like a bad patch job. Go from large to small or vice versa for a deliberate look.

A SERIES OF HOME-HUGGING OUTDOOR SPACES WERE DESIGNED TO LURE THE BUSY FAMILY OUT OF DOORS. A COVERED "MORNING PORCH" GIVES WAY TO AN OPEN TERRACE, WHICH IN TURN STEPS DOWN TO A GROUND-LEVEL SITTING AREA FRAMED BY POTTED PLANTS AND HERBS. SITTING OUTSIDE, EVEN IF FOR ONLY FIVE MINUTES, CAN BECOME SOME OF THE MOST VALUED TIME OF THE DAY.

grills, like Viking's, with 25,000-BTU infrared burners alongside refrigerated beverage centers, have moved the entire kitchen outdoors. Besides the practical benefits of feeding the family, you don't heat up the kitchen, and the dog does the vacuuming. The outdoor kitchen should be covered, even if the rest of the patio isn't, to keep rain from soaking everything on the grill. You should have at least 3 three feet of workspace on both sides of your grill. And the area around the kitchen should be made of fireproof materials that can take the heat and support the weight. Thankfully, the preferred patio/terrace surface is stone, inherently fireproof and strong.

A natural extension of the outdoor kitchen and a true delight is the outdoor fireplace. People have always congregated around a place of fire. Today, manufacturers make all kinds of outdoor heating units fired by gas, electricity,

TRADE TIP

IF YOU ARE CONSIDERING A POOL, THE NATIONAL SPA AND POOL INSTITUTE (NSPI) SUGGESTS THAT YOU COMPARE BUILDERS. GET SEVERAL ESTIMATES, LOOK AT THEIR WORK, AND CHECK REFERENCES. ASK IF THEY'RE CERTIFIED BUILDING PROFESSION-ALS (CBPS), MEANING THE BUILDER HAS GONE THROUGH A RIGOROUS AND COM-PREHENSIVE TRAINING PROGRAM DEVELOPED BY THE NSPI.

wood pellets, and propane. Chimineas and copper bowl burners sell for as little as $50. Gas-powered fireplaces, in contrast, start at around $2,500. Our own firepit, dug by our young sons, has provided the family with many hours of entertainment and just as many amusing anecdotes.

POOLS AND SPAS

The backyard swimming pool has long been a key component of the American Dream, and the demand for pools and spas is on the rise. Growing up, I remember the friends who had swimming pools and how much time we spent there, first playing and later sunning. Our family now has a pool, and it's not about luxury; it's about lifestyle. A pool means that family and friends visit often during the summer months.

Contrary to conventional wisdom, swimming pools are also now viewed as a positive selling point for homes. As we've become more health-conscious, we've gained a new appreciation for pools. Swimming is a great low-impact aerobic exercise. Fully 20 percent of all homes priced over $250,000 have a swimming pool, and an even higher percentage of homes over $1 million have one.

As with all else, pool design is susceptible to the vagaries of fashion. Kidney-shaped 1960s pools were supplanted in the 1980s by free-form pools built with rocks and natural materials and, perhaps, incorporating a waterfall. Lap pools or sports pools were the 1990s status symbol. This decade, infinity designs are ubiquitous. They make pools seemingly stretch to the horizon or disappear into the ground—so serene, we could call them yoga pools.

Like any building project, pools have their own set of regulations governed by local jurisdictions, including setbacks limiting how close you can put a pool to your property line, fencing requirements, and insurance. Where you put the pool in your yard, providing you have a choice, is largely a personal matter. If you put a pool close to your house, it's a shorter trip with a tray full of drinks, but if your children and their friends will be using it, then you have to consider the noise factor.

For the actual pool construction, homeowners have three general options:

A POOL PROJECT CHECKLIST

If you need major pool repairs or are embarking on a new pool project, refer to the following checklist.

1. Hire only licensed contractors.
2. Get references and review past work.
3. Get several bids.
4. Get a written contract, and don't sign anything until you completely understand the terms.
5. Pay 2 percent or $200 down, whichever is less, for swimming pool projects.
6. Don't let payments get ahead of the work.
7. Don't make the final payment until completion of the final plastering phase of construction, if the pool is concrete, and until the installation or construction of equipment, decking, or fencing required by the contract is also completed.

Cool Pools

When siting your pool, keep in mind that it is not always (or even often) a thing of beauty. In season, it's a picture of soggy towels, limp alligator inflatables, and chairs rotating with the sun. Out of season, a blue plastic pool cover is your centerpiece for nine months or more.

Study the way the sun moves around your proposed pool site and plan for the surrounding pool surface to be largest at the place where the sun hits in the afternoon—prime pool time.

Do you want a play pool (one with constant depth) or one with varying depth (a deep end)? Will it be used mainly for entertaining, or do you plan to use it primarily for exercise? In-ground pools with a small patio surround and fencing start at around $20,000. Custom designs run between $40,000 and $100,000 or more, depending on size, design, materials, and extras such as spas or waterfalls.

Water features like spillways, waterfalls, or fountains in a swimming pool not only mask sound but also maintain the quality of the water by aerating it.

If you don't want your pool area to be a litter-strewn mess of masks, goggles, and limp inflatables, plan for pool toy storage. Good-looking storage bins in pressure-treated teak and laminate finishes are available through outdoor entertaining catalogues.

[BELOW] A FENESTRATED FRETWORKLIKE FENCE ADDED SCREENING FOR THE POOL AREA. [OPPOSITE] THE DENSITY OF THE TRELLIS DETERMINES THE DEGREE OF SUN-SCREENING AN ARBOR LIKE THIS WILL PROVIDE. WIDELY SPACED LATTICE ALLOWS JUST ENOUGH SUN TO FILTER THROUGH.

concrete (also known as gunite), fiberglass, and vinyl-lined. Gunite, a sprayed concrete with a plaster finish coat, is the traditional method. Fiberglass pools are gaining in popularity because of their versatility, resilience, and lower cost. Vinyl-lined in-ground pools work well if you are constrained by price. As a rule of thumb, your house should dictate your investment in a pool. If you live in a million-dollar property, building a $10,000 vinyl-lined pool makes no sense. Many experts recommend opting for a smaller pool with better-quality equipment and finish rather than going with a bigger pool and skimping on equipment and finish.

What's next in line as pool style of the month? Spas or hot tubs. Forget the debauched hedonistic image. Relatively inexpensive (especially when compared to a pool), easy to maintain, and space-saving, they can be dropped into a wood deck or recessed into the ground.

In my neighborhood, the rectangular pool with attached spa reigns supreme. Heating a pool is expensive. A spa not only extends the season but also keeps down heating costs. More than swimming laps, a pool is about a quick dip. A spa adds a sybaritic soak.

Custom-built spas can be any size or shape, but generally spas range from 6 feet, 6 inches to 8 feet, 4 inches in diameter, including seating, a footwell area, and room for steps. You need room to relax and stretch out without bumping into everyone else. There are no hard and fast rules on where the spa should be positioned if it's being added as part of your pool. Basically it should be near the shallow end, but it can be on either the house side or the yard side of the pool.

Whatever form your water feature takes, I promise it will afford many hours of fun and entertainment. To me, it's a much better investment, in terms of family fun, than redoing the master bedroom and bath.

Somehow adding to or investing in an outdoor living space just seems right. Organic, authentic, and ever so human.

LIGHTING

If you plan to spend on an outdoor space, you want to be able to enjoy your investment even when nature turns out the lights. That's why lighting should be a key element of your design. Consider these factors: What purposes will the lighting serve? Is security one of your goals? How about safety? Most of all, think about mood and ambiance—always. Lighting can be used to draw attention to important features or create street presence.

Consider uplighting, a technique that places a light source below the object you want to illuminate and directs the beam upward. Uplighting a beautiful tree creates a visual outdoor room by adding depth and dimension to your nighttime view. In planning a pool, patio, or porch, be sure to incorporate lighting as part of the plan; consider an oversized exterior wall sconce mounted over an outdoor grill, a post-mounted lantern out by the pool, or an ancient hanging pendant under your covered porch.

Nuts and Bolts

It's not the most glamorous part of a project, but choosing an architect, finding a contractor, negotiating the fine print of a contract, and managing the process are key to a smooth and happy renovation. Here, advice culled from the experts: the professionals and the families who hired them.

THE ARCHITECT

SIZING UP THE PROS

- Visit recently completed renovations and look at the way the details are handled. Does the space feel appropriate and natural? Is there a sense of balance, a rhythm to the doors and windows?
- Ask if she or he has handled jobs of similar scale and budget. If the architect is accustomed to much larger projects, you may not be able to get his or her attention; if the architect's expertise is with smaller projects, he or she may not have the manpower or savvy to design or oversee your project.
- Look for passion. If the architect doesn't start with it, he or she is unlikely to feel passionate as the job unfolds. The initial passion carries through all the dreary details and unending delays.
- Do you click?
- Is the architect able to adjust his or her vision for your home to accommodate yours?

FIGURING OUT THE FEES

Architects work under various financial arrangements. Some charge a fixed price for the design drawings, with a contingency for follow-up—great if you are skittish about ill-defined expenditures on the front end. Other architects charge a fee of anywhere from 8 percent to 25 percent of the total construction costs, always a moving target.

To get a realistic budget, make sure to include filing fees, permits, surveys, and engineer's reports. These numbers can fall through the cracks when bidding and budgeting but can add up to tens of thousands of dollars. Ask your architect what you should anticipate.

THE CONTRACTOR

SIZING UP THE PROS

- Visit a current project and look at the condition of the job site. Is it strewn with empty bottles and lunchtime litter? A sloppy site can reflect sloppy workmanship.
- Interview the contractor yourself; don't leave it to the architect or the designer. He's going to be living in your house, not theirs, for many months.
- Ask for references—and check them. Ask previous clients if the contractor showed up on time. Was he or she in touch with the customer throughout the project? Would they work with him or her again without

reservation? Were they happy with the tradespeople/sub-contractors? Were they able to communicate easily and effectively with the contractor?

- Ask the contractor how many similar projects he or she has taken on in the last two years (too few, and he or she must be doing something wrong; too many, and your renovation may get caught in a logjam).
- Ask to see the contractor's license and paperwork stating that he or she is insured with full liability and workman's compensation insurance.
- Confirm that the contractor you meet with is the one who will actually work on your project. Make sure to meet the contractor's key tradespeople.

FIGURING OUT THE FEES

There are several accepted and standardized payment arrangements, each with its own pros and cons.

STIPULATED SUM

Establishes a ceiling on costs. A fixed price is set for your job. You pay the same price whether the job ends up costing more or less. On the plus side, there are no surprises. A $100,000 job costs exactly $100,000. On the negative side, there's the chance the job will come in under budget and you'll still be stuck paying the fixed fee (this is less of a risk if the bid is in line with others you've received). Even a fixed price isn't ironclad. While the price won't waver for anything *specified* in the contract, if you encounter a bombshell problem lurking behind closed walls—for example, a floor that can't support the tile you plan to lay—then all bets are off. If you choose this method, it works best to schedule monthly payments so you are paying for work that's just been completed. The risk of paying one-third up front, one-third halfway through, and the last third on completion is that somewhere along the way you've paid for work that hasn't been finished. If this is the case, you can tie payments to what is called substantial completion of specific

phases: foundation, framing, windows, and doors. This gives the contractor incentive to complete a phase and receive payment.

COST PLUS

Essentially, cost plus means you pay as you go for time, materials, and contractor's profit. This arrangement usually involves a fixed percentage fee of the overall project cost ranging from 15 percent to 30 percent. Customers are typically billed monthly or bimonthly to cover overhead. On the plus side, you know what you pay for every nail and every shingle; the transaction is transparent. On the downside, if the project drags on, the labor costs can skyrocket. And because there's no cap, it's hard to anticipate the total.

Whichever method you choose, as the project is winding down, experienced renovators suggest holding back a small but significant percentage of the final payment as incentive to get the job wrapped up. If you're satisfied with the job, withhold 5 percent of the contractor's profit until he or she finishes; if you see larger issues, hold back 10 percent.

WHAT NOT TO DO

- Let painters pick paint colors or volunteer to faux paint your dining room. That requires an artist, not a painter.
- Let electricians do a lighting plan, as they tend to be concerned with maximum overall lighting rather than mood, ambiance, and romance.
- Let carpenters do on-site cabinetry—carpentry only, please. Cabinetry should be built in a cabinet-making shop with special tools and finishing techniques.
- Let plumbers do HVAC design and work. HVAC (heating and air-conditioning) requires special training. People go to school for it!
- Discuss work with subcontractors—do this only with the builder and the architect.
- Criticize in public. Instead, praise in public and com-

AND TO THINK THE OWNERS BELIEVED IT WOULD BE A SIMPLE MATTER OF BRICKING OVER A FEW WINDOWS TO CREATE ADDITIONAL WALL SPACE IN A NEW MUDROOM. AS IS OFTEN THE CASE, THE NEW BRICKS DID NOT MATCH THE OLD. THIS PROBLEM LED TO A SERENDIPITOUS DECISION TO SAND-BLAST THE ENTIRE HOUSE, CREATING A NEVER-NEEDS-TO-BE-PAINTED ANTIQUE SPECKLED BRICK FINISH.

plain in private; otherwise, you undermine your contractor in front of the subcontractors. In the end, it's your renovation that will suffer.

TIME LINE

THE PRE-RENOVATION PROCESS

Renovations inevitably start with a problem that is unique to you and your home. Defining and resolving that problem is what drives us to renovate time and again. From the time the problem is identified (kitchen's too small, don't have any closets, or no place to put the computer), a series of working steps must take place in logical order.

1. Identify the problems.
2. Round up your ideas and references. Magazines, books, and drives through neighboring communities will help you research your ideas.
3. Get a guesstimate, a preliminary budget (usually calculated on a square footage basis), to decide whether you're even in the ballpark. This rough number is illuminating and is usually followed by a period of adjustment to the cost realities.
4. Locate, interview, and identify your team: architect, contractor, and designer.
5. Budget for the project.
6. Work on and develop your design plans and construction drawings.
7. File your plans with the municipality (permits can take up to three months).
8. Begin construction.

WHAT THE PROS DON'T KNOW

Elements beyond your contractor's control (only three) can blow the budget and wreck the time line. The uncontrollables are the weather, the customer's work change orders, and unseeables such as termites, mildew, understructured foundations—and, in one case, a leaky oil tank. The cleanup cost tens of thousands of dollars and took two months of construction time. Renowned renovator Terry Ross says, "Expect the worst and hope for the best."

THE PROJECT

STEP BY STEP, HOW THE RENOVATION PROCESS UNFOLDS

DEMO, OR DEMOLITION. The demolition stage is fast and furious. Renovators get false hopes seeing how quickly their home is taken down to the studs and expect the rest of the project to unfold at the same pace (it won't). (Deconstructing a house, whereby you systematically strip away plumbing, mechanical, and electrical systems, is more laborious and time-consuming.)

FOUNDATIONS. Pouring a foundation is contingent on weather, since cement should not be poured in freezing temperatures. Your project will sit until spring if the soil is frozen. Inclement weather can also slow initial exterior work.

FRAMING. With the new foundation poured, the contractor will begin framing the new structure. Framing, depending on the size of the addition, can be the lengthiest portion of the renovation process, as you are basically building the new sections.

FASCIAS. Once your framing work is complete, fascias and soffits are applied to the roof. Once these are done, the roof is ready for finish roofing and flashing.

ROOFING. Roofing, a specialty trade, is next. The contractor wants to get the finished roof on so the shell (the structure thus far) is dry.

EXTERIOR DOORS AND WINDOWS. The next carpentry process is to fill the exterior openings with windows and doors and apply exterior trim that must be installed before the exterior finish material can go on. (Exterior finish materials are siding, stone, brick, etc.)

EXTERIOR SIDING. With windows and doors in, the exterior finish materials can be installed and finished to the windows. The exterior of the structure is always ready to be finished before the interior is ready to start. While the HVAC contractor, plumber, and electrician are doing their rough-in work on the interior of the shell, all of the exterior work can be in progress—including painting.

ROUGH PLUMBING, ELECTRICAL, HVAC. Now that the windows and doors are up, the exterior is basically dry. Work begins on putting in the guts inside the walls: security, phone systems, audio/visual, rough heating and air ducts, mechanical equipment. Before the walls are closed up with drywall and preferably before insulation is installed, the owner, builder/architect, and designer should do a walk-through with the electrician, plumber, and HVAC contractor to review all of the rough-in systems and wiring, including light fixtures. Vents, air intakes, switches, outlets, surface lights, and thermostats must be in the right places. Now is the time to make changes.

INSULATION. Once the rough work is done and inspected, insulation follows. Insulation must also pass an inspection. Postinspection, the walls are closed up with drywall.

DRYWALL (OR SHEETROCK). Drywall is the interior surface of your home; it is what the eye sees. Care and attention must be paid to the taping of the seams and to sanding prior to painting; if not properly taped, your walls will have ridges.

INTERIOR PRIMING AND FIRST FINISH COAT. A good contractor applies a primer coat and a first coat of paint prior to installing interior trim. As there is not yet any trim, the finish paint can go behind the area to be trimmed with wood. Wood shrinks, and this ensures that there will be no exposed or unfinished lines down the road.

INTERIOR DOORS. Hang interior doors and then run the base molding and other interior trim pieces.

INTERIOR TRIM. At this point, all of the interior openings are completed and the walls are primed and first-coated. Now, trim carpenters install the base casings and case the doors and windows. Decorative paneling and moldings are also now applied (installed).

CABINETS. Kitchen and bath cabinets and all built-ins go in at the same time as the trim phase.

COUNTERTOPS. Your countertops, whether stone or synthetic, can be installed once your cabinets are set in place. Typically, the counter manufacturer will first make a template of the counter. The finished counters will arrive one or two weeks later.

A SIMPLE QUESTION—WHAT COLOR SHOULD THE FLOORS BE REFINISHED?—CAN HAVE MANY ANSWERS. EVEN MATCHING THE OLD MIGHT MEAN MIXING MULTIPLE STAINS. HERE, A REFINISHER APPLIED NUMEROUS COMBINATIONS OF MINWAX STAINS IN SEARCH OF THE PERFECT COLOR. BEFORE THE OWNERS DECIDED, THEY WET THE COLOR WITH A PAPER TOWEL—A BETTER REPRESENTATION OF HOW IT WILL LOOK ONCE IT IS POLYURETHANED.

TILE AND WOOD FLOORING. Tile and wood floors are installed but neither grouted nor finished.

FINISH PAINTING. The process is simplified if the finish (final) paint is applied before you have switch plate covers, light trim kits, radiator and floor grilles, door hardware, and handles installed.

FLOOR FINISHES. The floor is sanded to clean off any construction damage, then stained and polyurethaned. The house should be completely empty of all workers during this phase if you do not want dust and grit to settle into your floor stain.

FINISH ELECTRICAL, PLUMBING, HEATING, AND TRIM OUT. Grilles, thermostats, security panels, and door hardware are installed.

KITCHEN APPLIANCES, AUDIO/VISUAL, AND PHONES. These are installed.

PUNCH LIST. Walk through the house with the architect and the contractor. Note dings, missing hardware, broken windowpanes (inevitable), and so on. Don't let these little to-do lists cloud your perception of what we hope has been a rewarding collaborative experience.

Resources

AMMIRATI

CONTRACTOR:
HAROLD R. REEVE
  & SONS INC.
P.O. BOX 1441
MATTITUCK, NY 11952
631-298-4713

BLATT

ARCHITECT:
JUSTIN F. MINIERI, AIA
P.O. BOX 1439
NEW ROCHELLE, NY 10802
914-576-7087

CONTRACTOR:
JARY CONSTRUCTION CORP.
5 BEVERLY ROAD
PURCHASE, NY 10577
914-694-4111

MATTHEWS

ARCHITECT:
NORMAN DAVENPORT ASKINS P.C.
2995 LOOKOUT PLACE NE
ATLANTA, GA 30305
404-233-6565

CONTRACTOR:
BREIDING CONSTRUCTION
6310 HILLCREST WAY

DOUGLASVILLE, GA 30135
404-863-3267

DESIGNER:
JACKYE LANHAM
LANHAM DESIGNS
472 EAST PACES FERRY ROAD NW
ATLANTA, GA 30305
404-364-9472

QUINLAN

ARCHITECT:
G. CHRISTOPHER POWELL
231 WEST 16TH STREET 19
NEW YORK, NY 10011
212-645-7180

CONTRACTOR:
RAUL MONGES
37 JAMES DRIVE
BREWSTER, NY 10509
914-837-6547

ROBERTSON

CONTRACTOR:
PHILIP WOODS
PHILIP WOODS HOME
  BUILDERS, INC.
1425 RICHARD ARRINGTON JR.
  BOULEVARD. S
SUITE 106
BIRMINGHAM, AL 35205
205-933-2373

SAMFORD

CONTRACTOR:
FRANCIS A. BRYANT & SONS
58 VINE STREET
BIRMINGHAM, AL 35213
205-802-7700

DESIGNER:
LAURA LEE SAMFORD
LLS FURNITURE DESIGN
728 SHADES CREEK PARKWAY
SUITE 120
BIRMINGHAM, AL 35209
205-871-0675

TOMASSO

ARCHITECT:
HAWTIN JORGENSEN
  ARCHITECTS, P.C.
P.O. BOX 1682
265 EAST KELLY STREET
JACKSON, WY 83001
307-733-4365

CONTRACTOR:
BONTECOU CONSTRUCTION
(PROJECT MANAGER: TERRY ROSS)
P.O. BOX 862
JACKSON, WY 83001
307-733-2990

HOME THEATER:
ACOUSTIC INNOVATIONS
1377 CLINT MOORE ROAD
BOCA RATON, FL 33487
800-983-6233

WHITNEY

ARCHITECT:
PETER A. COLE
75 S. GREELEY AVENUE
CHAPPAQUA, NY 10514
914-238-6152

CONTRACTOR:
D&R SCHAPPACH, L.L.C.
74 N. MOUNTAIN ROAD
BROOKFIELD, CT 06804
914-447-8178

INTERIOR ARCHITECT:
ROSAMUND A. YOUNG
THE YOUNG COMPANY
6 NORWOOD ROAD
SCARSDALE, NY 10583
914-723-8637

LANDSCAPE ARCHITECT:
RICHARD F. HEIN ARCHITECT, P.C.
138 LARCHMONT AVENUE
LARCHMONT, NY 10538
914-834-1414

BATHS

BEST PLUMBING TILE AND STONE
JONAS WEINER
TONI ANN FRANCOMANO
830 CENTRAL AVENUE
SCARSDALE, NY 10583
914-723-2002
WWW.BESTPLG.COM

KITCHENS

BILOTTA KITCHENS OF MT. KISCO
PAULETTE GAMBACORTA, DESIGNER
175 MAIN STREET
MT. KISCO, NY 10549
914-242-1022
BILOTTA.COM

CRAFTSMAN KITCHENS
3591 SOUTH 300 WEST
SALT LAKE CITY, UT 84115
801-293-8001

MILLENNIUM STONE
JIM SPADER
1 MILL STREET
PORT CHESTER, NY 10573
914-939-0999

LIEBERTS ROYAL GREEN APPLIANCE
   CENTER
228 EAST POST ROAD
WHITE PLAINS, NY 10601
914-428-5363

JEFF MAZIN
CHRISTOPHER PEACOCK BESPOKE
   ENGLISH CABINETRY
4 DEERFIELD DRIVE
GREENWICH, CT 06830
203-862-9333

ARCHITECT:
HAMLIN GOLDREYER ARCHITECTS
BART HAMLIN, AIA
102 BRITE AVENUE
SCARSDALE, NY 10583
914-472-4724

MISCELLANEOUS

MILTON GARTH JAMES
MGJ DESIGN CONSULTANT/
   DRAFTING SERVICES
70 VIRGINIA ROAD
WHITE PLAINS, NY 10595
914-288-9898
FLOOR PLANS FOR BOOK

THE COMPUTER NERDS, INC.
JOSEPH G. MINOVICH, PRESIDENT
P.O. BOX 31
BRONXVILLE, NY 10708
914-779-7952
JMINOVICH@THECOMPUTER
   NERDSINC.COM

Index